Journalist, writer and TV and radio presenter, Stuart Maconie is the host of *Stuart Maconie's Critical List* on Radio 2 and has written and presented dozens of other shows on BBC Radio. As a DJ, he regularly deputises for Johnny Walker on Radio 2 Drivetime and on Richard Allinson's late night show. He presents the DVD Collection on BBC 4 and appears on Radio 4's Saturday Review. His books include *3682 Days*, the official history of Blur, and *Folklore*, the official James biography. He was The Sony Awards Music Radio Broadcaster of the Year in 2001. He lives in Birmingham and is happiest fell walking with his dog Muffin.

Cider With Roadies

STUART MACONIE

Cider With Roadies

EBURY
PRESS

5 7 9 10 8 6 4

First published 2003 by Ebury Press,
An imprint of Random House,
20 Vauxhall Bridge Road, London SW1V 2SA

Random House Australia (Pty) Limited
20 Alfred Street, Milsons Point, Sydney,
New South Wales 2061, Australia

Random House New Zealand Limited
18 Poland Road, Glenfield, Auckland 10, New Zealand

Random House South Africa (Pty) Limited
Endulini, 5a Jubilee Road, Parktown 2193, South Africa

The Random House Group Limited Reg. No. 954009

www.randomhouse.co.uk

A CIP catalogue record for this book is available from the British Library.

Cover designed by Jon Gray
Typeset by seagulls

ISBN 0 091891115 9

Printed and bound in Great Britain by
Mackays of Chatham plc, Chatham, Kent

Contents

Introduction

According to an opening gambit much better than this one, Laurie Lee tells us he was 'set down from the carrier's cart at the age of three'. It's the first sentence of *Cider with Rosie* and I've read it many times.

I have no idea what it means though. It seems to suggest that his family bought him from Argos.

Whatever it means, I love *Cider with Rosie*. It's one of the few books to have survived a thousand draughty classrooms and come through unscathed. I loved it even though Laurie Lee's evocation of a Gloucestershire childhood struck no chords of recognition with me. I never 'carved a switch' or 'scrumped' an apple or tickled a trout, although I did once empty some tropical fish into the drainage culvert of the Leeds–Liverpool canal.

My first memory finds me at three years old as well. But there are no 'white roads, rutted by hooves and cartwheels, innocent of oil and petrol'. All the roads of my childhood have rainbows of petrol in every gutter. There was also little sign of horses in the streets, though much evidence of dogs. But maybe there are similarities. We both grew up in working-class homes far from the centres of cultivated learning and we both dreamed of being writers, a dream that came true. Laurie Lee wrote about the glories of nature, the quasi-spiritual truth of early experience and the myriad complexities of love. I wrote about Shaun Ryder and Kraftwerk's curious dress sense.

Our love of words led us both far from home. Laurie Lee walked across the Pyrenees to fight for the Republicans in the Spanish Civil War. I once spent four days in a van in France with Napalm Death. I do not know what it is like to share an Andalusian cell with battle-hardened Ukranians. But I do know what it's like to share the changing room of a Dusseldorf leisure centre with MC Hammer. I feel Laurie and I are brothers beneath the skin.

1 With The Beatles

George Orwell wrote that 'only by resurrecting our own memories can we realise how incredibly distorted is the child's vision of the world'. If you've read *The Road to Wigan Pier* you may remember Orwell also claimed that people who drank orange juice were the henchmen of Satan so he wasn't always right. I have read *The Road to Wigan Pier*, partly because of a keen interest in sociopolitical British class analysis and partly because it's got 'Wigan' in the title. That's where I'm from, you see, and that's where a lot of what follows takes place. Not this first bit though. Excitingly, that takes place in Swinton.

I'm in bed in my auntie's house in Swinton, a suburb of Manchester. The room is airy and filled with light. It's a sunny day, the windows are open, curtains are billowing and the bedspread is fluffy and white. Of course, bearing in mind Orwell's words, it's possible that I've mentally mixed the whole thing up with a Daz advert. For instance, in my memory the bedspread is a duvet although logic dictates that this can't be true, the duvet not making its incursion into British bedrooms till some years later, along with other racy innovations like radio alarms and the works of Dr Alex Comfort.

In the room though, definitely, are my cousins Eileen and

Elizabeth. They'll be about eight or nine I'd guess. They're obviously teasing me in some pleasant girlish fashion as I can picture a smiling blonde female face above me and some tickling under the chin. But most memorably, and this is the one element of this tableau that I can't have subconsciously filched from a Daz advert or George Orwell, Laurie Lee or *A Taste of Honey*, somewhere nearby a record is playing. And the effect is utterly electrifying. Even I, a romper-suited toddler, can feel the sheer visceral thrill of it. Every time I've heard it since, a shivery echo of that first encounter grips me.

The Beatles recorded 'Can't Buy Me Love' on 29 January 1964 at the studios of EMI Pathe Marconi in Paris; knocking it off swiftly in an hour remaining at the end of a session that was devoted to German language versions of early hits. I didn't know this. But I was in love.

Instantly in love, and I've never been the same since. I loved it so much that I decided to 'check out the buzz' and catch this hot new band live. The fact that I was three years old, and almost certainly not on the guest list, would not deter me.

We didn't live in Swinton. We lived in Wigan and the trip to my aunt's must have been some glamorous, cosmopolitan weekend break. Throughout my childhood the Mancunian branch of the family would always seem exotic and thrilling, particularly when, a few years later, Eileen was asked out by George Best. Blonde, pretty, stick-thin and a girl about town, it's not surprising she caught George's eye, although in the family legend George 'must have felt sorry for't lass and thowt she could do wi'a good feed'. That's what they were saying over in Wigan anyway where we weren't quite as steeped in showbiz.

From the earliest of ages, I was dimly aware that there was something funny about my home town. The name cropped up in all kinds of seemingly unrelated contexts on telly. Mirth would always be evinced when it was mentioned and once I saw it referred to as a 'music hall joke' in my dad's *Daily Mirror*. Even today, comedians will say things like, 'It was like a wet Wednesday night in Wigan', with that chortle in their voice that is the trademark of the chillingly humourless.

Mention Neasden, Wilmslow or Cirencester and the mind is a blank slate. Mention Wigan and a host of images flash across the screen of the mental multiplex in quick, grimy succession. Darkened mills belching smoke, men in flat caps hawking up phlegm into spittoons in pub vaults accompanied by the maudlin clack of domino on Formica, scrawny whippets, hard-faced women in aprons dolly-stoning the steps of terraced houses in a thin drizzle, dirty-faced urchins eating tripe in the street, shin-kicking contests, canal boats, rickets, possibly a ukulele.

I don't know when our last case of rickets was in Wigan, but I know that factory chimneys haven't belched smoke for about two and a half decades. I can understand why the image endures though; it's a great deal more poetic and evocative a visual cue than, say, the car park of a software company or the reception area of a leisure centre or any of the other ways Northerners are more likely to be gainfully employed these days. The only way blokes come home sooty-faced from work these days is if the toner cartridge had leaked while they were printing out their presentations on stock control innovation or the future of portable air conditioning

If these conceptions of my home town are wrong then, what is Wigan truly famous for? Rugby for one. Even though our utter, unquestioned dominance in the sport has ended, all Wiganers secretly believe that we are really just indulgently letting the other teams win for a while in order to make it more interesting. When I say rugby of course I mean rugby league, not the other sort wherein wheezing off-duty policeman, solicitors and dentists bite each other's noses off, watched by retired headmasters in driving gloves. A friend of mine once said, perceptively, that rugby union has but one saving grace, namely that it's always nice to see coppers getting knocked about a bit on their day off.

Rugby then ... and pies. Wiganers are known to the rest of Lancashire as 'pie eaters' for their prodigious enthusiasm for this noble foodstuff. Lobster thermidor, kangaroo, lychee, truffle; there is no foodstuff so unusual or arcane that Wiganers will not attempt to encase it in a crust and eat it at a bus stop. Here's a local joke: a sophisticated man of the world, possibly from Chorley or Bolton, is attempting to entice his Wiganer workmate to the pub at lunchtime.

'They've got a lunchtime special on; a pie, a pint and a woman, eighty pence. Eighty pence!'

'Ah,' replies the Wiganer, eyes narrowed in suspicion. 'Whose pies are they, though?'

So, to recap, pies, the pier, the rugby – and, of course, soul music of which more in due course. Back in 1964 though, Beatlemania, a kind of collective insanity affecting toddler, show-girl, duchess and politician alike, has Britain in its vicelike grip. Returning from Paris, they barely had time to work out a new press-conference routine of witty, oblique, self-effacing bon mots before jetting to New York for more TV and concert appearances. Two weeks later, they were back home to shoot their first major motion picture, *A Hard Day's Night*. In between they nipped into Abbey Road and recorded 'You Can't Do That', the B-side of 'Can't Buy Me Love', in four takes. Then they had lunch, smoked a quick duty-free Chesterfield or Lark and came back and did 'And I Love Her' before teatime. On a daily basis, breezily, and with the minimum of fuss, The Beatles were changing the world like most people change their socks.

Life as a toddler in Wigan was much quieter than life on the road with The Beatles, I would imagine. But ever since hearing 'Can't Buy Me Love', I was with them in spirit. Moreover, our two worlds were about to collide. Hot on the heels of 'Can't Buy

Me Love', the title song of *A Hard Day's Night* was Number 1 through most of August while The Beatles toured the States again, having already visited Australia and New Zealand in the early summer. Then on their return, they announced a 36-date tour of the UK and right there, in black and white in the itinerary, in the very first week, between Birmingham and Manchester, was an appearance at the ABC cinema, Wigan, 13 October 1964.

It was to prove a momentous week for all kinds of reasons. The back pages were full of the Tokyo Olympics and long jumper Mary Rand taking gold for Britain cheered on by millions in front of grainy monochrome TV sets. The front pages were dominated by the General Election and Harold Wilson's attempt to put an end to what Labour were calling '13 years of Tory misrule'. Nowhere was this more eagerly awaited than in Wigan, a town where, as was often said, 'they'd vote for a pig in a red rosette'. And then probably put it in a pie.

But Harold Wilson, a lugubrious pipe smoker in a flasher's mac, was no impish moptop. Young Wigan was understandably more excited about the forthcoming visit of the most famous, sexy, glamorous guys on the planet. They were coming down from Olympus, or the Olympic Theatre, Paris, at least, trailing clouds of glory, to our town, to our cinema, the ABC or 'the Ritz' as the townsfolk knew it, where excitement was usually confined to the back row or the Saturday morning 'minors' when tiny kids would throw penny chews at each other and smoke illicit Park Drive oblivious to the antique Flash Gordon serial on the screen. I was only three but I was still going to be there.

Naturally, I have many reasons to be grateful to my mother but none more so than taking me to see The Beatles. Down the years, I've relished that moment in pub conversation when someone says 'OK, what was the first band you ever saw live?' and after others have chipped in with Haircut 100, Carcass or the Icicle Works, I sip thoughtfully at my beer and say, 'Oh, Focus at the Southport Theatre, 1974 ... unless you count The Beatles of course.'

And who doesn't count The Beatles? The most important pop group ever, perhaps the most important cultural force of the twentieth century, harbingers of global change. And I saw them. Thanks, Mum.

My memories of the show are a little vague. I'd only been walking upright for a year and my vocabulary at the time wouldn't have stretched to 'amplifier' let alone 'Aeolian cadences'. So in order to evoke the experience for you, dear reader, I thought I should really interview my mum on the subject. What follows is an interview with her in the Q & A format beloved of well-established music journalists since (a) it affords direct access to the subject unmediated by the writer's implicit or explicit bias or subconscious shaping or editing; and (b) because it's a piece of piss. Here it is, conducted by phone in September 2002 and presented here pretty much in full:

Q: Was it big news when The Beatles came to town?

A: I'll say!

Q: How exactly?

A: It was in the papers and everything.

Q: Were you a Beatles fan?

A: Oh yes. Well, actually I preferred Cliff. But The Beatles were, you know, very good.

Q: How did you find out about the show?

A: Erm, it must have been in the papers.

Q: Was there a support act?

A: Pardon?

Q: Was there another group or singer on as well?

A: Oh, I'd have thought so. Can't remember who though.

Q: And what did they play, The Beatles?

A: Oh, you know, all the hits. Beatles stuff.

Q: And what about the crowd. Was there screaming?

A: Screaming! God, you couldn't hear yourself think. *You* loved it. We had you stood up on the back of the seat in front of you, dancing.

Q: So how did we get the tickets?

A: Ah, right, well. I was working part-time at Eckersley's Mill in the afternoons so we were able to go along in the morning. You had to queue up. It was chilly and actually very foggy, early autumn. Me and you, your Auntie Kathleen and her neighbour's little girl. The queue stretched all the way down Station Road and it was very cold as I say and just opposite the ABC there was a little café. Always open. People used to call in when they came out after the pictures. So the people waiting for Beatles tickets started to go across for a coffee to pass the time in this enormous queue. You'd save the place of the person behind you and they'd go off and get a drink and a warm and then when they came back, they'd do the same for you. I remember what you had – a milky coffee and a piece of toast, and they let you use the toilet. And then after The Beatles show had finished, we went to that chippie by your nana's, the one behind Madge Makin's pub.

So to recap: I went to see the most important pop group ever. And I know pretty much bugger all about it; songs played, support act, notable moments, solos, banter, choreography, etc. Nowt. But we do know, thanks to my mum, a great deal about the weather conditions, our own circumstances, what refreshments were consumed prior to the show and where we ate afterwards. Obviously I was destined to be a music journalist. It runs in the family.

Even I, a man who learned his journalistic trade on what is laughingly called the music press, and where turning up at the right venue with a working pen counts as hard-nosed reportage, couldn't have let it drop so easily. I had to do a little legwork at least. I'm feeling quite pleased with myself actually.

As was customary, The Beatles performed two shows that autumn evening, one at 6.20 and one at 8.35. I'd have thought we'd have been at the earlier one although – *quelle surprise* – my mum can't remember. The show was a package of sorts, featuring several other Epstein charges, namely The Rustiks, Tommy Quickly and Michael Haslam and Sounds Incorporated – later to feature on Beatle tracks like 'Got To Get You Into My Life' – plus Mary Wells, whose 'My Guy' still reappears in the charts at distant though predictable intervals like Halley's comet. The compere was one Bob Bain and the Beatle set list comprised a brace of crowd-pleasing covers ('Twist And Shout', 'Money', 'Long Tall Sally') and a slick selection of their new material: 'Things We Said Today', 'I'm Happy Just To Dance With You', 'I Should Have Known Better', 'If I Fell', 'I Wanna Be Your Man', their most recent chart-topper 'A Hard Day's Night' and, yes, three numbers in, my personal favourite 'Can't Buy Me Love'. Who knows? Perhaps I turned to my Auntie Kathleen and pointed out the light acoustic rhythm and bluffly asexual lyric. More likely though, I asked if we could get some chips on the way home. One thing is sure, the show must have moved along at a fair lick. Ten tunes by the Fab Four, a compere and five other performers. No wonder they called him Tommy Quickly. He must have been going like the clappers, predating those four-second Napalm Death songs by decades. I hope they weren't paying him by the hour.

Though he had the whole bill pretty much in his pocket, Epstein wasn't there that famous night in Wigan. He was in London recording readings from his *A Cellarful of Noise* book with George Martin. He did find time though to send a telegram to Harold Wilson on the eve of the General Election: 'Hope your group is as much a success.' They certainly were, and in Anthony Wedgwood Benn, Wilson had his own John Lennon, charismatic, awkward, prone to insane political affiliations.

So Britain had a new government, and what's more one that didn't look like their natural apparel was plus fours and a shoot-ing stick, and there's a new mood abroad. The nation is running a temperature, with Beatlemania pushing up the feverish hormonal high. The kids are frugging and watusi-ing like demons to Tommy Quickly. The Sixties, I suppose, are beginning to swing, although, like Ringo, it took the North a long time to wash the grease out of its hair. To my three-year-old eyes, adult men still looked more like Albert Finney in *Saturday Night and Sunday Morning* than George Harrison, endlessly combing back lustrous, oily hanks of hair, and they were more likely to be seen clutching a pint of mild than a Scotch and Coke.

Morrissey is a few years my senior but generationally I guess we are cut from the same cloth. The milieu he mournfully celebrates – the cobblestones and rain-bleary streets, factories, football, funfairs, canals and chippies – have always resonated with me.

Child of the Sixties has come to mean a pony-tailed Grateful Dead fan or an aromatherapist from Hebden Bridge; Anita Roddick, Rosie Boycott, Tariq Ali, Tony Blair even. But I dispute this. They weren't children of the Sixties, they were teenagers, students, twenty-somethings of the Sixties. I, let me tell you, was a genuine child of the Sixties. A toddler of the Sixties. Their battle cry was 'Never trust anyone over thirty.' Ours was 'Never trust anyone over six', closely followed by 'Don't swallow your Bazooka Joe chewing gum or it will curl round your intestines and kill you.' My generation were not going to Marrakesh in a Dormobile. We were going to Cubs. Watching *Stingray*. Taking our first communion. Going to see The Beatles with our mums and having some chips on the way home.

If you remember the Sixties, 'they' say, you weren't really there. And for once, 'they' are absolutely right. I was there, and I hardly remember a thing.

2 All Kinds of Everything

The first objects that I can recall being imbued with anything approaching mystery and beauty, objects that I coveted with what clearly bordered on the fetishistic, were the vinyl records in the darkened, reverential space inside my nana's radiogram.

We lived with my nana when I was a kid and, like any good Northern working-class family then or now, we acquired new consumer durables on HP as a badge of our social status. Some years earlier, Harold Macmillan had told the workers that They Had Never Had It So Good, by which he meant that they now owned a toaster as compared to, let's say, salmon fishing rights over a twenty-mile stretch of the River Tay. But in essence, he was right. The factories hummed night and day, overtime was plentiful, and Grundig, Hoover and Electrolux were the must-have designer labels of the day.

Of these brave new consumer totems, by far the most exciting was the radiogram. Ours was made by Philips of Eindhoven. It was incomparably wonderful. The telly was OK, when it wasn't merely showing a picture of a girl futilely endeavouring to teach long division to a gonk. But to tell you the truth, I'd developed a curious phobia where I had become irrationally frightened of the little white dot that shrank in on itself in the centre of the screen when you turned the set off. Not that we did that a great deal.

The radiogram though was a daily source of wonder and majesty, not least because of its bulk. It was roughly the size of a cara-vanette and you had to squeeze up against the opposite wall to slide past it into the kitchen. It was made from what must have once been a goodly sized Brazilian copse of solid teak, apart from the speaker grille which was a faux gold latticework. I would spend whole hours of the day lying on the carpet, staring at this interesting textual effect, mainly as I had discovered that after about half an hour's intense scrutiny, something mildly hallucinogenic happened and then you were sick. How touching to think that, in my own way, I was reflect-ing the pioneering psychedelic experiments of Kesey and Leary on the other side of the world at roughly the same time.

Inside it was even more intoxicating, though I can see that ours served as a kind of Hades of eternal damnation for 45s and EPs that had been wicked in a previous life. The singles were largely naked, their gorgeous laminated picture sleeves consigned to the wind or perhaps the dustbin. Occasionally, a prized record might be afforded the protection of a paper sleeve on which some-one – me, I imagine – had biroed a stylised dog or crazed battle scene. They were stored upright in a wire rack to afford maximum abrasion and warpage. They were played by being scratched by what amounted to a drawing pin wired to a flimsy Bakelite arm and this only after being stacked for hours like tortillas in an unpopular cantina and then dropped with a splat onto a judder-ing, ribbed turntable rotating erratically between 4 and 97 revolu-tions per minute. Still they were only records.

I remember almost every one; its look, its label design, even its smell. Although in a vain attempt to protect these hard-earned artefacts I was not strictly allowed anywhere near the radiogram, naturally I was right in there, jammy-fingered and desperate for kicks as soon as an adult back was turned.

There was 'Mac The Knife' by someone called Bobby Darin: weird and scary – all sharks and teeth and murder in goosestep waltz time – especially if you're three going on four. 'Here Comes Summer' by Jerry Keller was far nicer. There were a couple of Elvis records lurking in there: 'Good Luck Charm' and 'Can't Help Falling In Love With You'. I adored these. I had no clear idea who Elvis was. I'd seen his pictures in newspapers and magazines and these suggested he was a bit of a show-off with a penchant for dressing up as racing drivers or soldiers. But 'Can't Help Falling In Love' was so beautiful it made my neck prickle as I sat entranced on the Axminster, head bowed to the giant golden speaker. These days I know that this ravishing tune was filched from a piece of early nineteenth-century French music, Plaisir D'Amour by Giovanni Martini. Back then, if anyone had asked the residents of our street about Martini's music most would have started singing 'Any time, any place, anywhere ... there's a wonderful drink you can share.' But whether knowingly or not, I'd been introduced to classical music and found it good.

There were traces of levity elsewhere in the bijou collection. One of the singles was by Ken Dodd, the comedian whose face when glimpsed on TV I found only marginally less traumatic than the white dot. However, there was nothing 'tatifilarious' about 'Pianissimo', a tender, appropriately quiet ballad which cast Doddy, unconvincingly, in the role of sensitive, emoting lover. Funnier even than this was the single I had won at some very early age at the ABC minors for collecting silver paper that somehow, magically, became guide dogs for the blind; this, I imagine, on the stern but somehow alluring instructions of Valerie Singleton. At odds with the altruism of the whole enterprise, my prize was a seven-inch single of the gormless theme from a TV advertisement for gents outfitters John Collier. This consisted chiefly of thunderous tympani and a male voice choir bellowing 'John Collier, John Collier, the WIN-DOW TO WATCH!!' It was rubbish, but it got a spin on slow weekends as a conversation piece when neighbours called round for sugar.

Too young to read properly, I grew to recognise the tunes I craved through the label logos and other visual clues. Daft Ken Dodd bore the deep royal blue of Decca, Elvis wore the coal-black livery of pre-Seventies Orange RCA, the John Collier Theme still had its laminated sleeve featuring a giant Trilby. My favourite, though, the sight of which always quickened the pulse a little, was the very emerald green of a goalie's jumper, the word Columbia grandly embossed in silver above the little hole.

I can tell you now, having just looked it up, that *The Shadows to the Fore* EP was released in June 1961, a conflation of two single releases that had both charted high in the Top Ten over the previous year. Nothing of the records history mattered to me back then. What mattered was that sound, eerie, penumbral, metallic. It sounded like the future. 'Fireball XL-5' rather than *Two Way Family Favourites*. It was, I've since found out, the sound of a Fender Stratocaster, 1959 model. An electric guitar. There was no turning back now.

Of course The Shads did their fair share of toe-tappers and shindigs, bouncy tunes for church socials and coffee-bar twist sessions. They were no Led Zeppelin. Not for them selling their souls to Beelzebub and buying Aleister Crowley's old gaff on Loch Ness. No, The Shadows' speciality was a cute little dance whose simplicity was almost touching; left foot forward, right foot over left, return to original position, smile. Add to that the incipient Jehovas Witnessism and the glasses and here was a band who set Cliff into relief as a volcano of rank animal lust. You can laugh. But does anyone remember Led Zeppelin's little dance?

Luckily though, I'd dropped on The Shadows at their most, well, shadowy. Though the title *Shadows To The Fore* obviously alludes to the guys stepping out from Cliff Richard's, err, shadow, the tracks are clearly themed around some notion of danger, suspense and exoticism. For me, to whom a new flavour of Farley's Rusk was a voyage into the unknown, it was unspeakably thrilling.

The four tracks were 'Apache', 'Man Of Mystery', 'The Stranger' and 'FBI'. 'The Stranger' I have no recollection of, but I bet it was a bit spooky. 'Apache' must surely still be their biggest hit, sending Jimmy Page, Eric Clapton and a whole generation of future axe heroes rushing to their full-length wardrobe mirrors with a tennis racket.

My faves were the other two though. 'FBI' is still a cracking tune, though its always seemed a little jaunty as the theme for an organisation devoted to counter-intelligence, global espionage and the defence of the world's biggest superpower. I just can't see J Edgar Hoover doing that little dance. Best of all though was 'Man Of Mystery'. It had a wonderfully cloak-and-dagger, moustache-twirler of a melody and, as I started to read and pick up words over the next year or so, I realised it had a great title. In brackets, it said 'Theme from the Television Series "The Edgar Wallace Mysteries"'. You may have seen this on UK Gold in the middle of the night. The credits feature a bust of crime king Edgar Wallace rotating, very slowly, in a thick fug created either by dry ice or a cameraman smoking furiously just off camera. It goes on for about ten minutes as The Shads twang on. How innocent, or if you prefer, primitive TV was then.

So, who had bought these records? Naturally, my mum doesn't know and even if she did, would you trust her evidence, m'lud? Well, it wasn't my nana obviously. Or my grandad, dead just before I was born and still hanging in the air, dark and heavy as soot, for most of my childhood. Their pop music was Marie Lloyd and 'Faith Of Our Fathers', saucy ditties and sacred hymns. So it must have been one of the kids – Molly, the eldest, or my mum, or Mo and Maureen the twins. Delving back now, with the benefit of pop reference books Grandad would have harrumphed at, we can piece together a photofit cum psychological profile. The records were all released and purchased between 1959 and the summer of 1962; the two Elvis singles were consecutive releases. To me all the evidence points to Uncle Mo. He'd returned from national service in Malaysia in 1959 where young British conscripts had been charged with putting down what was known as the Malaysian Emergency. Coming home, he'd obviously decided to start catching up on irresponsible youthful pursuits.

The tunes all have a robust rock 'n' roll feel too; there's no Adam Faith or Cliff in there, no evidence of swoonsome girly infatuation. But The Shadows are the conclusive piece of evidence. Instrumentals have always appealed to boys. Down the years, lads have always been able to indulge in their equivalents of teen crushes, whether the subject be Jimi Hendrix, Rick Wakeman or John Squire by founding them on supposed technical ability rather than dimples or a nice bum. As for the other discs, there is of course the troubling aberration that is Ken Dodd. Maybe that was Molly's. Or maybe the trauma of spending two years fighting armed guerrillas in the Asian jungle was manifesting itself in strange and disturbing ways.

Come what must have been the long-awaited weekend, my mum and dad would go to the pub or Labour club and I would sit newly scrubbed in candy-striped cottonelle pyjamas on the settee with my nan and watch the array of cathode entertainment which, come to think, has hardly changed in thirty-odd years – talent shows, inane games, cop drama, men in drag, people playing pranks on unsuspecting folk at bus stops.

Several of these Sixties TV staples would feature the music of the day. We watched everything, my nan and me, and would no more have turned the telly off and made small talk than we would have arm-wrestled or composed a haiku. So I can only imagine that I missed Jimi Hendrix's famed appearance on *The Lulu Show*, where he dismisses his own number with a snort and goes into

Cream's 'Sunshine Of Your Love', because I was having borax rubbed into my scalp, something my nan did dispiritingly often as part of her one-woman campaign against nits. I did see the Stones on *Sunday Night at the London Palladium* when, controversially, they wouldn't appear in the show's finale. This involved all the guests standing on a giant revolving cake-stand, waving and grinning as they turned to face the audience. The Stones thought it looked stupid. They had a point.

Since the invention of TV, the function of the older generation has been to embarrass youngsters by making derisive comments whenever a contemporary pop act was featured. I imagine when Edison invented the phonograph and first played that famous recording of 'Mary Had A Little Lamb', his dad stood behind him muttering, 'I can't tell a word he's saying ... Is it a boy or a girl?'

I learned to dread the frequent appearances of a luscious-lipped singer called Kathy Kirby as it was the cue for my nan to start muttering darkly and hinting that she was 'no better than she ought to be'. The night the Stones wouldn't go on that revolving London Palladium stage she was incandescent with frail rage; she'd tolerate the hair and scruffy clothes and drug busts. But no one dissed Norman Vaughan. The Beatles drew no comment. My friend John has told me that whenever The Beatles came on telly his dad would watch in contemptuous silence for about half a minute and then, and he would do this every single time, say the same five-word mantra, 'That John Lennon's a bum', before returning to his *Football Pink*. But whatever Wigan thought of Lennon, we were distraught when we heard about Paul McCartney

I can remember exactly where I was when I heard Paul McCartney was dead. I was in the hall of St Jude's Roman Catholic Primary School, Tyrer Avenue, Worsley Mesnes, Wigan, in short pants, waiting for Mr Kane to start morning assembly, a start delayed because of a bout of vomiting by David Lavin.

It was Anne Ruddy who told me and I was shocked. Anne

Ruddy often told me things, mainly dealing with problems and situations that were still some way off for me. She told me that you could hide a love bite by putting toothpaste on it. She told me that if the police ever stopped you for under-age smoking, you should tell them that you had the toothache. Any good, decent policeman, satisfied that there was a humanitarian reason for the misdemeanour, would send you on your way.

The shocking news affected me badly. Perhaps David Lavin had been told and hadn't taken it well either. I haven't been in a primary school for some time so I can't say whether it's still like this, but back then they were like dysentery wards. Our caretaker Mr Canley was engaged in a doomed struggle against a tide of bodily fluids. The school was usually dotted with little molehills of sawdust from his bucket and the ubiquitous smell of a bleach mop, grim reminders of the spot where Ian Parkinson had wet himself or Steven Barry had 'had an accident'. This was accepted as the normal state of affairs. Boys spontaneously expelled internal fluids. Girls fainted. I reckon in total Pauline Johnson was unconscious for a whole term in 1969.

David Lavin was a lugubrious but likeable boy about a foot taller than me with gigantic bat ears. Again times change but in the Sixties and Seventies it was compulsory by law for every school class to contain one boy who looked like the FA Cup when viewed face on. David was also notable for his voice. When we were singing 'Kumbaya' or 'Poor Old Parson's Cow', you would slowly become aware of a mournful, dissonant low rumble, like something out of late-period Bartok, and a look of genuine pain would cross Mr Moore's face as he sat at the piano. 'Tone deaf' is a phrase often bandied about as a cheap insult. But the actual condition is quite rare. David Lavin had it. He couldn't have carried a tune in Mr Canley's bucket.

David's baritone would bring out hidden undercurrents of menace in otherwise amiable tunes like 'If You're Happy And You

Know It', 'May Is The Month Of Mary' or that curious African one we used to sing about the goat shaving, 'Misser Ram Goto'. You know the one? No? Well, maybe Mr Moore was a pioneer of world music. He was a thoughtful man, certainly thoughtful for someone who also coached the junior rugby league team. I remember him, one afternoon, prefacing a new song we were about to maul with a little speech that went roughly, 'The words of this song won't mean a lot to you now. But as you grow older you'll understand why they're so beautiful and true.' Then he commenced with a tune so gorgeous and sad, it was evident even to an oik in ankle socks and a snake belt that it was leagues ahead of 'Misser Ram Goto' and the rest. Ralph Vaughan Williams's 'Linden Lea' is still one of my favourite pieces of music. Every time I hear the words, 'Let other folk make money faster in the air of dark-roomed towns / I don't dread a peevish master though no man do heed my frowns' – I think of old Joe Moore trying to explain the proto-hippy message of liberation from capitalism to a class of vomiting, fainting nine-year-olds. And succeeding.

Paul McCartney wasn't dead of course but Anne Ruddy assured me that by 'dinnertime' – possibly even 'breaktime' around eleven when we ate cold toast brought from home wrapped in greaseproof paper (was this just a Wigan thing?) – the news would be everywhere. Ashen-faced, though not as ashen-faced as David Lavin, I sat and waited for the grim announcement. It never came of course. Paul was not only not dead but 'on a motoring tour somewhere in England with his wife, two children and a dog' according to a spokesman for Apple. McCartney himself later issued a statement saying, 'I am alive and well and concerned about the rumours of my death. But if I were dead, I would be the last to know.' Though her reputation as a news source was in ruins, Anne Ruddy did not seem unduly concerned. She went off to the playground and joined some other girls who were engaged in a collective rendition of 'Sugar Sugar' by The Archies.

The Archies did not really exist. They were not a proper group. They were just cartoons. News of this travelled the playground bush telegraph as speedily as reports that Paul McCartney was dead and that hundreds of violent thugs called greenjackets were going to attack the school tomorrow (nearly every school in the UK fell for this at some time). But The Archies' rumour was true.

The Archies came from a Saturday morning kids cartoon that first aired in the States in September 1968. Each episode featured a song and dance segment performed by the titular band. The show's music was supervised by Don Kirshner, the man behind The Monkees assisted by bubblegum genius Len Barry. 'Sugar Sugar' actually knocked the Rolling Stones off the Number 1 position in America and sold six million copies there. Here, it was Number 1 for two, long months.

Long for me anyway. I hated 'Sugar Sugar' by The Archies. I hated its dorky little xylophone riff. I couldn't stand the guy's voice, which was both wholesome and insinuating at the same time. I couldn't stand the lyrics, which made me hotly embarrassed by their gooey intimacy. Worst of all, and here we see the first stirrings of the archetypal elitist underground music snob and rock hack in waiting, I couldn't stand its ubiquity. Everyone else loved it. The girls at school formed ad hoc ensembles to sing it. My mum took to singing it when she was washing up. OAPs sang it on the way to bingo. Barbara Castle probably sang it at cabinet meetings. I cringed every time I heard it.

In Granadaland – as we rather quaintly termed our local television region, essentially the north-west of England – we also didn't get The Archies. But we did keep getting the little clip of them performing 'Sugar Sugar'. I hated that too. The animation was rubbish, involving about four repeated 'dancing' gestures. The singer, who looked like Superman's berkish chum Jimmy Olson, wore a kind of neckerchief-cum-cravat thing, which I found irredeemably poncey, even though he was only a felt-tipped daub.

I should say here a little more about those schoolgirl vocal performances. Again I don't know whether this was a localised phenomenon but hardly a day went by without one. Sometimes they would just be massed playground singalongs. But more often they would be rehearsed routines. Someone, usually Kelly Carter or Mary O'Riordan, would ask Mr Moore or Miss Hart whether they could 'do a show' at the end of the day. Surprisingly often, the answer was yes. And so, as the teachers did the usual end of school day housekeeping – tracking down lost anoraks, asking us to put chairs on desks, piling mounds of sawdust on patches of sick – five or six girls would assemble on the raised portion of the room by the Solar System wallchart and perform a little dance number of their invention while singing The Equals' 'Viva Bobby Joe', Freda Payne's 'Band Of Gold', Pickettywitch's 'Same Old Feeling' or Edison Lighthouse's 'Love Goes Where My Rosemary Goes'. All these songs were hits between late 1969 and mid-1970, the heart of my junior school years. I remember all this vividly, perhaps because of their ground-breaking routines, but more likely because I was romantically involved with both Kelly Carter and Mary O'Riordan, the latter with whom I'd once spent a very informative hour in a concrete pipe over by the Red Pond, the bleak sheet of water by the railway line that was the nearest our estate got to rural idyll.

The Swinging Sixties, the decade of peace and love, the Age of Aquarius, the beatific high summer of the Flower Children, ended three weeks early. On 6 December 1969 to be precise, when Hell's Angels went on a vicious rampage at the Rolling Stones' free concert at Altamont, San Francisco, killing one Meredith Hunter, and injuring scores of others. Elsewhere, there was widespread looting, arson and sexual assault. In April, Paul McCartney had issued a writ in the High Court which effectively dissolved The Beatles and thus ended the most significant creative alliance of our time. A month after The Beatles split, the last embers of the Summer of Love were put out in a hail of gunfire and young women's screams on the campus of Kent State University in Ohio. There, the National Guard turned on an unarmed crowd of anti-war demonstrators with bayonets, tear gas and rifles. They killed four students, two of them girls, and the massacre is commemorated vividly in Neil Young's scathing 'Ohio'. As a symbol of the end of the hippy dream, nothing could have been more stark than US military personnel slaughtering their own children.

In the UK though, we had other things to concern us. The Eurovision Song Contest for one, and Bobby Moore's shopping habits for another.

The Eurovision Song Contest held in Amsterdam on 21 March 1970 was won by the Irish entry, 'All Kinds Of Everything'. Perhaps we can see in Dana's surprise win – an unaffected young woman in simple garb singing a song about daffodils and fishermen – evidence of a new downbeat simplicity in pop, a post-Vietnam, post-Altamont re-embracing of the traditional and sustaining. Or perhaps it was just 'My Favourite Things' steeped in Guinness. Whatever, it was a big, big hit with the Maconies.

We took our lead here from Granma Coney, my dad's mum, who'd come here from Cork as a young girl and grown into a classic example of what Scousers call a 'shawlie'; a much-adored Irish matriarch, swathed in headscarves, rosary beads and rugs, spending her days playing cards, nibbling at soda farls and arguing about dogma with the local priest. She loved Dana and her winsome little song for reasons that I now see were completely extra-musical and entirely sectarian. The kid from the old country had given the English what for. Granma Coney was no shrinking violet; to the horror of my assembled family, she once tried to explain the rhythm method of contraception to me when I was about seven over a light salad of boiled egg, lettuce and corned beef with piccalilli.

English self-esteem was taking knocks down Mexico way as well as in Amsterdam in the early summer of 1970. The national football team, then champions of the world, were off to defend their title in the testing heat and thin air of South America. For weeks, the papers were full of 'altitude sickness', 'acclimatisation', 'Montezuma's revenge' and other dauntingly long words and alien concepts. Hopes were high. The squad was a solid one; there were the prematurely aged but stalwart Charlton Brothers, the elegant, overlapping fullbacks Keith Newton and Terry Cooper, the violent berserkers Norman Hunter and Nobby Stiles. Piping-voiced Alan Ball, with his translucent freckled alabaster skin and hair the colour of Lucozade, we hoped had packed some Factor 50.

Within days of arrival, we were in trouble. Bobby Moore, Olympian captain of 1966 – he who had wiped his muddied hands on the red velvet upholstery of the Royal Box before shaking the hand of the Queen and hoisting aloft the Jules Rimet Trophy; he whose innate decency shone like a beacon, whose scrupulously fair but resolute defending made him the best in his position in the world – had been fingered for half-inching some tacky gold necklace in a Bogotá jewellers.

I was nine and Bobby Moore was a golden god. It was obviously a fit-up. As it was, Moore played a blinder in the next match against the mighty Brazil. I was an altar boy at this point, dragooned in what was a kind of national service for pre-teen Catholic lads (or a kind of papal roadie if you like). On the fateful Sunday of the game, Father Toibin came 'backstage' as it were, into the vestry where we where polishing the chalices, checking the incense and donning our daft costumes. He beckoned us to him – don't worry, it's not that kind of vestry anecdote – and said,

'Don't hang about tonight, lads. No undue reverence. We need to get this finished in under half an hour then everyone can get home for the match.' And thus was celebrated the fastest 6.30 mass in the history of the Catholic Church; communion wafers were tossed Frisbee style into waiting mouths as we passed by at a brisk trot, sacred words were gabbled at racing commentator pace, incense was flung about with gusto till the air was blue and thick. Coughing and dabbing at their eyes like anti-war protesters in a CS gas haze, the parishioners of St Jude's emerged onto the street stunned. But they were all safely home, feet up, Double Diamond to hand in time for kick-off.

It seems hard to credit when you look now at their comb-overs, their goofy, toothy expressions, their gauche public demeanour and Man at C&A leisurewear but the England World Cup Squad of 1970 were not just football icons. They were pop stars. Their uncomplicated ditty 'Back Home', more redolent of a German bierhaus than the groovy UK pop chart, was nevertheless Number 1 during May when hopes were high and the jewellers of Bogotá slept easy.

Number 1. Top of the Pops. I had started to realise what this meant, started to become aware of the primacy, the semi-sacred status of the singles chart. It would be a year or two yet before I was fully conversant with its catechisms and writ. But here's the beginning of the indoctrination into what would become my church. It spelt the end of my days on the altar. A man, OK, a boy, cannot serve two gods. Mine were in direct competition, since both expected me to give them their undivided attention at teatime on Sundays. Something had to give, and it was the cassock. From now on, the Top Twenty chart rundown on Radio 1 would be my one true faith, and Alan Freeman would be my shepherd. Amen. Not 'arf.

In case you don't know how the actual football panned out; well, a dodgy burrito laid low the exemplary custodian Gordon

Banks and the Germans knocked three past us. Back home they indeed came, to find 'Yellow River' by Christie had knocked them from the Number 1 slot. They were doubtless as sick as parrots.

So that was the bummer of my summer. While I was learning fast about pop music, able to whistle the odd Mungo Jerry number, vaguely aware that Jimmy Savile was frighteningly strange, I was still only nine. I wasn't to know that, for rock's cognoscenti, the year continued to bring forth bleak reminders that, as Lennon sung that year, 'the dream is over'.

In September, Jimi Hendrix died, choking on his own vomit – where was that conscientious caretaker when you needed him? – and the next month, also abed, Janis Joplin followed him into the afterlife. News of these tragedies didn't reach St Jude's Primary School or, if they did, they didn't have the same currency as the whisper that Paul was dead or that Mr Charnock and Mrs Lavender had been seen snogging in his car after late rugby practice.

While I was helping that very same hot-blooded Mr Charnock fill in Class Five's World Cup Wall Chart – first goal of the tournament scored by Ladislav Petras, Czechoslovakia v. Brazil, it's all still there – Britain was having its very own mini Altamont. No one got killed at the second Isle of Wight pop festival of July 1970. But people got really very, very annoyed, and some fences were quite badly damaged. Lured perhaps by the Isle of Wight's global reputation as a powder keg of political unrest, a loose amalgam of politicised hippies, anarchists, acid-heads and French and German student revolutionaries tried to commandeer the festival. Their self-styled leader stormed the stage and gave an impassioned address calling for the fences to be cast down and for the weekend to become a spontaneous free gathering and rebel freak out rather than a capitalist entertainment. The audience, largely happy-go-lucky garage hands from the shires of England who'd paid 15 bob for a weekend's camping,

3 Electric Warrior

It's S. For Six. One, Two, Three, Four, Five, Six. Give yourself a pat on the back if you worked that out. You could have gone to grammar school, you know.

The eleven-plus hung over our youthful, tousled heads for much of our school lives in the same way that the spectre of nuclear destruction hung over the world during the Cold War. At the age of ten, I'd have welcomed the friendly bombs if it had meant that the eleven-plus, or 'scholarship' as some called it, could have been postponed.

It was essentially an IQ test and, like all IQ tests, it proved nothing except that you were good at IQ tests. The man who pioneered its use as tool for educational grading, Cyril Burt, was later found to have cheated with most of his research. Thanks to him, generations of British kids were rubber-stamped at 11, allocated grammar school places or branded subnormal for life on their ability to do spot-the-difference tests. Nice one, Cyril.

It didn't bother me back in Miss Hart's class though. I just wanted to spot those differences, complete those numerical sequences and see how quickly A could fill that bath. All through my youth those wastrels A, B and C, fellows with way too much time on their hands evidently, were challenging each other to pointless races, usually featuring bizarre and plainly unfair handicaps. C would have to run blindfold or with his legs tied together. In the much-loved bath-filling contest, B's bath would leak at the rate of one pint every two minutes. They accepted these difficulties stoically though, just as I accepted my fate, which was to have to calculate the winners and losers.

If you passed your eleven-plus you went to Wigan Grammar School or St John Rigby. If you failed you went to St Thomas More Secondary Modern, or Tommy More as it was known to all. This, I imagine, is the only time the great English martyr was ever referred to as Tommy.

All of this mattered a great deal back then. Pauline Johnson's dad told her that if she passed, she could have a bike. Steven Hickey's dad told him that if he failed, he'd get a good hiding. Such threats and inducements were commonplace. My mum and dad weren't so primitive but I could still feel the burden of expectation, heavy as a wet donkey jacket.

In the end I passed. Laurie Lee talks of leaving village school 'with nothing in my head more burdensome than a few mnemonics, a jumbled list of wars and a dreamy image of the world's geography'. I was marginally better equipped than this. I left junior school with the self-same mnemonics I imagine, some Lakeland pencils, an Oxford Instruments tin containing the arcane tools of geometry, a posh Parker fountain pen given to me as an exam-passing present which, needless to say, I lost almost immediately.

And I almost forgot – a stupid uniform. They say the intention of school uniform was to act as social leveller; well-meaning educationalists fancying that, left to their own sartorial devices, the middle-class child would come to school in spats swinging a silver-tipped cane while us council estate oiks would wear a barrel supported by braces as the bankrupts in the *Beano* always did. In one sense though, the John Rigby School uniform, a

Fauvist riot of maroon and silver, did act as a leveller. Rich and poor, we all looked shit. Also included was a vermilion felt cap intended, presumably, to alert local troglodytes to the presence of a grammar school ponce in the vicinity. After a few bruising encounters, everyone's cap went in the canal.

But I can hear music. The month I started St John Rigby Grammar School, Gathurst Road, Orrell, 'Coz I Luv You' by Slade was Number 1. Right behind it at Number 2 was 'Jeepster' by T. Rex. The symbolism is just perfect. For in that heady, anxious, hormonally raging first year at grammar school, Slade and T. Rex stood like giants, eyeball to eyeball, locked in eternal conflict like Thor and Loki, Thatcher and Scargill, *Blue Peter* and *Magpie*.

In my school you were Slade or T. Rex. This, in fact, was the faultline that ran though the town's youth. Copies of *Slade Alive* or *Electric Warrior* were shibboleths, badges of allegiance.[1] I was T. Rex and the reasons for this were partly historical, partly cultural and partly musical. The first grammar school friend with whom I shared any musical enthusiasms was Peter Conlon. He lived near the park, so his house was a convenient spot to 'warm down' after a thirty-a-side kickabout, relax with a can of Top Deck shandy and listen to records. Conlon – he was always known by his surname, boys are like that – had an enviable bit of kit; a Sony cassette recorder with built-in radio! (Those hover jet packs were surely just around the corner!) Via this technological marvel, he recorded the chart rundown on a Dixons C90 every Sunday and also had a small but first-rate collection of T. Rex albums on, get this, Dolby stereo pre-recorded cassettes. It was

---

1 Years later I was having a conversation with Matthew Priest, drummer in the Midlands band Dodgy. Finding out that I lived in the suburb he'd grown up in, he demanded, 'So, what are you, a Quinton Mod or a Brandhall Boot?' He was joking. But I knew what he meant. The instinctive desire to find out whose side you were on was still lurking in the psychological make-up. I'm a Quinton Mod by the way.

through him that I was educated in and ultimately converted to the T. Rex camp.

All over Britain, in bedsits, crashpads, squats and university common rooms, hippies were bemoaning the fact that eleven-year-olds like me were becoming the new T. Rex constituency. Marc Bolan, the former Marc Feld, ex-catalogue model, former Mod, child actor and soi-disant poet, had been making records since 1965. In 1967, he'd joined the infamous anarcho-hippie collective John's Children and, upon leaving them, created Tyrannosaurus Rex and made a succession of albums of delicate acoustic Tolkienish folk rock called things like *My People Were Fair and Had Sky in Their Hair but Now They're Content to Wear Stars on Their Brows*; *Prophets, Seers and Sages, the Angels of the Ages*; *Unicorn*; and *Beard of Stars*. In this he was abetted by a percussionist called, appropriately, Steve Peregrine Took and later with Mickey Finn. These records, full of elvish chicks, royal crocodiles and people called Aznageel the Mage, attracted a small but devoted following of gentle 'heads', including John Peel who often contributed sweet, fey poems to their albums.

In October 1970, though, he discovered electricity. Not literally; that was Edison of course. But his next single, 'Ride A White Swan', while keeping all the gubbins about Beltane fires, tattered gowns and spells, was driven by a fat, fuzzed-up Les Paul riff. People went mental, 'Ride A White Swan' went to Number 2, and T. Rextasy began.

Peter Conlon had two albums that we played over and over again, till the cassettes grew encrusted with oxide, till Bolan sounded like he was singing underwater. These were *Electric Warrior*, their transition album, and *The Slider*. In retrospect, it's not hard to see why pubescent boys would go nuts for them. Just like Lara Croft, anime and fantasy fiction, they combined two keen interests of the young adolescent male: preposterous all action hero fantasy and smut. The recipe was irresistible.

Electric Warrior is the better record; 'Jeepster', 'Get It On', 'Life's A Gas', the ludicrous, wonderful 'Cosmic Dancer' with its 'what's it like to be a loon / I liken it to a balloon' refrain. And it had a great title – Electric Warrior – essentially meaningless but hinting at something profound. I had no idea what a slider was, unless it was that ruler thing you worked out square roots on. But I fancied it was something saucy. That's because sex, and in particular baffling, quite scary-sounding sex, covered every inch of *The Slider* as lubriciously as baby oil. Rudest, most confusing of all was 'Baby Strange' in which Bolan groaned of 'wanting to ball ya' and stated 'in waves of passion / my whip is lashing'. He sounded like he had toothache as well. It was all a bit worrying for those of us poised on the edge of the great adventure of adulthood.

Some of the lads at school looked like they'd got there ahead of us. Alan 'Foz' Foster was six feet tall and built like Bjorn Borg, Dylan Sharrock had a full set of mutton chop whiskers at twelve. Why? Why on earth would a schoolboy want to affect full Rhodes Boyson mutton chop whiskers? Because so did Noddy Holder.

Noddy Holder was not, as I originally thought on hearing the phrase, some kind of bizarre Enid Blyton-related implement, but a jolly, worryingly raucous individual from Walsall. His trousers were generally too short, the better to display his 12-hole oxblood docs, the footwear of choice for the man about town with a great many heads to kick in. He had a penchant for long multicoloured patchwork jackets of the sort favoured by Dr Who and Jesus' stepdad Joseph, although there the similarities with leading religious figures ended. Like Gary Glitter he looked permanently, antagonisingly startled and he had adopted the aforementioned riotously verdant 'sidies' last seen on Jimmy 'Wacko' Edwards.

Best of all though was his hat. He nearly always sported a top hat with small circular mirrors attached. It was the kind of thing desperate mums make for their offspring just before fancy-dress parties when they have no clear idea what to send them as.[2]

Amazingly, though Noddy Holder was not the most ridiculously dressed person in Slade. That honour has to go to Dave Hill. Dave was the group's second guitarist and had a guitar that bore the legend Superyob. He usually wore a jumpsuit made of the foil that you baste turkeys in and platforms of oil-rig-derrick height. All of this though paled in comparison with his coiffure, a sort of demented tonsure with a great scooping fringe. He looked like a glam rock version of a medieval monk.

Noddy's co-writer in Slade was Jimmy Lea[3] with the line-up being completed by the brooding, taciturn drummer Don Powell. Not much to say here other than, at the height of their fame, Powell was injured in a car crash and afterward suffered bouts of short-term memory loss. I don't intend to make light of this but even then I used to wonder what it must have felt like to 'come to' in the middle of a set and realise, 'Well, I'm obviously a drummer of some sort. Wait a minute, isn't that Noddy Hol— bloody hell, I'm in Slade!'

Slade were not popular with teachers or parents. There was the outlandish appearance for one; they had only recently transmogrified from the skinhead band Ambrose Slade and still bore many of the bootboy trappings. Then there was the spelling. Slade's gimmick – sorry, among Slade's armoury of gimmicks – was deliberate, contrivedly moronic misspellings in their song titles: 'Coz I Luv You', 'Gudbuy T'Jane', 'Cum On Feel The Noize',

---

2 When I got to know Noddy in the Nineties, he told me that the hat is still on a shelf in his garage between the half-empty tin of creosote and the Rawlplugs. He is, I should add, one of the most splendid fellows I have ever met in the music business.

3 Now, amazingly, a psychotherapist. In 1973 the thought of being psychoanalysed by a member of Slade would have been hilarious and terrifying, rather like Liam Gallagher being the Chancellor of the Exchequer.

etc. Nearly every day a headmaster would complain about the damage being done to the English language and the general literacy of Britain's youth. We, the kids, cuddent get enuf of it.

Generally when Slade weren't Number 1, T. Rex were. Slade fans thought T. Rexers were 'puffs'. This led to the odd bout of fisticuffs around my school. Rogue splinter groups would also sometimes emerge. David 'Sully' Sullivan allied himself with leathery Leicester Fifties revivalists Showaddywaddy. He wore half-mast trousers, pink socks and would nut you if you dissed 'A Little Bit Of Soap' within earshot.

Who else was in the frame? Well, there was Mud. Mud wore turquoise drape jackets and played songs of primeval simplicity – the work of glam's uber-writers Chinn and Chapman – with unfathomable lyrics. What were Tiger Feet? What Mite Dyna do exactly? Why did the Cat Creep In … and then creep out again? These were interspersed with rock 'n' roll revival numbers sung by leader Les Gray in a cod Elvis delivery. The rest of the band comprised drummer Dave Mount, bassist Ray Styles and guitarist Rob Davis[4] who wore flouncy bell-bottomed chiffon ensembles and gigantic earrings and whose oddly feminine air was much at odds with Styles and Gray's burly blokishness. They were even named after Seventies footballers.

The Rob Davis role in The Sweet, another Chinn and Chapman act, was played by Steve Priest. While all around him, the other members of The Sweet, tyre-fitters to a man, looked fantastically uncomfortable in their cerise lurex catsuits, Priest seemed to the manor born. Usually wearing some camp, vaguely militaristic garb, and caked in eyeliner, he is best remembered for being the man who lisped 'we just haven't got a clue what to do' to camera during 'Blockbuster'. Steve reappears in our narrative a little later in conjunction with the problems of posting a live panther.

---

4 Now a top dance pop producer, the man behind pert Kylie Minogue's recent hits.

There was the Glitter Band and their leader Gary, over whom we shall draw a veil, except to say that 'Rock And Roll Parts One and Two' (on the silver Bell label) is still a minor masterpiece of glam rock – menacing, primitive, immense. There was The Rubettes whose thing was scrotum-tightening falsetto and red berets. There was Alvin Stardust, a man who you could well believe had enjoyed a previous career as a rock 'n' roller called Shane Fenton. I could have believed that he'd enjoyed a previous career as someone who sent children up chimneys, such was his air of great antiquity and malevolence. He sneered at the camera from beneath a towering, raven-black quiff and beckoned with the crooked finger of a gloved hand to the terrified listener. My cousin Christopher who'd lost an arm as a child wore just that sort of glove to cover his prosthetic limb, adding for me a certain frisson to Stardust's already sinister ambience. His big hit – Number 2 in March 1973 – was 'My Coo-Ca-Choo'. The line about laying down and grooving on the mat is surely still the creepiest attempt at a musical chat-up line ever.

Similarly leather clad but more interesting and palatable to me was Suzi Quatro, a pint-sized rocker from the US who sang a range of exciting, totally incomprehensible Chinn and Chapman numbers called things like 'Can The Can', '48 Crash' and 'Devilgate Drive'. There was something kinda cute and sexy about a girl in leathers who played an electric guitar, certainly more so than a guy who looked like Elvis's funny uncle, probably had a false arm and sang about 'grooving on the mat'.

If we don't count Kelly Carter, Mary O'Riordan and the other girls in my class, or the Yugoslavian girl I had once seen in a BBC documentary about 'people from other lands', or Venus off 'Fireball XL-5', which I was briefly convinced took off from behind the cooling towers over by Scotmans Flash Lake, then Suzi Quatro may have been my first crush.

I don't really remember puberty. It moved in slowly across my adolescence like a weather system bringing with it sudden storms, glowering depressions and the occasional brilliantly sunny day. I began to experience profound feelings of confusion and a kind of discomfort while watching the blonde singer from Abba in her blue satin jumpsuit. Jenny Agutter's obligatory nude scenes in all films – she even gets her knickers off in *The Railway Children* – were similarly a source turmoil.

But there were real girls too. In American movies, kids 'dated'. This seem to involve borrowing their dad's Ford Pontiac – in America people learned to drive in junior school – and going to the drive-in. The film on the giant screen would usually concern a giant newt running amok in Des Moines but this wouldn't concern the dating couple who would spend the time 'necking' or 'petting'. I had no idea what necking was, but petting I knew something of. Along with running, diving and bombing, it was one of the forbidden activities at the swimming baths and it was illustrated poolside with a cartoon of a shifty, acned youth bearing down lasciviously on his buxom girlfriend.

We, though, called it snogging – along with some more colourful, less genteel expressions. These furtive encounters took place not at the drive-in – nothing was drive-thru then except the council tip and car washes – but usually round at some complete stranger's house while babysitting. Babysitting was one of the preferred leisure activities of all the girls I knew. Some, I'm sure, were committed and responsible in their approach, seeing each assignment as essential training before they broke into the high-pressure world of professional child-minding. Most though saw it as an excuse to drink someone else's advocaat, play someone else's David Essex records, have boys round and earn about three pounds fifty. You, the ardent young suitor, hung around somewhere within signalling distance of the house, watching as the owners set out for the Labour club, cinema or disco. After a while – just about long enough to read a toddler two pages of a Mr Men book and tuck them up with a glass of Ribena – the babysitter would signal you (and sometimes a whole throng of your pals) into the house for illicit fun. Illicit fun with one eye on the clock of course as you would have to be a dot on the horizon before the householders returned.

On one particular warm summer night I ended up at a loose end. No babies to be sat evidently and I'd somehow managed to lose my mates. I had made a circuit of all our usual meeting places – the swings in Newtown Park, the toilets at the corner of Little Lane, the Ben Jonson pub – and drawn a blank. It was only half seven. I set off for home, resigned to an evening of *Mind Your Language* and a cheese bap.

I walked back through the grim concrete of the estate, from Baucher Road then across to Tyrer Avenue and up towards Fisher Close. On the other side of the estate, the first to be built, they had named the streets and tower blocks after poets; I had friends in Eliot Drive, Keats Avenue and the high-rise flats Dryden, Masefield and Byron House. By the time they built my patch, their golden Sixties optimism and lyricism had evaporated. My world rang with the names of local councillors past and present. Baucher, Tyrer, Fisher.

That night though, even Tyrer Avenue looked magical. Low sun over the high-rises and, as I turned into Fisher Close, there, sitting on the step of her house, having a crafty Number 6, was Angela Thomas.

You have to know what a stroke of luck this was. Angela Thomas was widely regarded as the cutest girl on the estate – small, dark and flighty in a good way. She also had a broken leg, though this state was temporary while the others were more permanent.

'Hey, Stuart, hey…' Springing to attention rather more rapidly than a cooler young man might have done, I crossed the street to her door. She was bored, she explained, in a sulky way that was insanely attractive. 'Have to have this on for six weeks,' she said, indicating the plaster that encased most of her lower leg. 'Bastard,'

I said charmingly and examined the leg and its plaster with a diligence not entirely medical in nature.

'Why don't you come in? I've got some cigs and a bottle of Cinzano. My dad's gone down the club. He won't be back till half eleven.' Mention of a night with Angela Thomas and a bottle of cheap vermouth was compelling, but the thought of her dad was not. He was a fabled creature – Celtic, short-tempered and fiercely protective of his daughter. He had once thrown Colin Chambers from an upstairs window when he had caught him with Angela in her bedroom doing nothing more shocking than revising for a test on world capitals. I mulled it over.

'Great,' I said, and helped her to her feet. 'Let's put that bottle on ice and get to know each other a little better.' I didn't say this last bit actually. I was too busy trying to breathe normally.

I had in the past nursed the thought that Angela and I might share a certain rapport but then quickly put this down to wishful thinking. But it turned out to be true. The evening passed by blissfully in a haze of Cinzano and *Aladdin Sane*. More than that I will not say. Ten o'clock found us draped across the settee, watching Tommy Cooper with the sound off. Because of this I could hear quite clearly the front door open and a rich tenor singing the 'Rose Of Tralee'.

Even before Angela had stammered, 'Jesus, it's my dad' I was on my feet, spruced up and headed for the door. He came through it just about the same time I got there.

'A-ha, and who's this fine fellow?'

'This is Stuart, he lives round the corner. We were just...'

'I'll bet you were. Well, Stuart, tell me one thing, and tell me honestly.'

Time slowed down so you could hear the cavernous gaps between ticks from the mantelpiece clock.

'Do you play cards?'

'Not really,' I said truthfully.

'Excellent.'

We sat at the kitchen table, the three of us, drank whisky from mugs and played black jack, rummy, poker, possibly even canasta and happy families. I was hopeless and my incompetence was a source of genuine mirth to Mr Thomas as he relieved me of every penny I had on me.

Luckily I didn't have far to walk home. He was still chuckling in the background as Anne pushed me out the door, kissed me and said, 'I've never seen him like this before.'

Maybe it was a rare conjunction of the planets, maybe it was the Cinzano but it was a never to be repeated night. Angela's plaster came off and we drifted apart. Her dad went back to throwing people out of windows. I went back, I imagine, to Suzi Quatro.

I borrowed Mickey Worrall's cassette of her first album, having by now acquired my very own combined radio compact cassette for my twelfth birthday, and would admire her alluring picture on the cover while trying to ignore her band who, as was customary, all looked like binmen. Then I would try and work out just what might constitute canning the can, or indeed what a 48 Crash was; Chinn and Chapman's lyrics merely offered that it was akin to a lightning flash or a silk sash bash. I wondered whether I would ever get invited to a silk sash bash, presumably a glitzy trade function for soft-furnishing salesmen.

Suzi's heyday was the summer of '73 when she was in the chart almost continuously with a succession of daft mock-biker anthems; can anyone now remember how 'Daytona Demon' goes? Among pubescent males, the other talking point of the summer was Abba, a group of Swedes whose insanely catchy 'Waterloo' had won the Eurovision Song Contest and whose blonde singer in her blue satin jumpsuit had caused widespread feelings of 'confusion' among twelve-year-old boys.

Glam rock pervaded my first couple of years at grammar school. Major talents like David Bowie went for it, hard rockers like Mott the Hoople and Alice Cooper tried to get into bed with it, Elton John fell for it. Sadly no one has told Elton that it's finished. Like that Japanese soldier who didn't know the Second World War was over, Elton still thinks pink leather suits and feather boas are really cool.

Everyone else moved on at length. The last desperate fling of glam, I guess, was the most successful of the lot – the Bay City Rollers. They had got their name after sticking a pin in a map of the USA and so, theoretically, could have been called the Dinner Station Nevada Rollers.

Their take on glam was very Scottish, very homemade, in that it involved wearing some tartan scarves and trousers that were slightly too short, thus making them look really poor. Girls though fell upon them like they were gods come down from Olympus rather than some daft-looking blokes come down from Airdrie. And who can blame them? After Alvin Stardust, the Rollers were the very stuff of teenage dreams, a summer love sensation in half-mast keks.

It was perhaps the Rollers, a group who polarised male–female opinion like no other before or since (did the Rollers sell one solitary single to a bloke, I wonder?), that began to push me towards stranger, stronger stuff. That and a bloke called Prof and a funny newspaper called *Sounds* that turned your hands and face black.

4 Hocus Pocus

Yodelling has no place in pop music. Frank Ifield was all a terrible mistake on the part of our forefathers. If it has a place at all, it is in the high Alpine pastures, something to amuse the Swiss and relieve the monotony of their bland dairy-heavy diet and half a century without a decent war. And yet 1974 finds me, a moderately bright grammar school boy, modishly long-haired, flared of trouser, listening of my own free will to a man yodelling. A Dutchman yodelling. Yodelling like a goodun, if that's not a contradiction in terms. Not just me either. Great swathes of the record-buying public. How had it come to this?

In my case, a few incidents, small but cumulatively life-changing had happened in quick succession. The first of these had occurred not on the road to Damascus but in a council house in Worsley Mesnes one Thursday evening just after I'd turned twelve. My mum and dad had popped to the Labour club for a pint, leaving me, I'd guess, supposedly swotting up on the decline of the Ottoman Empire or the New Zealand steel industry. Instead, obviously, I was watching the telly. Channel-hopping was very different then and involved lying on one's stomach on a throw rug, head five inches from the TV, so close the static made your hair stick to the screen, and going through the buttons manually. As there were only three channels, this didn't take long. I must have already dipped into and rejected *Love Thy Neighbour* on ITV or a *Panorama* special about the Cod War or *Sportsnight with Coleman* on the BBC when I found it – something of such jaw-dropping weirdness that even at this remove I remember the effect it had on me.

It was a concert of some sort. Five or so blokes were on stage in a TV studio; behind them was a logo of a man made of little lights kicking at a star Norman Hunter style. The blokes didn't look like any pop group as I knew them. They were multiracial, knotted of brow, their garb was distinctive, involving a lot of what I later found out to be cheesecloth and kaftans along with ripped, faded denims. They were about as far removed from Mud as it was possible to be.

They didn't have a singer. But where the singer should have been, there was a strange bloke playing the most mental guitar I had ever seen. It had two necks. That's *two* necks. I was no virtuoso but I knew this was one more than was strictly necessary. It looked more like something you would milk a cow with than a musical instrument. As he played it, its owner – who looked appropriately like a milkman in his white suit and short back and sides – was pulling faces as if he had caught himself in his zip. He looked like those blokes in the Lake District who take their teeth out and pull faces with a bog seat round their neck. He looked nuts, frankly. If my dad had been in the room, he would have had an explanation for the facial contortions. It would have been because of the agonising and distressing music, he'd have reckoned.

Because that music was another thing again. It was the kind of music you might have expected to be made by someone like this on an instrument like that. It was inhumanly fast and had no discernible tune whatsoever. Occasionally the first suggestions of a melody could be heard but they would be immediately extinguished in a typhoon of ensemble hammering and sawing. From time to time, the drummer would go into a paroxysm of thrashing, making a sound like a man trying to beat his way out of a locked wardrobe. Then it would all stop and a violinist – no really – would do something on his own for a few seconds before everyone joined in again at twice the original speed. This went on for about twelve minutes and then it stopped. The chief nutter smiled and put his hands together as if in prayer. Then a bloke with a beard came on and whispered, so quietly you could hardly hear him – come on, mate, speak up – 'fantastic set there from the Mahavishnu Orchestra'. I tried to commit the name to memory immediately, as it was the most exciting thing I had ever seen in my life. It was thrillingly strange and faintly menacing. I had taken my first steps into the impossibly exciting demi-monde of rock. Leo Sayer, Suzi Quatro, Kenny; none of them would never look the same again.

Slightly stunned, I went back to the Ottoman Empire and the many, boring reasons for its decline. I had been given a glimpse of a world just as exotic and strange as the bazaars and minarets of old Constantinople. But it was a fleeting glimpse, like the views you see from airplanes before the clouds close in again. I'd be back though, with a guide and a passport.

When it comes to nicknames, schoolboys are rarely imaginative and never flattering. Alan Foster, I have mentioned, was nicknamed Foz. Similarly, David Yates was known as Yaz. Paul Morrison was Morri, John Howarth Howie, John Hamersley Hammy, David Sullivan Sully. Peter Houghton was known briefly and daringly as Debe, before common sense prevailed and we rechristened him Houghtie. Dylan Sharrock was Shaz. Do you see a pattern emerging? A simple but effective system when flushing each other's heads down the toilet or playing thirty-a-side football in dense fog with a cricket ball.

Our school had several kids of Polish parentage whose dads had come over to work in the Wigan pits at the time of the Nazi occupation (of Poland, I should add, not Wigan). They had fabulously exotic surnames: Cwiakala (pronounced Sweerkala) and Ciaputa (Chipyuta). Such flamboyance clearly could not be tolerated. They became Sweer and Chips. Mark Johnson, who was fat, became Slim; Terry Stokes who was thin was known as Stocky (clever stuff, this last one, a kind of double reference). Paul Manley, a pale, puny kid with National Health specs, was known as Muscles. Chris Brown was known as Rastus for reasons no one could ever explain.

Martin Browne – because he was clever and wore glasses and had an abstracted and academic mien – was Prof. And because he could often be spotted at breaktime reading a newspaper. That's a newspaper. Not one of Richard Allen's lurid Skinhead books or a three-year-old copy of *Mayfair* someone's older brother pinched from the newsagents. No. A newspaper. A weird-looking newspaper, yes – smudgy and usually featuring some wild-eyed 'freak' with an afro on the front, but a newspaper.

It was called *Sounds*. It said so in crazy writing on the front, the font they used for short-lived boutiques in Wigan town centre. I was not so naïve that I hadn't sussed it was a music mag. I was reasonably familiar with the oeuvre. I had read *Jackie* over girls' shoulders, learned about David Cassidy's favourite colour and the kind of girls that Merill Osmond went for (Mormons, I'd imagine). I also had my own copy, purchased for 5p at St Jude's jumble sale, of the very first Radio 1 annual, featuring profiles of John Peel, Kenny Everett, Dave Cash, Keith 'Cardboard Shoes' Skues and, of course, Tony Blackburn.[1]

---

1 The John Peel profile was headlined Candid Peel. In years to come I would spend far too many afternoons thinking up such punning headlines for a living but right now it went completely over my head. I had never heard of candied peel. I would have gone for Taking the Pith anyway.

The Radio I annual also had screeds of those mini-question-naires in which you find out that Lulu needs nine hours' sleep a night and that the singer out of Edison Lighthouse's pet hate is photo sessions. But none of this adequately prepared me for the jaw-dropping experience that awaited within the badly printed, smudgy pages of *Sounds*.

There was scant information about The Rubettes' favourite meals or the pet hates of the Glitter Band. It seemed to be devoted to a version of pop music from a parallel universe, a universe populated with exotic names that were completely unknown to me but here bandied around with an easy, hip familiarity – Clapton, Beefheart, Zappa, Crimson, Gabriel.

Beefheart, on whom there was a substantial piece, turned out to be a Captain. I had scant experience but this Captain seemed unlikely to pass muster on even the most liberal of Dutch army parade grounds. Crimson was a group, apparently. Gabriel was a singer who dressed like a hyacinth. With some relief, I eventually found a piece on Neil Young who I had at least heard of. He'd had a hit some months earlier with 'Heart Of Gold' and they'd shown footage of him on *Top of the Pops*. Once I'd realised that it wasn't a joke, I'd found it compellingly odd; a lank-haired fellow on a stool alternately wheezing into a mouth organ and singing weirdo poetry in the reediest, weediest voice imaginable. There was also in this here *Sounds* thingy an interview with Hawkwind. I fell upon this eagerly as well, knowing Hawkwind from their brief dalliance with chart fame with the insistent rocker 'Silver Machine' and which Peter Conlon's sister Ruth had thought was called 'Sewing Machine'.

I was abruptly arrested when right there in the middle of the second sentence of the interview was the word 'motherfucker'. Even now, it's a word excised for mass consumption from gangsta rap and X-rated movies. Back then, it was possibly the most shocking thing I'd ever seen. I almost dropped the paper and hid.

Surely, the world would fly off its axis, and horses would eat each other in the street.

When I got over the shock, I decided then and there that this was for me. I had 'found my brand'. Here was another world, rich with the heady blend of the anti-establishment craziness of Monty Python, the subcultural cool of rock 'n' roll and a juicy dollop of sex; for, yes, the Hawkwind piece featured prominently their onstage dancer Stacia, a statuesque girl who took with surprising enthusiasm to the unenviable task of dancing naked at various sodden, windswept free festivals in Lincolnshire for the edification of Hell's Angels.

It's too pat, too glib, too neat to say that then and there I decided I wanted to be a music journalist. I think that came a few issues of *Sounds* later, by which time I was dropping the names of Fripp, Sabbath and Joni with the practised ease of a Ladbroke Grove 'head', even if my record collection still consisted chiefly of hours of tapes of *Pick of the Pops* and my bootlegged copies of Conlon's T. Rex albums. Bootlegged I should add not via the Internet or double decks or even something as prosaic as a connecting lead but by the primitive technique of placing my cassette recorder alongside Conlon's and taping via a little plastic microphone (supplied, unlike batteries). Sound quality was awful and you could hear my mum washing up during 'Baby Boomerang' off *The Slider* but it felt at the time like the very frontier of science. All this was about to change though as Prof led me, like a trusty sherpa, up the daunting but exhilarating sheer face of rock.

This new music was called progressive rock. Or underground rock. Or heavy, although that was a specific sub-genre also known as hard rock or metal. Purple, Zep and Sabbath were heavy, ELP, Yes, Genesis and Focus were progressive. The Mahavishnu Orchestra (whose name I mispronounced badly, drawing a derisive snort from Prof) were jazz rock and the head nutter with the double-necked guitar was John McLaughlin who was maybe the best electric guitarist in the world, with the exception of Jan Akkerman.

Prof talked of Jan Akkerman in the kind of tones reserved for a combination of George Best, the Pope, Morecambe and Wise and John Cleese. He was all these things and more. He was the world's leading 'axeman', which was not to be confused with 'mad axeman' or possibly 'forester'. In the arcane parlance of rock, an axe was a guitar. I had no idea why. The whole of the underground scene was a semantic minefield to be negotiated at one's peril for fear of blowing one's cover, revealing that one was not a 'groovy head' or 'prog freak' at all but a thirteen-year-old from Wigan who was actually quite worried about his mocks. Mouth organs were 'harps', ace keyboard players – Wakeman, Emerson, Banks – were 'wizards' or 'merchants'. It always amused me in the Eighties that 'keyboard merchant' Rod Argent actually did become an actual keyboard merchant with a shop on Denmark Street in London where you could buy a nice Yamaha home organ.

LPs were 'albums', groups were 'bands', concerts were 'gigs'. It made your head swim. But it was terribly exciting. Like being inducted into a secret society without all the bothersome trouser-rolling or balaclavas or objectionable political goals. Prof's favourite band was Focus, the band Jan Akkerman was in. These were the progressive records I came to know and love first. Focus had been the resident band in the Dutch production of *Hair* before branching out on their own and enjoying considerable success. Their breakthrough here came with the album *Moving Waves*, a record I quickly became immersed in to a ridiculous extent, utterly submerging myself in it with all the zeal of a new sect member at a mass baptism.

All of one side of the album was taken up with one long piece of music called 'Eruption'. One song. Except, hey, it wasn't a song, it was a track, man. Twenty-odd minutes! Mental! Such lunacy appealed to me conceptually almost as much as it did musically.

I loved the music, though. Well, it had monkish chanting, thunderously loud electric rock, some pretty quasi-classical doodling on the piano and some full-on synthesiser wig-outs. I mean, how could anyone not love it?

Of course, plenty of people didn't love it. Frankly, they hated it then and now. They thought it was overblown, pompous and against the true verities of pop (economy, catchiness, danceability). Most of my classmates thought it was weirdo crap and would forcibly remind me of this at the bus stop with an accompanying ear tweak or Chinese burn. It certainly wasn't 'Get Down And Get With It'. But it felt like enlightenment, initiation into a secret realm beyond the understanding of mere mortals with their oxblood Docs and half-mast trousers. There was a certain snobbery involved, I'll admit that. Already I was acquiring many of the traits we associate with the music journo, I guess. High-mindedness and no sense of rhythm.

But guess what? Unthinkably, the other side of *Moving Waves* was the home of the hits. Smash Hits! Monsters! Chart-bound sounds, as Tony Blackburn would have had it. There was 'Sylvia', a catchy guitar instrumental that I still sometimes strum on the guitar to the mild, largely feigned interest of family and friends. And there was 'Hocus Pocus'. This started like your bog standard hard rocker, you could even imagine The Sweet essaying it in one of their wilder moments, perhaps after a few pints when singing about Little Willie not going home nightly had finally pushed them over the edge.

But then came the yodelling. There was a whole lotta yodelling going on. Plus what could only be described as 'pom pom-ing'. Balding Dutchmen called Thijs yodelling and pom pom-ing is, you'd think, no one's idea of the sexy, windswept, glamorous, irresistible spirit of rock 'n' roll. Certainly not a young lady's idea of it anyway, not when you had David Essex being all impish and gypsy-like or Donny being all puppyish or even Alvin being all leathery and seedy. So we can only imagine that the scores of thousands who bought 'Hocus Pocus' when it was issued as a single in January 1973, who made it a Top Ten monster smash (Emperor Rosko ibid.), the legions of consumers who put these hairy oddballs from the Low Countries on *Top of the Pops*, were all blokes. Men are from Mars, they say, and women are from Venus. Focus were beardy geezers from Holland, and I doubt that David and Donny ever had to make wall space for them.

5 *Brain Salad Surgery*

My new bible was the youngest of the UK's big three weekly music papers, the 'inkies' as they were known in the trade. Even for those of us not in any kind of trade, it was an apt description. The one thing *Sounds*, *NME* and *Melody Maker* had in common was a shared casualness vis-à-vis print quality. All of them appeared to have been printed on Izal toilet paper with a potato and ink pad ensemble with the result that even the most cursory of perusals would have you looking like Al Jolson or one of the day shift at Bickershaw Colliery.[1]

Melody Maker was the daddy of them all, and by the time I started reading the rock press, it was about as cool as the average dad too. It began in 1926 and its first cover blazoned 'THE BANJO IN THE MODERN DANCE ORCHESTRA'. It quickly established itself as the industry bible with a must-read situations-vacant column if

---

1 Bickershaw, a mining village on the outskirts of Wigan, was briefly the epicentre of rock culture when, for one sodden weekend in 1971, it had hosted a free festival where Captain Beefheart and the Grateful Dead had both played along with many other luminaries of the scene. How they must have pined for sun-drenched California as they watched the rain pour down the windows of their luxury Dormobiles. I was far too young to go to Bickershaw though I did hang around the fence one afternoon looking at girls in Afghan coats walking gingerly through the quagmire.

you were a session man looking for work – perhaps a banjo player looking to break into those modern dance orchestras. After thirty years of unchallenged dominance, though, and having sewn up the hipster trad jazz end of the market, a promoter named Maurice Kinn took over the running of a new and already ailing competitor, the *Musical and Accordion Express*. Perhaps wisely, Kinn cut back heavily on the accordion bias of the coverage and went for the pop market instead. The *NME* or *New Musical Express* took off and fought a war for cultural superiority with *Melody Maker* all though the Fifties and Sixties. Then, the *NME* appropriated the best of the late Sixties underground press writers, 'scribes' like Charles Shaar Murray and Nick Kent who'd come to prominence via the anarchic pages of *IT* and *Oz*.

But then in 1970, a group of disenchanted *Melody Maker* journalists and editors broke away to form *Sounds*, billing it as 'a left-wing *Melody Maker*'. What this slick and empty slogan actually translated into was a more street version of the venerable *Maker* with more emphasis on pictures, politics and progressive rock and hardly anything about banjos, a much more enticing proposition for the teen hipster. On any given week, *Melody Maker* would picture a tiny cover shot of a bearded fellow in an Aran sweater or a lead story about Lionel Hampton performing at Ronnie Scott's, while *Sounds* would have a full cover action shot of Keith Emerson setting fire to a roadie. It really was no contest.

Keith Emerson was the keyboard player in a trio called Emerson, Lake and Palmer. Though they sounded like a firm of Shrophire solicitors but were in fact the undisputed titans of progressive rock. 'You're so prog, it's unbelievable', we might have chanted, à la North Bank or Stretford End, if rock bands had had football-style fans. E, L and P had all served time in various rock, soul and jazz bands but had now come together to make the ultimate progressive rock racket accompanied by the ultimate in prog rock theatricality. Emerson would sometimes levitate, turn upside down suspended in mid-air and rotate perpendicularly while still playing some bamboozlingly complicated solo. Even on a quiet night, perhaps when he had fluey symptoms and really fancied getting tucked up with a Lemsip and *Parkinson* back at the hotel, he would still attack and run the keyboard through with giant carving knives.[2] P stood for Palmer, Carl, the drummer who would batter the daylights out of a kit the dimensions and complexity of Jodrell Bank. Then he would pull on a massive rope that hung behind him, thus effecting strikeage on a gong that could be heard on Neptune. L was Greg Lake, the guitarist and bassist who contented himself with always playing on a Persian rug the size of Lincolnshire which was rumoured to cost £2,000 – then roughly my dad's yearly income. Come to think of it, if it was a carpet it must have been 2,000 guineas. Carpets always came in guineas, as did a handful of other items like horse races and buried treasure.

Even at this remove, I could still sing you every track from any of Emerson, Lake and Palmer's first five albums. Sing implies words actually, and many of ELP's most glorious, imperishable moments were wordless. But I can still ner-ner, la-la and generally ba-bum you through every keyboard flourish and drum para-diddle. But I'm not going to. For one thing, you never know, there might be ladies present. I have never met a girl who liked Emerson, Lake and Palmer. Did I say that the Bay City Rollers polarised male/female opinion like no other group before or since? Well, I was wrong. I've met a girl who liked Steely Dan and a girl who cried when Steve Hackett left Genesis and I even moved in with a female Rush fan. But has anyone ever mooned over a picture of Greg Lake in their bedroom while listening to *Tarkus*? I really hope so. But I doubt it.

---

2 I now know that they were not in fact carving knives but genuine Nazi daggers supplied by Emerson's one-time roadie, Lemmy.

It wouldn't stand up in a court of law but here's some circum-stantial evidence. At around this time, the school had a field trip to Aviemore, the Scottish skiing resort which some of the more well-heeled kids went on. Somehow, after a couple of halves of après-ski bitter shandy in the teenies disco, Mark Lowton managed to entice a local girl away from The Wombles and 'Crazy Horses' back to his little chalet room. He'd brought with him a half- bottle of Tia Maria from his dad's drinks cabinet and all seemed set for a night to remember. Remember that this is a thir-teen-year-old boy who has had the unbelievable good luck to find himself in a James Bond scenario on a school trip: chalets, booze, ladies, snow fluttering gently against the window.

'How about a little music?' he said, moving towards his portable cassette player.

'Great,' says she, possibly arranging her coltish limbs seduc-tively on the Dralon settee, undoing another button and hoping for a little Chet Baker, Dean Martin, or at least one of The Rubettes' less terrifying outings.

He put on the second side of Emerson, Lake and Palmer's *Brain Salad Surgery*. Not the first side, not the one with the short-ish songs that he might have got away with. Not the side with 'Still …You Turn Me On'.

Oh no.

No. Side Two. 'Karn Evil 9'. Three Impressions. Twenty-five minutes of frightening, quasi-operatic electronic hokum about the future enslavement of humanity by a race of hyper-intelligent computer-controlled robots. And the world's longest drum solo. By the time Mark Lowton had turned around, toothmug of Tia Maria in hand, she'd gone. Gone in a cloud of Charley by Lentheric, a dot departing towards the snowy horizon in search of a Cherry B with a ski instructor.

Her loss I reckon. Have you heard 'Karn Evil 9'? It's great. Honestly. OK, I could do without the drum solo but you don't get anything like enough terrifying post-apocalypse dystopias set to Bartók-inflected techno-rock on Jo Whiley or *Later with Jools Holland* these days.

The lyrics to 'Karn Evil 9' were written by one Pete Sinfield, itinerant wordsmith and one of the true characters of progressive rock. Sinfield, remarkably, later went on to write 'The Land Of Make Believe' by Bucks Fizz and most of Five Star's hits. In 1973, though, he was to all intents and purposes the fourth member of ELP, contributing doomy, silly, grandiloquent lyrics that we thought the last word in poetic insight. Daft though I now realise many of his original lyrics were.

The lyrics of fellow prog giants Yes were the work of their diminutive Napoleonic leader Jon Anderson. Anderson was an ex-milkman from Accrington, but you would not have guessed this from his adopted persona within the band: guru, sage, avatar, short-arse Dalai Lama with flat vowels. Anderson's lyrics baffled everyone, including the other members of Yes. Drop into his canon anywhere at random and you will find gobbledygook that nonetheless has the ring of high cosmic truth.

Yes's keyboard 'merchant' was Rick Wakeman. Nowadays Rick's every inch the down-to-earth, born-again Christian, reformed-alcoholic rock veteran. Even then, he stood out among his colleagues with his predilection for Watney's Red Barrel and birianies. But this aside, he too was very much a creature of the times. He wore his hair long and flaxen and his capes long and sort of silvery. When not singing with Yes, he had a sideline going in high-concept solo albums based around, to take them in order, *The Six Wives of Henry VIII*, *Journey to the Centre of the Earth* and *King Arthur and the Knights of the Round Table*. I loved these records dearly, fool that I was, but even then I knew that the lyrics were pants.

My copy of *Brain Salad Surgery*, complete with H.R. Geiger's fabulous foldout sleeve, cost £1.49 on cassette from Whelan's supermarket in Wigan. Whelan's staple fare was savoy cabbages, Angel Delight, Marmite and the like. However, they did have a tiny revolving cassette rack at the rear of the store where you could sometimes find prog rock bargains in among *The Very Best of Roger Whittaker* and *The Golden Hour of Chicory Tip*. It was one of the few places in town you could buy rock records. I knew every one of these few vendors by heart, a Saturday afternoon itinerary usually window-shopped but sometimes browsed excitedly with pocket money burning a hole in the pocket of your Wranglers.

There was Smiths across the market. Not WH Smiths, just a local family called Smiths. It was here that I bought *Moving Waves* and *The Best of Tyrannosaurus Rex*, thinking it was *The Best of T. Rex* and thus became happily acquainted with Bolan's pre-fame folky whimsy which I still love. Unlike vinyl albums, the rock cassettes shifted so slowly that some became much loved friends, monuments like the town hall clock that you were always reassured to see after time spent away. I swear that Smiths copy of Neil Young's *Time Fades Away* and *The Kinks Kontroversy* gathered dust there behind the propelling pencils and refill pads for three years.

Tucked away in the market hall itself, with its sawdust floor and ever-present stench of raw meat and offal, was Roy Hurst's records. Here I bought *Sgt Pepper* and Pink Floyd's *Obscured by Clouds*. They too had their permanent fixtures, notably a copy of that Barclay James Harvest album with the baby in a plant pot which was probably still there when they knocked the old market hall down in the mid-Eighties. I liked the shop for two reasons: for the silver-haired proprietor Roy who would chortle dismissively at your purchases while recommending an LP of military marches or cha-chas and for the fact that it was here that John Howarth pointed at a copy of The Who's live masterpiece *Live at Leeds* and announced, 'Do they really live at Leeds? I thought they were from London.'

Best, or worst, of all was Rumbelows on Standishgate.

Primarily the store sold washing machines and those huge teak-effect TVs. Downstairs, though, in a dim, moody cellar where you expected to see Tommy Steele blowing the froth off a cappuccino, was the 'record bar'. Tiny and badly lit, with walls festooned with sleeves and posters, it was marginally trendier than anything found in any of its competitors. But only marginally. White goods floated Mr Rumbelow's boat. His subterranean record outlet was a grudging concession to the town's hepcats and longhairs, while upstairs there was brisk, sensible trade in Indesit spindryers and Moulinex food processors.

Nonetheless I did get some bargains below ground here; *Tubular Bells* for £1.50 minus inlay card on the old white Virgin label. I'd marvelled at a film on the *Whistle Test* in which men had skied downhill to the strains of this haunting, ethereal music. Out of loyalty to Focus, I bought a solo album by their guitarist Jan Akkerman, a jazz-rock freak-out called *Profile* which is nearly as distressing and unlistenable to today as it was then. Sometimes after school, I'd go in and stare at the cover of Lou Reed's *Rock and Roll Animal* just to scare myself.

There were two young assistants who alternated shifts. If you were lucky, you got the bloke, a fey soul in a greatcoat and cloud of pachouli oil who would generally smile approvingly at your purchases. If you were unlucky, you got the girl. Sharp-featured, long, lank black hair, a kind of cross between Morticia Adams and a young Edwina Currie, her air of contemptuous disdain never eased or warmed for a second. I bet she really, really liked Lou Reed's *Rock and Roll Animal*. She was probably only twenty but when you're fourteen, this is a great age conferring a position of sere authority and power. She was also well known for her waspish wit. My friend Nigel – another prog ally – once went in hoping to find an album by the cult Swedish keyboardist Bo Hansson.

'Have you got Bo Hansson's *Magician's Hat*?' he asked, innocently.

'No,' she sneered, adjusting a display of Emitex record cleaner pads, 'did he leave it here?'

That was the sort of thing girls said about progressive rock. Remarks like this hit home woundingly because they implied, in a sensible, deflating, acerbic, girlish kind of way, that the whole thing was monumental guff. They knew that, for all our talk of axes and concept pieces, the whole kit and caboodle was a bit, well, silly, like a great many other male hobbies, such as vintage traction engines or civil war re-enactments. I can even imagine Mrs Emerson or Lake or Wakeman or perhaps Madame Akkerman – in her wooden clogs rustling up a pancake with melted gouda – welcoming hubby home.

'Good day at work, dear?'

'Not bad, we began work on a rock opera questioning the notion of human progress if, as I very much fear, it results in a future dictatorship of super-intelligent robot technocrats.'

'That's nice, dear,' says the wife absent-mindedly. 'Now, any chance of getting those shelves put up this weekend?'

By the way, if you think that such subject matter is far-fetched, I swear that around this time I saw a band play at Bolton Tech, then very much our Fillmore East or Roundhouse, who concluded their set of epic noodlings by saying, 'We'd like to finish with a song which is a sort of potted history of the earth from its creation through the various evolutionary stages of man to the present day … and with a few thoughts towards the future. Cheers.'

Girls saw through this sort of stuff much quicker than we did. And what girls thought was becoming increasingly important in my young life. Things were stirring deep within, itches that yodelling Dutchmen and Barclay James Harvest just could not scratch. And right on cue, into my life came the perfect soundtrack; a music that spoke not of robots, trolls, Guinevere and giant hogweed, but of girls, dancing, money, work and the complex, gritty, sexy matrix that bound them all.

Soul music the sound of the streets, the sound of youth, the sound of passion, freedom, the night. To be fully attuned to the pulse of soul music in the 1970s, to feel its beating rhythm and heartbeat in the sounds of the metropolis around you, in the traffic, in the bars, the schools, the clubs, the songs of shop girls and factory boys at downtown bus stops, you had to be living in one of only a handful of places; Memphis, Detroit, Chicago, New York ... or Wigan.

This, you have to admit, was a real stroke of luck.

6 Out on the Floor

I spent the best part of 1974 dancing. And it was the best part too, give or take the odd dicey moment. In this I wasn't alone of course. A lot of people danced away the dreary, strike-bound, economically blighted, candlelit 1970s. They danced with tears in their eyes, danced in the city, danced with the captain, danced away. They danced, danced, danced (Yowsah, Yowsah, Yowsah!). Maybe they haven't stopped dancing yet.

I was different, though. I had, in effect, joined a religious cult devoted to dancing. I was a Moonie of the dance floor. I danced when I should have studied, danced when I should have slept. Dancing brought me some of the best fun I have ever had and it nearly got me killed on several occasions.

The legacy of my dancing days is still with me. Call me simple, call me shallow or snobbish, but I still don't trust men who don't dance. There are no excuses. As a heterosexual white man, every last smug double helical strand of my DNA has always conspired to keep me off the dance floor. But if we let ourselves be prisoners of nature, then we'd still be gnawing on bones and dressing in pelts. I'm no terpsichorean elitist, mark you. I don't think people should have the flying feet of Fred Astaire or Gene Kelly. Get on that floor, cut a rug, shake a leg …

literally if that's all you can manage. But shame on you, if you can't dance too, as Shirley and Company had it.

Or rather, if you won't dance too. What I mean is I don't trust people who look down on dancing as if it's a lower form of musical appreciation. Dancing, said Thomas Beecham, is the vertical expression of a horizontal desire, which is pretty good you have to admit. Looking back at my own time on the floor, a lot of it was sublimated sex, yes. But there's more to it than that. As anyone who's ever danced alone in an upstairs room, or found themselves shuffling in their seat at a traffic light or tapping a foot to a particular sprightly hymn at a funeral, will attest, music flicks switches all over the central nervous system not just in the groin or brain.

Actually, pace Gonzalez, I have pretty much stopped dancing. I'll still throw a shape or two at a wedding, or on the rare occasions I end up in a nightclub, even in someone's front room if we've reached the stage of the evening where the Brazilian liqueurs are being dug out from the cupboard under the sink. But the very particular dancing of my youth is behind me. Occasionally, when they learn just what kind of kid I was, someone will say, 'Go on, do a bit of the dancing.' And very occasionally, when in my cups, I'll try the kind of move that made me feared and respected across most of South Lancashire's dance floors. Sadly, these days, this normally ends with furniture being damaged, shattered glass, a displaced vertebrae and me being helped to my feet by solicitous friends while someone goes to get a cold compress.

Because I was a Northern Soul boy.

'Were you one of Wigan's chosen few?' as the chortling enquiry I've heard a million times has it.

Well, yes, I like to think that I was actually.

At this point, I could launch into a detailed, thematic analysis of what actually constitutes Northern Soul. But you wouldn't thank me for it. In fact, you'd be looking for a fork to jab into your eye after a couple of paragraphs. There are whole books devoted to just this subject and no one has yet arrived at any comprehensive technical definition. That's not how pop music works. Suffice to say that Northern Soul is generally black American soul music, normally of the vintage 1964–70, characterised by the Tamla Motown sound but often on much more obscure imprints, generally with a fast, up tempo beat perfect for flashy, stylish, gymnastic dancing.

Lancashire's Mods were the first Northern Soul boys, saving their weekly wages during the new-found prosperity of the early Sixties to buy import R&B 'sides', Italian fashions, scooters and a bewildering array of amphetamine-based stimulants; 'bennies', 'dexys', 'bombers' and 'blueys'. The Twisted Wheel on Manchester's Whitworth Street was their temple where, zealous police raids allowing, they danced the night away, grinding their teeth all the while, to Donnie Elbert's 'A Little Piece Of Leather', Ramsey Lewis, Bobby Bland and Major Lance. I don't know what happened from there: spores carried on the wind, maybe it got into the water supply, but for as long as I can remember you heard soul music wherever you went in Wigan. Not just Wigan, obviously. I remember the shock of chatting to people who grew up south of the Walsall M6 junction and of realising that not everybody was familiar with Al Wilson's 'The Snake' or The Marvelletes' 'Jimmy Mack', the shock of finding out that not every disco, by law, had to finish with a slow dance and a furtive grope to Jimmy Radcliffe's 'Long After Tonight Is All Over'. How had these people got through their teens?

This will sound fanciful but you'll just have to trust me. Kids in Seville and Cadiz must grow up with flamenco clicking in their ears; teenagers in Ulan Bator must assume that the whole world loves that clanking goat bell and throat singing groove. In Wigan, we were raised on soul. You didn't even realise it was soul. It was just that music, the one you heard in every pub, at every youth club. As we've seen so far, I knew there were other kinds of music available, to paraphrase the mortgage ads. On the radio, there was Showaddywaddy and Leo Sayer. On the telly, there was Marc Bolan and, if you were lucky, the Mahavishnu Orchestra or, if you were unlucky, Dave Lee Travis doing something unfunny dressed as a womble. But you would no more have danced to any of these or put them on at a party than you would have bumped to a Bartók string quartet or sashayed to the Swingle Singers. All social gatherings were soundtracked by Northern Soul. It didn't mean a thing if it didn't have that swing. I was at this stage a lank-haired disciple at the church of the Holy Mellotron of course. But I was about to have a crisis of faith. Unusually for a crisis of faith, it came in the concert room of Wigan Athletic's Supporters Club.

The mid-Seventies were not exactly halcyon days for sport in Wigan. Wigan Rugby League Club had dominated their sport throughout the Sixties but the Seventies saw them losing ground, unbearably, to hated local rivals such as St Helens, Warrington and Leigh. Their position was almost an exact parallel of the one that local football legends Manchester United found themselves in at the same time. Once the undisputed, swaggering colossus of their sport, they were now languishing in the doldrums and, thus humiliated, could only assuage their wounded pride through violence. I had by now acquired from somewhere a clutch of older mates who actually worked for a living, although from what Brownie told me, squinting through the updraught of blue smoke from the Number 6 clamped between his lips at all times, most actual mechanical work down at the garage took second place to the hectic daily round of goose-greasing each other's genitals and putting ball bearings in each other's tea. It was a tough job and at weekends Brownie liked to relax by kicking hard and repeatedly the ribcages and heads of rival rugby teams' supporters. In fairness to Brownie (whose real name was Leonard, not that you would ever risk calling him this obviously) they were every bit as keen to do the same to him.

I preferred football. Wigan Athletic were not actually in the Football League at this point. They played in the Northern Premier League and on an almost weekly basis enjoyed glamour clashes with the lowliest of neighbours across Lancs and Yorkshire. Even these afforded many an opportunity for blood-shed. Midweek clashes with Goole Town, Macclesfield and Barrow were, strangely, not as lucrative as the committee might have hoped, so any given night of the week the Latics Supporters Club was given over to some other activity – slimming club or drum majorettes or bingo. Wednesdays at the Latics though was Northern Soul night.

I knew what Northern Soul was by osmosis, and I knew that the Northern nights at the Casino were becoming a cult event. I should explain. The Casino was not where Wigan's dinner-suited playboys risked their wet fish and tripe fortunes on the turn of a hand of baccarat but a huge, prewar ballroom on Station Road between Waring and Gillow's furniture store and the municipal baths.

I knew of all this back in 1974. But I'd never actually been to a proper Northern Soul night. This wasn't a proper Northern Soul night either, not the sort those snobs in *Blues and Soul* magazine would recognise anyway. Admittance was 20p and there was nothing stronger than Vimto for sale. But the DJs were a real draw; Russ Winstanley and Richard Searling, two of the Casino's star names. It would make a change from eating chips and gravy in a freezing bus shelter anyway, arguing over who was the better drummer, John Bonham or Carl Palmer. We made our way 'up town', over Seven Stars bridge, across the canal, through Gillibrands factory yard, past the abattoir (I'm not making this up, honest) and cut through by Sacred Heart Church to Springfield Park, home of Wigan Athletic Football Club. The San Siro it wasn't but a run-down sports ground that has been in use since the late nineteenth century for horse-trotting and local police athletic meets.

Inside, it was a grimly typical Seventies disco. You paid your 20p and got your hand stamped by an emphysemic ex-miner who collected the coins in a blue Senior Service ashtray. Then you made your way into the 'big room' collecting a bottle of Barrs Cola and a packet of ten Number 6 on the way, jointly paid for and thus owned by four of you. The mobile disco system was on the stage in front of the organ and drum set-up that was used to pound out 'Yellow River' and 'Viva España' on a Saturday night. Some tube-effect lighting flashed in time to the beat. The two DJs stood onstage above and aloof from the teenage throng, silent, lifting and marking records in cardboard sleeves from their DJ boxes. Compared to the Casino Allnighter or Friday sessions when 2,000 people might cram that huge sprung dance floor, this must have been very small beer. Perhaps they were keeping their hand in or earning a bit extra to buy a new bowling shirt, or Adidas bag, or jumper with stars on.

These were the de rigueur fashions of Northern Soul. Everyone on the dance floor, male or female, was wearing some or all of the above, along with Oxford or Birmingham high-waisted baggies. This was pretty much the ubiquitous look of 1974 actually; I'm sure it's how Harold Wilson dressed at Chequers at weekends. What struck you much more vividly than the clothes was the mood of sheer exuberance.

The music was vibrant, pulsating, irrepressible. And the dance floor was alive with energy, with individuals each performing their own variations on the classic Northern moves and steps, crossing the dance floor at speed, shuffling, sliding, occasionally breaking into a spin. At key points in the track, the whole dance floor would clap their hands in time to a certain pivotal drumbeat and the crack reverberated around the room like gunfire. It was intoxicating, not least because the place was full of girls.

Then a particular track came on and the dance floor cleared, a couple of the dancers hanging around at the edge of the floor with an expectant look on their faces. Out of the dark by the bar corner, a young bloke of about nineteen stepped forward. He wore voluminous bags and a sleeveless vest showing off muscled arms dotted with tattoos and with a sweatband at the wrist. He sported the regulation 1974 David Wilkie page-boy/feather-cut hybrid and the kind of moustache later favoured by members of Frankie Goes To Hollywood. Obviously this was his song, and it was a funny old one.

It began in a haze of sitars and tablas and then exploded into life with a maniacally fast stomping drumbeat. And he was off, criss-crossing the floor at implausible velocity, his feet resembling that abstract whirly illustration that denoted extreme speed in Billy Whizz's adventures in the *Beano*. He did the claps of course, extravagantly too, flinging his arms open wide and then across his chest like a Cossack who'd drunk a bottle of potato vodka. Then, just when he seemed to have spent himself like a Roman candle and you were thinking it was safe to get near him, he flung himself several feet in the air. Descending, he fell into a kind of backward reclining crab shape on the floor, then sprang forward laterally like Gordon Banks going after Pele's far post header and went into a series of leisurely ad hoc press-ups before flipping over again on to his back, leaping to his feet and rocketing off towards the corner of the floor, spinning and clapping as he went. Within a second or two, the track had ended[1] and, wiping his brow with his sweatband, he made his way to the cool darkness by the bar, lighting a fag as he went. I couldn't help noticing that a few cute young women looked admiringly in his direction as he passed.

---

[1] I would later learn it was a cover of the Rolling Stones' 'Paint It Black' by the Love Sitars, a West Coast psychedelic outfit with the lifespan of a mayfly.

If you tried that kind of thing on a dance floor today, a burly shaven-headed man in a black zip-up satin jacket would be propelling you towards the exit with great force before the intro was over. If you went for the full repertoire of Northern Soul moves on the wrong dance floors even back then, as I was to discover, you ran the risk of ending the night in casualty. Described baldly in print, the performance sounds like someone having a massive, distressing seizure and just as sexy. But I tell you, we were gobsmacked. It combined the natural exuberance of dancing with the athleticism and show-offiness of a parallel bars routine. It wasn't remotely camp either. That was always a danger with regular dancing, unless you did that thing Mud did where you found a partner and both tucked your thumbs in your belt, jerking violently forward and backward in a kind of stylised head-butting ceremony. Moreover, the music was weirdly compelling, irrepressible, sexy and obscure. Clearly I was about to become a Northern Soul boy.

Most of us *were* actually. Brownie and Nidge never took to the dancing, I think fearing that even this masculine a variant of the dance was but a few short steps from liking Ethel Merman and wearing a feather boa.[2] But with the zeal of the convert again, I went for full immersion baptism. I bought the clothes; or rather my mum did. I bought the sew-on patches ('Keep The Faith', 'Night Owl' 'Heart Of Soul'). I bought the Adidas bag, in which hardened dancers kept Johnson's Baby Talc – to make the floor slippier and better for dancing – and a change of clothes as a couple of hours spinning and backflipping and you could wring

---

2 It's a curious thing this about the Seventies that Brownie, a brown 'n' bitter drinking, street-fighting greasemonkey, saw no contradiction in being a devoted, obsessive Bowie fan and also being utterly steeped in the comedy homophobia of the day, all that 'get you ducky', 'shut that door, Everard', 'watch your backs, lads' stuff. That *Clockwork Orange* vibe of mascara and ultra-violence was ever present in real life as I recall.

the sweat out of your bowling shirt. I learned the holy writ, starting with the names of the clubs.

Wigan was, of course, the capital of Northern Soul: in 1977, in a *Blues and Soul* survey of the world's best nightclubs, Studio 54, New York's ultra-exclusive hedonistic high temple of disco, came second. Wigan Casino came first. I felt, and still feel, strangely proud of this arcane fact. But it was considered gracious to acknowledge the importance and influence of earlier venues – the Twisted Wheel, the Torch in Stoke – as well as the existence of other contemporary clubs – the Blackpool Mecca, Va Va in Bolton, the Catacombs in Wolverhampton.

And of course I bought the records. Buying Top Forty records was merely a swift commercial transaction, you handed your 59 pence to the Saturday girl in Woolies and she gave you the new one by David Essex or The Arrows. Buying Northern Soul records was a ritualistic journey into the dark heart of the cult. Most of these records had been flops when originally issued. They were obscure discs on obscure labels made by singers who promptly disappeared without trace into the US hinterland. By now, they'd be pumping gas or filing invoices in Pensacola or Spokane, unaware that they were revered as gods across the Atlantic on dance floors in the industrial North.

The top DJs and opinion formers would make pilgrimages to the States, to thrift stores and bargain bins and long-defunct record-label offices, seeking out the singles that they would bring back and 'break' at Wigan. Often they'd cover up the artist and title with a bit of sticking plaster and invent a fictitious name, the intention being to throw other DJs off the scent and preserve the exclusivity of the track. Thus the floor-filling instrumental 'Double Cookin'' by the Checkerboard Squares was known as 'Strings A Go Go', 'Little Ann' was known as 'Rose Valentine' and, most famously, Frank Wilson was credited as Eddie Foster on the first plays of what is often regarded as the best and certainly the rarest Northern Soul tune, 'Do I Love You (Indeed I Do)', one copy in existence, current asking price £15,000. More important than the price, it is utterly wonderful. If you want to know what the magic of Northern Soul is, get yourself a copy (it's readily available on CD compilations, only the vinyl is worth the price of a terraced house in Whitehaven) and allow yourself to be swept away by its life-affirming, luminous, lump-in-the throat beauty and effervescence. As far as I'm concerned, there is no ailment or depression so profound and weighty that two and a half minutes in the company of this fabulous tune won't lift and banish. Excuse me while I go and put it on.

The two DJs who I'd seen at that Latics club event turned out to be real grand fromages of the scene, movers, shakers, opinion formers, revered figures. They were Russ and Richard, Russ Winstanley and Richard Searling, the two best known of the Casino DJs. As well as spinning the discs at club nights, they jointly ran a record shop on Mesnes Street called, unsurprisingly, Russ and Richard's. The atmosphere in here made Nick Hornby's Champion Vinyl or the virago in Rumbelows seem like a particularly cuddly branch of Sue Ryder. The walls were covered in handwritten sheets proclaiming the wares on offer. There were tranches of 50p stuff but anything half decent involved severe lacerations of the pocket; 'Paul Humphries Cochise Nine Pounds. Mike Post Coalition Afternoon Of The Rhino (in-demand stomper) ten pounds. Luther Ingram Exus Trek (acetate demo) offers'. Come Saturday afternoon, the shop was always packed with soul boys – and it was mainly boys – flipping through the boxes of seven-inch singles, making deals, arranging lifts to and from out-of-town venues. It all felt severely intimidating and implausibly exciting.

At the time, I wrongly assumed that the whole scene had been this fertile and vibrant for years, an underground river that I was taking my first tentative dips into. Northern Soul had certainly been a cult for some years – indeed it's still going strong – but with hindsight 1974 was its annus mirabilis. The Casino's Allnighter started on 23 September 1973 ushering in Northern Soul's halcyon era, at least from the point of view of popularity and profile. Later, soul purists would say that 1974 was where it all started to go wrong, where kids like me got involved and when the newspapers and documentary makers stared to trek up the M6 to make silly, patronising films which juxtaposed cloth caps and smoking chimneys with shots of the Casino's patrons, wired on cheap speed, whirling like dervishes to Judy Street's 'What'. 1974 was the year when the record companies descended like vultures in Vauxhall Vivas on the scene. There followed a slew of embarrassing novelty Northern Soul hits – the execrable 'Footsie' by Wigan Chosen's Few, Wayne Gibson's 'Under My Thumb', Wigan's Ovation's 'Ski-Ing In The Snow'.

Tracks like this last one really stuck in the purists' craw even then; a bland, modernised, easier to license version of a classic Northern tune originally by US artists. Pye's Disco Demand label were the worst culprits here, regarded by true Northern Soul disciples as a combination of Rio Tinto Zinc, Exxon and the Burmese government.

All of this made shopping for records a challenging and interesting experience to say the least. I once saw Russ practi-cally spit at some foolish punter who made the mistake of asking for the superb instrumental 'Sliced Tomatoes', not in its groovy Sixties original by the Just Brothers but the horrid synth version by the Sounds of Lancashire, clearly made by a bloke in a shed in Chorley with a cheap Korg keyboard. But you could see the lad's point. The Sounds of Lancashire version cost 50-odd pence, the original was eight quid. Also, if these new versions were so awful, why sell them? Well, sound business sense obviously. It's a funny old thing; specialist record shops are the only emporia on earth that will sneer at you for buying something. Can you imagine a butcher's where the owner wipes his bloodied hands on his apron and says, 'Lamb chops? Lamb chops? You're not serious are you?'

Russ and Richard's was not so much a record shop as a testing ground for one's personal status and self-worth. If Richard said 'great track' as you parted with a week's spending money for Earl Jackson's 'Soul Self Satisfaction', then you would leave the shop not just light of pocket but light of step, tacitly welcomed into the faith. Maybe you were indeed one of Wigan's Chosen Few.

You had to get to know all these records intimately to know where exactly the claps went. Two in the middle of the first line of Gloria Jones's 'Tainted Love'. One right before the chorus of Al Wilson's 'The Snake', best accompanied by a yelp and a quick drop into the splits if you could manage it. By now, I actually could manage most of the manoeuvres. I was becoming quite a proficient dancer. I had the general repertoire of moves, plus a few of my invention. The one thing I could never master was the spin. The really brilliant dancers could deftly execute a hundred-mile-an-hour rotation just like Katerina Witt and Robin Cousins but without the benefit of ice or skates. The trick, Neil told me, was to keep your eyes fixed on some point in the distance, a beer pump or mirror. Whatever I did though, I always ended up heading straight off the dance floor at an unplanned trajectory until a nearby table halted my progress. Eventually I gave up with the spin. It was costing too much in replacement drinks.

Neil, by the way, was the ace dancer from the Latics club. We had got to know him by now. He was a nice guy, surprisingly shy and lugubrious away from the dance floor. He worked at Middleton & Wood's funeral directors and would tell blackly comic tales of breaking limbs stiffened by rigor mortis in order to get folks in the coffin or ladling random handfuls of dust and shavings into urns instead of loved ones' ashes.

Armed with my rolls, dives, shuffles, stomps and backflips, if not spins, it was time to try out these moves in the ultimate arena, the Casino itself. I was fourteen. Going to the Allnighter stood about as much chance of parental sanction as me buying a motorbike or going to live in a Danish commune. Fortunately though, Wiganers always having an eye for the commercial consideration, the Casino's management had realised that many of the scene's new recruits were just slips of kids and couldn't attend the over-eighteens-only Allnighter. So they introduced the early sessions – seven till eleven, Mondays, Wednesdays and Fridays. Even these, though, demanded that you be sixteen. And so, three times a week, you'd fetch up, all unconvincing, unconcern and ashen pallor, beneath the basilisk gaze of Hilda Woods, the Casino's legendary doorlady. There was the usual embarrassing interrogation, me being the most baby-faced and, indeed, youngest of the gang.

'You're not sixteen.'

'Yeah, I am honest.'

'Date of birth then?'

The response to this you would have practised expertly but fear and anticipation would inevitably cloud the mind. 'Thirteen of the eighth, 1874 … no, 1974 … no nineteen sixty … er, two, I mean one.' I found myself back out on a freezing Station Road many times. After a while, Hilda softened and would wave me though with a roll of the eyes and a shake of the head. It was a wonderful feeling, acceptance, joy, liberation. I can remember it still.

The Casino had long been a local landmark, a huge First World War era ballroom that had briefly and excitingly been the second biggest billiard hall in Britain before reverting to a *palais de danse* during the Big Band era. It was called the Empress or 'Emp' at this time, and all our grans or mums could tell tales of putting gravy browning on their legs and dancing with GIs to 'In The Mood' at the Emp. In the Sixties, the Stones, Tom Jones and other luminaries played there. Then an entertainments promoter from

Carlisle called Mike Walker helped set up the Allnighters with Russ Winstanley. The Allnighters soon became part of local folk-lore. The older generation regarded them with fear and revulsion; it was a den of vice and drugtaking according to my nan who could have been persuaded that human sacrifice and devil worship went on there too. In truth, it didn't even have a late licence so for most of the night people drank milk, the wilder element popping benzedrine or snorting sulphate.

It was a terrific place; three storeys and a huge balcony that overlooked the oak sprung dance floor. Dancers tended to find their own spot, the best ones over by the pillars stage left while newcomers would undergo an apprenticeship on the perimeter of the floor, moving to the middle as they became more confident and proficient. On the top floor, record dealers laid out their wares in boxes; the air was as full of haggling as a Tunis bazaar. In a draw somewhere, I have a tape that an anonymous soul fan sent me some months ago. It is labelled, simply, Wigan Casino 1974. It's a C90 recorded at an Allnighter. You can hardly hear the records, it's all atmosphere. The Casino inspired this kind of devo-tion; the sort that would compel someone to smuggle in a suitcase-sized mid-Seventies cassette recorder and fill an hour and a half of tape with random snatches of conversation, glasses clinking, the thumps of a faraway bass and kick drum.

This tape is now priceless in its way; living history, the Casino at its height on a hot Saturday night in 1974. A vanished world. In 1983 Wigan Council, in their wisdom, knocked the building down to make way for a civic centre extension that was never built and ultimately a car park. The men responsible for this should hang their sorry heads in shame. To them, the Casino was an embar-rassment. In fact, when every member of that Wigan Council is justly forgotten, people will still talk of the Casino.

As well as the Casino, we soon got to know the places around town where you could hear Northern Soul. There was the

Minorca in Hindley, Penson Street Social Centre and the Conservative Club in Scholes. There are Conservative clubs in Wigan, each with a little picture of the Queen above the bar, but patronage of these places is generally down to convenience or the availability of better-quality baize or mild rather than political affiliation. No one regards it as class treachery if you pop down to the 'Con' club for a pint and a frame of snooker on Sunday lunchtime. And anyway, a Conservative in Wigan is just someone who baulks at the idea that Surrey should be made into a collective farm.

The Con Club in Scholes has a particular significance for me. I nearly got killed there. Dancing at the Con Club on a Thursday night I'd met a girl three years older than me. In itself this was enormously exciting and attractive, even though I was warned she was 'trouble'. If this was supposed to put me off, it failed signally as it was bound to do. Unfortunately there was an irate not quite ex-boyfriend in the background who didn't approve of Northern Soul, my dancing or the fact that I'd nicked his girl-friend. There were a few hostile semi-encounters and then, one Thursday, it all kicked off as they say.

It was something or nothing that started it, as it often is. Someone tripped someone up, a bottle of Worthington E went flying over someone's jacket, someone lunged at someone else.

It spread like beer across a pub table. Suddenly it was a massed battle on the dance floor between my mates and the boyfriend's faction. It spilled out into the car park – as convention demands – and became a rolling maul comprised of swinging arms and legs but then common sense must have prevailed and impromptu peace negotiations were convened. During these, my gang drifted over to our chauffeur, Fat John from Swinley's, and his old boxy Hillman Avenger. By this stage, everyone was pretty much happy for the thing to be over with just the odd parting insult and hand gesture and with each reckoning themselves the victors. Unfortunately, as we were leaving the car park, one of the other faction, a notorious local nutter called Stan, ran over to us and jumped onto the boot of the car. Fat John hadn't spotted this and was continuing to manoeuvre out of the car park. 'One of them's on the back of the car,' we pointed out helpfully but this seemed only to spur Fat John on. Recklessly, and for reasons best known to himself, he put his foot down and sped out on to the main road. Down the hill into Wigan town centre we went, at around fifty, with Stan clinging grimly on, his face, from my recollection, contorted by G forces and his bullish aggression now faded, replaced by sorrowful reflection at high speed.

It was clearly an untenable state of affairs. It ended just between the baths and the police station when Stan lost his grip on the car and landed face first in the middle of the road. A chorus of expletives came from the rear seat of the car, as well as the confidently expressed and nervous opinion that 'the mad bastard's dead, we've killed him'. I'd never thought of Fat John as a man of great personal valour, and so it turned out to be. We roared off into the night, leaving Stan prostrate on the tarmac.

After a couple of hundred yards and a turn into Library Street, even Fat John's slender sense of morality got the better of him and we stopped. We ran down to the baths and peered around the corner. Our unwelcome passenger was gone but there did seem to be some commotion outside the police station. It had been, after all, a great spot to fall off a fast-moving Hillman Avenger. Unsure of what to do, discretion prevailed. We drove off in the direction of Pemberton.

We'd got about as far as Wallgate Station when a police car overtook us and slowed us to a stop. A uniformed PC came to the car window, which Fat John wound down with the best approximation of casual unconcern he could muster. 'I don't want you to talk about what happened, I just want you to follow me back to the police station.'

This we did. A curious old evening ensued. Stan wasn't dead but the stunt hadn't done him much good. He'd been taken to hospital and there he stayed for a day or two. I felt bad about this but then his decision to ride pillion on a moving car had been very much his own. The police, though, were having some trouble believing our story. Perhaps they thought, quite reasonably, that no one in their right mind would voluntarily sit atop the boot of a moving vehicle. One of them took me outside for 'a chat'.

'So you say this bloke climbed on the back and before you had a chance to do anything about it, he fell off.'

This, I admit, was not strictly accurate but a truer account would not have reflected well on Fat John.

'That's about it,' I stammered.

This seemed to annoy him. Next thing I knew I was up against the 'meat wagon'.

'Look son, I've been here since nine this morning and I'd like to go home. What really happened?'

'That's what happened. He's a nutter. He didn't like us 'cos we dance to Northern Soul and I pinched his mate's girlfriend!' I shouted.

And this seemed to do the trick.

Back inside a little later, the desk sergeant told us we could call our mums and dads for a lift home. Nervously I called mine.

'Hiya,' I breezed nonchalantly, 'errm, I'm in the police station. Could you come and get me?'

My mum and dad arrived, it seemed to me, at around the same time I was putting the phone down. The officer who'd got so exasperated with me earlier took my dad to one side.

'I'd just like you to know that there's just been a bit of an incident, a minor accident, horseplay, but your son has done nothing wrong whatsoever.' And then, catching my eye, he winked at me conspiratorially. Perhaps he was an old Twisted Wheel mod.

I had a day or two of enforced bedroom time to reflect on my lifestyle choice. It did seem to be getting me into quite a lot of trouble. Elaine was cute, but she wasn't worth going to prison for. We – the gang and I – decided we ought to lay low for a while. It was just as well. According to reports, the next week, Stan's brother lay in wait for us in the car park of the Con Club with a 12-bore shotgun resting on the partly wound-down driver's window. Evidently, placidity and calm good sense ran in the family.

A week later we did risk a visit to Gidlow Lane Community Centre's soul night, but Jamo Thomas's 'I Spy For The FBI' was the only Northern we could coax out of the DJ whose definition of soul included Hot Chocolate and Smokey. To cap it all, we got set on and chased out by a splinter group from the Scholes mob led by one Spadge, an enormous man with a square head.

As we legged it down Frog Lane – it's a real place, honestly – I noticed Brownie stoop as we passed a house. Ten minutes later we were cornered in the waste ground by Gillibrands factory. Things looked bad, Spadge stepped forward, smirking. Suddenly Brownie stepped into the pool of illumination cast by a flickering arc light on the factory roof and, reaching into his trenchcoat, produced a milk bottle which he swung and smashed against the iron railings. It glinted in the light. Even at this moment of high tension, I remember feeling that there was something distinctly Arthurian about this. Brownie really ought to have declaimed, Ian McKellenish, 'Come no further, thou foul spawn of treachery.' Instead he said, 'Come on, then, you twat.' The effect, though, was electrifying: Spadge and his minions dissolved like shadows into the night. We walked home by the canal and Robin Park deep in thought. For once, the travellers who lived on the waste ground didn't take pot shots at us with an air gun.

We were just in time for the last pint at Goose Green Labour

Club, notoriously lenient then with regard to under-age drinkers if you sat in the billiard room and kept quiet.[3]

We held our own council of war and decided that this had to stop. We were marked men; desperadoes if you will. Brownie, who didn't even much like Northern Soul and never danced, was getting a bit sick of his evenings ending in ambushes and mass fights over music he didn't understand and girls he had no stake in.

I didn't know at the time but Northern Soul itself was about to go back underground where it belonged. 1974 was its high watermark before it evaporated in that cheesy whiff of novelty records. But it had been fun while it had lasted. To quote that wonderful Northern Soul anthem by Dobie Gary, I had got my kicks out on the floor; and in more ways than one. But it was time to sit a few out.

---

[3] This is Goose Green in Pemberton, Wigan, I should say, not the one in the Falkland Islands. Later, when I was a student, I once dashed to the newsagent's in disbelief after catching part of a radio bulletin that said, 'There is fierce fighting and heavy artillery shelling in Goose Green which has fallen to the Argentinian army.'

7 In a Glass House

1975 was the calm before the storm. Calmish anyway. Cambodia fell to the Khmer Rouge, Patti Hearst joined the Symbionese Liberation Army, terrorism, be it the IRA, the Red Army Faction, the Bader-Meinhof gang or the South Moluccans, was all the rage across Europe and there was a constitutional crisis in Australia when PM Gough Whitlam was sacked by the governor general.

Most of this I learned at teatime from Reginald Bosanquet and Alistair Burnet while eating egg on toast; me, not them, obviously. Few of these events impinged much on me. I went to and from school, learned about the Anti-Corn Law League and Brownian motion and tried not to get 'strapped' by Brother Ring, the most sadistic of the bullying bog-trotters who taught me – or the Christian Brothers to give them their official name. When not thus engaged, I would be watching *Fawlty Towers* or *Ripping Yarns*, smoking furtively in a variety of toilets, parks and bus shelters or engaged, equally furtively, in a kind of amiable hand-to-hand combat with a girl from Orrell called Hilary. In an almost comical piece of good luck, Hilary turned out to be a teenage nympho whose dad owned an off-licence, a semi-mythical creature not normally found outside of the fantasies of Sid James.

We didn't have the Khmer Rouge. But we did have Dr Hook,

The Eagles and the Bellamy Brothers. I have grown to love the icy, affluent, coke-addled angst of The Eagles in my adulthood but back then they represented everything that was wrong with music. They wore stetsons, twanged smugly and drawled about places called Sausalito and San Antonio. I wasn't to know it but in little pockets around the country, and, in particular, in a clothes shop in London, others were feeling just as alienated from the diet of bland FM rock that had become the standard daily fare of pop music.

I didn't know what was happening on the Kings Road but I would tell anyone who would listen at the Station Road bus stop that we were in a cultural cul-de-sac. Some of this was my own analysis, most was borrowed from *Sounds* and *NME* and replayed verbatim. I did what bolshy teenagers have always done and immersed myself in various left-field stuff by various mavericks that other people 'just wouldn't understand'.

First there was poor doomed Syd Barrett. Pink Floyd were one of the giants of prog rock of course. Their album *Dark Side of the Moon* was still hanging around the lower reaches of the chart where it had been since the invention of the Spinning Jenny. It was a good record, I admitted. I had even bought it from Whelan's supermarket on the same day I picked up *Black Sabbath Volume 4* (no inlay card, swirly Vertigo logo, £1.25). But I had developed an affiliation with Syd Barrett, the ousted drug-casualty elfin poet who had formed the band. I would infuriate fans of the new, arena-filling, epic rock Floyd by claiming that David Gilmour, Barrett's replacement, was a foul usurper and that throwaway Barrett doodles like 'Effervescing Elephant' or 'Bike' were better than the whole of *Echoes* or *Animals*.[1]

---

[1] In this I may have been right, but I was wrong to slur Gilmour who in fact had been a staunch supporter and friend of Barrett and produced his spooky, tragic, nursery-rhymish solo albums.

That summer, you could often hear on Radio 1 – the station of the nation, as Noel Edmonds would inform us regularly – a single by a German band called Kraftwerk. It was a modernist slice of electronica that represented, pretty faithfully actually, a trip on a German motorway called, naturally, 'Autobahn'. Few records I'd come across before so polarised people. Some, me included, thought it a work of genius, sort of funny and beautiful and dour at the same time. Others thought it was soulless drivel that sounded like your fridge coming on. I'm pretty sure that the Hairy Cornflake, Dave Lee Travis's side-splitting soubriquet, did a comedy Nazi accent whenever he played it. Nearly thirty years on, Kraftwerk are still having this effect on people, and the same argument that divided critical thought in the artroom bogs in 1975 still rages or at least smoulders at candlelit dinner tables.

There was Deaf School from Liverpool, a band who'd won a *Melody Maker* talent contest and stood defiantly out of step with the long hairs and cowboys who dominated the cool music scene. Deaf School dressed flamboyantly in character. There was singer Betty Bright, a scarlet-haired vamp, the Reverend Max Ripple, a keyboard-playing vicar, Eric Shark and Enrico Cadillac, spivvish male vocalists and more; the songs were written by a studious-looking man in wire specs called Clive Langer. Deaf School were always gigging somewhere, and myself and a few similarly inclined friends would trek around Lancashire and Cheshire to see them, a splash of colour and wit in the drab landscape populated by David Soul, the Three Degrees and Billy Ocean. One night, they played at Wigan Casino – which had broadened its scope to include rock music – and the crowd was an unruly one with a heavy contingent of local boot boys and skinheads. Betty Bright took a volley of sexist abuse and leering nastiness from one guy all night until, frustrated beyond reason, she grabbed a bottle of Worthington E from the stage and hurled it at him, catching an innocent bystander full in the face. She looked down mortified, mouthing 'sorry, God, I'm so sorry' as his friends helped him, bleeding, from the venue.[2]

In a not dissimilar vein to Deaf School, another of my favourites of this funny old year were a gang of antipodean weirdoes called Split Enz who made Deaf School look like the shadow cabinet. They wore white face make-up, enormous suits cut to lines straight from *The Cabinet of Doctor Caligari* and colour schemes from Piet Mondrian. They were funny and sinister and oddly touching and their music bamboozled and delighted me; Cole Porter show tunes melded with frenetic progressive rock, Beatle balladry, lounge jazz, Hawaiian music and sci-fi soundtracks. The day I went to see them play live at the famous Erics in Liverpool and found a note on the door announcing that the show had been cancelled was one of the blackest of a black year.

I also became obsessed with an eccentric progressive rock group called Gentle Giant. That summer I took my final summer holiday with my mum and dad, a trip en famille with cousins, uncles and aunts to Butlin's holiday camp in Barry Island. On the day we arrived there were 90 mph winds, tables and chairs were thrown in the air and prams were blown along the seafront chased by horrified parents. My uncle Brian was lifted off his feet and dropped down some steps, breaking his foot and getting the week off to a bad start in a grim Welsh casualty department.

When I was a child I loved the bracing hedonism of Butlin's, the donkey derbies, the redcoats, the filmed horseracing from America, the cafés with the glass panels that offered submarine views of the swimming pool, the monorails. It was like a future metropolis designed by Le Corbusier and Andy Capp.

---

2 Twenty years after this, just a year or so ago, I met Betty Bright, now married to Suggs of Madness at a party. I told her of my Deaf School obsession and of the night there'd been an 'incident' at Wigan Casino. She blanched in horror. 'That was the night I hit the guy with the bottle,' she whispered. 'I've never forgotten it.'

But I was an adolescent now with a nascent interest in beer, girls, rock 'n' roll and Embassy Number 6. It was a slow week, enlivened only by a snog with a girl from Airdrie and the purchase of an album called *In a Glass House* by Gentle Giant.

It began with the unmistakable sounds of destruction, someone smashing windows and splintering wood which slowly formed itself into the rhythm track of the song 'Runaway'. As the album progressed, the band – of whom I knew nothing – turned their hand at whim it seemed to madrigals, hard rock, or jazz funk. A string quartet would break out in the middle of a blues jam or a five-part vocal fugue would emerge from a vibraphone solo.

Over the next few months, I would become slowly obsessed with this strange album, an obsession that has never fully left me. Fifteen, caught between child and adult, mixed up, it wouldn't be stretching a point to say that I was in a glass house of my own, a kind of open prison, and Gentle Giant's queer, off-kilter music provided the perfect soundtrack.

They were a quintet whose core, a pair of brothers called Shulman who had served time in a Sixties pop act called Simon Dupree and the Big Sound, whose big hit was 'Kites', a slice of prime UK psychedelia about hanging yellow paper suns in windows. Disenchanted with the fripperies of the Sixties pop scene, they had formed the most complicated, ornery band imaginable, dedicated to making music that made the listener's head swim. I adored it. Its austere and lovely medieval passages, thunderous rocking and tricky time signatures got me through several quiet nights in a Welsh chalet.

Because there was nothing else to call them, they were called 'progressive rock' in the rock press of the day and therefore destined to be sneered at and consigned to the ash heap of history when the storm broke in a few short months. But I still love them. Back then, it was the kind of love that gets you court injunctions and restriction orders though; my friend John once pointed out, accurately, that everyone who knew me had one Gentle Giant album as a result of my brow-beating. I scoured the press for details about them, which were scant. They had one supporter in the music press, a man called Phil Sutcliffe who instantly became my favourite writer. Now my friend Terry – one of the fellow passengers in the police chase and ejected passenger farrago – read the *Record Mirror*. Secretly, I regarded this as inappropriate and frankly embarrassing behaviour for a grown rock fan of fourteen, rather like buying David Cassidy albums or wearing lederhosen. But Terry's secret vice did have an unexpected benefit for me. One day, Terry waved a copy of *Record Mirror* under my nose as we shared an Embassy Regal on the steamroller climbing frame in Alexandra Park: 'Here, you'll want to see this.' He was right. *Record Mirror*, in a break from its coverage of the Glitter Band and Marie Osmond, was running a Gentle Giant competition. I can't remember what the question was but naturally I entered and, as I recall, the very next Monday, delivered to my door came a package containing a Gentle Giant T-shirt, a copy of their new album *The Missing Piece* and a promotional jigsaw (Missing Piece, geddit? – the marketing men at Chrysalis must have treated themselves to a good long liquid lunch after that morning's work).

I was stunned. Stunned and delighted. I played the album while wearing the T-shirt day and night. I did the jigsaw and found that it had, and you may be ahead of me here, a missing piece! It took me a while to realise that this was not the shoddy work of the GPO but the scintillating minds of the marketing dept again ('Another Sambuca, Trev? Don't mind if I do!'). At the time, I marvelled at my great good luck in winning the competition. With hindsight, it is tragically apparent that I was the only entrant. After all, how many Gentle Giant fans, most of whom lived in Helsinki and Bologna, were browsing for titbits of gossip about their favourite medieval jazz rock fusion experimentalist amidst the latest on Don Estelle and Windsor Davies?

'Whispering Grass' by these last two was Number 1 for a week in May 1975. God, it felt like more, didn't it? A glance at the chart for this, almost the decade's dead centre, reveals that pop music was in chaos, but not in a good way. There were some putative disco tunes by KC and the Sunshine Band and The Trammps; the fag end of glam as practised by The Rubettes; Alvin Stardust still plying his chilling trade; and a selection of establishment figures on autopilot – Elton John, Eric Clapton, Wings, et al.

One member of rock's glitterati who wasn't taking it easy was David Bowie. People were beginning to talk of him as the chameleon of rock, not because he lived under a rock and had leathery, camouflage skin but because every few months he looked and sounded completely different. Perhaps not completely different but at least as different as the average chameleon and certainly more so than the average rock aristocrat. At around this time, I rushed out and bought a Bowie single called 'Golden Years'. For everyone but Bowie, this was not the case. The three-day week, candlelit evenings and picket-line violence were behind us but Britain was still very much the sick man of Europe. On a weekly basis, Dennis Healey suffered the dual humiliations of having to go cap in the hand to the IMF and having to endure Mike Yarwood's impression of him. This basically consisted of Yarwood donning bifurcated furry draught excluders for use as two fake eyebrows and saying 'silly billy' a lot. Millions tuned in for this. When not watching Mike Yarwood or *The Two Ronnies*, most of the populace drank awful fizzy keg beer like the late un-lamented Worthington E and Watney's Red Barrel and kicked each other senseless at football matches. Tough times.

Bowie was thriving though. They were certainly his golden years. Look at his diary for the couple of years in question, starting early 1975; experiments with 'relentless Plastic Soul'; does it rather well; has American Number 1 with 'Fame'; moves to Los Angeles and stars in Nic Roeg's *The Man Who Fell to Earth*. While in LA records *Station to Station*; moves into darker, colder territory but still can't stop selling records viz 'Golden Years'. Decides LA is too boring and moves to Berlin to live with Iggy Pop; gives up drugs and popularises electronic music with his fabulous Eno collaborations *Low* and *Heroes*. On his days off he revives Iggy Pop's career by producing *Lust for Life* and *The Idiot*. You have to say that compared to Leo Sayer's achievements over the same period, it's pretty good work. Even his cock-ups brought forth positive results. When, at the frantic height of his cocaine paranoia, he started giving Nazi salutes and praising Hitler, the outcry led to the formation of Rock Against Racism and the Anti-Nazi League.

During the lean years of the mid-Seventies, Bowie was joint leading light of a minor scene in the North West often called Roxybowie and based around Bowie's work and that of fellow art rock dandies Roxy Music. I thought Bowie was pretty cool and getting cooler by the day but I never really went over to the Roxybowie cause. It was too much trouble for one thing. You had to wear trenchcoats which look stupid if you're five foot eight. In truth trenchcoats look stupid on everyone but if you're six foot three like my mate Terry you can at least look down threateningly on people who tell you so. You had to smoke Gitanes or Gauloises which smelled and tasted like the floor of a parakeet house. You had to get your ear pierced and dye your hair. You had to wear a bolero jacket which was every bit as stupid as a trenchcoat but in a subtly different way, i.e. it was way too short instead of far too long. Worst, you had to pretend to like the rotten *David Live* album with all those Earl Slick guitar solos that sound like a ferret being garrotted. Bowie by the way is wearing a bolero jacket on the front. Guess what? He looks stupid. He also, having taken all the cocaine in the world, looks like he could do with a large pie and two slices of bread and butter.

The good thing about the Bowie and Ferry look, though, was that it got you into over-eighteens discos. There's something very levelling about suits, cummerbunds and slicked-back hair. You all look rubbish but you all look about forty. Inside, you'd hear 'Ziggy Stardust', 'TVC 15', 'Pyjamarama' and 'Love Is The Drug'. Everyone did a variant of that dance that Bowie was very keen on at the time, the 'Boys Keep Swinging' one, where he sways his upper body from side to side and slightly backwards and forwards with a pained expression on his face, like a man with false arms whose shoes have been nailed to the floor trying to shake dandruff off. I tended to sit these out. I was a soul boy, and I knew the trouble that dancing could get you into. It still did too. After one Roxy/Bowie night at Cassinelli's in Standish, another friend, Paul Moran, got 'banjoed', as we said then, in the car park by a local tough called Skull. The Americans have a saying, 'Never eat at a restaurant called Moms and never play cards with a guy called Doc.' To this I would add, never pick a fight with a bloke called Skull.

Perhaps my reservations with this proto-futurist retro camp glam chic Roxybowie thing stemmed from my suspicion about the integrity of it all. I doubt it though. Later in life, lack of integrity was one of the things I would most look for in pop records and pop people. Van Morrison really means it, Kylie probably doesn't. Who would you rather go canal boating with? Perhaps I was disappointed with the lack of recorder duets or jazz madrigals. But perhaps, just perhaps, I was jealous. Let me explain. They say all rock critics are failed musicians. I was embarking on the long road to failure in a parlour in Upholland, Lancashire, armed with the most primitive tools imaginable.

8 Hey Mr Telephone Man!

You won't find Mammoth Frog in any of the standard rock reference works. We should be there right between The Mamas & The Papas and the Manic Street Preachers. But we aren't, a fact that still rankles. You won't find us on the Internet either, although you will discover, as I just have, that a Mammoth Frog is a kind of really expensive, rather superior violin bow.

None of this is any surprise really given the shallow, formulaic nature of the music industry. Back in early 1976 the world wasn't ready for a drummerless ensemble with an upright piano and three lead guitarists.

I'd entertained ambitions of being an actual musical performer for as far back as I could remember. I think that every music obsessive must do at some level, even if it's only drifting into a reverie where they imagine themselves being the sixth Westlifer or playing air guitar to 'She Bangs The Drum' in front of the wardrobe mirror. In my family folklore, mention was often made of the time at Janet Lake's wedding when, as a tiny tot, I had eschewed the normal child-at-a-wedding-disco etiquette of sliding from one side of the dance floor to the other and instead did the twist for about an hour before, my dander up, leaping on stage and commandeering the drumkit. I don't remember any of this.

My earliest musical recollection, bellowed hymns aside, is standing in front of the class at some Christmas thing, singing 'Born Free'. The reason I remember it so well is that I had only the sketchiest acquaintance with the lyrics – it was a poor choice, I now acknowledge – and thus had to repeat the bit about 'wherever the wind blows' over and over again and add some unconvincing stuff about lions improvised on the hoof. Or paw, even.

Somewhere at the very limits of memory, which would make me about two or three, I have a very dim and murky recollection of owing a huge white guitar with a picture of Elvis Presley on it, or perhaps it was The Beatles. Whatever, I think we can be fairly sure that this was a novelty item out of a Christmas catalogue rather than the handiwork of Messrs Martin or Gibson.

Time passed. My musical development was restricted to playing along on the chime bars to selections from Prokofiev's *Lieutenant Kijé* on that schools programme with the sinister puppets. I did enrol for violin lessons in the second year at grammar school but this was only because it absented you from double maths on a Wednesday afternoon. My violin teacher was tremendously discouraging. At the first session, he glanced at my hands and shook his head sadly.

'Entirely the wrong type of fingers,' he said. 'You should try the piano. Or the guitar. A violinist needs short, stubby fingers. Look at David Oistrakh.'

He indicated a poster on the music room wall; a severe-looking Russian man with fingers like new potatoes. I didn't want to be David Oistrakh though. I just wanted to avoid simultaneous equations and vulgar fractions.

Today, whenever I hear Vaughan Williams's *The Lark Ascending* – music of such elevated loveliness that it always brings tears to my eyes and I have to pretend to be having trouble with my contact lenses – I thank God that some brave and dedicated souls persevered with the violin. Like sex and glass-blowing, there must be a point at which it stops being a taxing, traumatic ordeal forever poised on the edge of disaster, and starts becoming really fantastic.

I never reached that point. The violin and I existed in a state of angry, sullen, tuneless combat. I had a school instrument which meant that scores of hands, some even grubbier and less dextrous than mine, had had their mitts on it before me. The case was a canvas sack bound with a discarded belt. The violin itself, to me, was less a musical instrument than a piece of Victorian farm equipment. There were pegs that couldn't be turned, bits of wood forever dropping off and rolling under the bed, strings made from cat's innards. Before you could even play the bloody thing, you had to ferret out the block of hardened wax that was stored in a special compartment of the rudimentary case and rub it in on a tiny yellow duster. Then you had to buff the violin bow with the duster so that even more stray hairs would come adrift, though the bow already looked like Paul Daniels in a high wind. Now there are a couple of activities for which I am prepared to spend twenty minutes applying lubricant greases for but playing the violin isn't one. It never made any difference anyway. Whatever I played, it all sounded like the shrill, atonal shrieking that challenging modernists like Penderecki and George Crumb worked so hard to achieve. To me, it came naturally. I'd sit on the edge of my bed playing 'Merrily We Roll Along' and people from neighbouring postal districts would knock at the door begging me to stop.

One evening after practising I came downstairs to talk to my mum and dad. I told them that I was never going to make a violinist and would they mind awfully if I gave it up and took the bloody thing back? My dad said nothing, but something about the way he gently squeezed my hand in gratitude suggested he wouldn't be overly disappointed.

Around this time a guitar appeared in the house. Someone at my mum's works had been getting rid of it and I was the lucky recipient. I say guitar, though the similarity to other existing guitars was purely unintentional. It had strings and a neck and a body but beyond that it was hard to say. The strings were like cheese wire and the 'action' (the distance between strings and neck) so high that it took superhuman digital strength to hold them down long enough to get a note. The neck was about as wide as a cricket bat and the machine heads would wind down in mid-solo. But let's not be too hard on my first guitar. It was, after all, my first guitar and evenings would find me hunched over it picking out with glacial slowness and arthritic dexterity the riffs to 'Paranoid' or 'Jean Genie'. It wasn't great, but after my violin playing it must have sounded like the St Matthew Passion sung by seraphim.

About a year later, I got an electric guitar. It was a Stratocaster copy made by Zenta, a company who have offered scant challenge to Fender or Gibson in the folklore of rock 'n' roll. I imagine they were a Polish company who generally made gas turbines or milking machines. But, again, it was my first electric guitar and I loved it, despite its enormous weight. The amplifier I played it through was made by Winfield, the shadowy nomenclature for Woolworth's own brand goods.

Armed with an electric guitar, there was a grim inevitability that some form of band would ensue. And so the Mammoth Frog story begins. The name? God knows. Clearly the influence of Monty Python melded with, I vaguely remember, an anecdote from a fishing trip to the Red Pond.

The line-up went thus: on guitar and vocals me; on acoustic guitar and vocals Peter 'Josh' Jones; on guitar (again) Andrew 'Wally' Walsh; on bass Nigel 'Nig' Power; on piano Martin 'Prof' Browne.

Technically we had all bases and abilities covered. Prof was a pretty fair classically trained pianist, able to sight-read and knock out a Bach fugue at the drop of a hat. Nigel P was a pretty fair bassist for a fifteen-year-old, and he had a Vox AC30 amp, the same sort The Beatles had used and thus he would have been in even if he'd only had one arm. Wally was competent enough, and bringing up the rear were Josh and me, who were still having trouble getting past the tricky E flat chord.

The absence of a drummer and the surfeit of guitarists made it an unbalanced line-up to say the least. But what really made us as unstable as a decommissioned Russian nuclear reactor was the warring musical influences within what we might charitably call the music. Prof liked Bach, Focus, Peter Hamill, Miles Davis and, increasingly Jimi Hendrix. Nigel hung out with Hell's Angels and liked Jethro Tull and The Groundhogs plus the odd funk track. My tastes were, by now, unfathomable even to myself.

Wally and Josh had very definite musical identities, ones that they were keen to stamp on the nascent group. Wally had a Gibson SG copy and a tight mop of blond curls. He also had a Deep Purple fixation. Richey Blackmore was God to him and no amount of assertion that Blackmore looked ridiculous in the Welsh buckled hat that was his visual trademark would dissuade him. Josh was coming at things from a different angle. He liked craft and balladry. His favourite act was Elton John and his lyrics owed a slight debt to Bernie Taupin. One of Josh's songs that he brought to practise was called 'Hey Mr Telephone Man'. You get the idea.

That one didn't make it into our slim repertoire. But here's a few that did. We had a song called 'Cancer Dying Blues'. Yes, it was about smoking. No irony here, this was a straightforward barrelhouse piano blues about the dangers of tar inhalation. In the central section, Wally played a fair approximation of the solo from 'Smoke On The Water'. We had a song called 'Messiah' which was basically a big, grandiose piano flourish out of Bruckner with a cute but flimsy chord sequence of mine tacked on the end. Very near the end, jarringly, Wally played the solo from 'Highway Star'.

As a unit, we made The Who look cosy and familial. Wally would berate me for not being able to control the feedback from my Woolworth's amp and I would respond tetchily, 'Put your hands on the strings!'

'I have got my bloody hands on the strings! Stop trying to be Ritchie Flipping Blackmore!'

Josh, sensibly, would try to rein in our instrumental excess and we would mock his cute balladeer aspirations. Nigel would play Groundhogs riffs at top volume until Prof would throw an ashtray at him. At every practice someone left.

Eventually, the Frog (as I'm sure our fans would have called us) settled around the trio of Prof, Nigel and myself who were at least relatively similar in our tastes. Now we sounded like Jethro Tull playing Brahms really badly on children's instruments. Every shred of our combined musical knowledge and dexterity went into a magnum opus called 'Triangle'. Essentially 'Triangle' was about a very tepid relationship I was having with a nice girl from Swinley, the posh end of town. However, what with me being in the grips of a Camus and Auden fixation, I was loathe to admit that it could be about anything so prosaic and everyday as a girl. So the lyric was an exercise in cryptic symbolism and pretentious literary allusion. Here's a sample verse:

Derelict now, we are you see
Empty rhetoric but no regrets
Who saw the music in our diarchy?
As...

Whoa! Whoa! If pushed I could just about defend that opening word, a reference to a cool chapter in my English set book, D.H. Lawrence's *Sons and Lovers*. I might even begin to justify 'empty rhetoric', a phrase I'd picked up from F.R. Leavis. But diarchy? Diarchy?

Some words are destined to have their moment only once in

the annals of pop. The Human League's 'Being Boiled' is surely the only song to feature the word 'sericulture' or silk cultivation. Warren Zevon mentions the cattle disease 'brucellosis' in 'Play It All Night'. And I feel sure that 'diarchy' ('government by two states or individuals' according to Chambers) is never going to turn up in the chorus to a Justin Timberlake song. Why, you may ask, had I become the default lyricist? Well, I was doing English.

As if the lyrics weren't daunting enough, the musical accompaniment to 'Triangle' would have driven away even more of the potential audience; a jolting series of cod-classical episodes in a succession of insane time signatures. At a loss what to do in the second half of the song, we simply lifted wholesale a charming piece of music called 'Saturday's Child' by the composer Richard Rodney Bennett from the pages of one of Prof's piano theory books that was conveniently to hand in the piano stool. Then we set about it with our rudimentary instruments till it was dead. If Mr Bennett is reading this, which I doubt, I can only apologise. We acted out of love but we loved not wisely but too well.

'Triangle' never got finished for two reasons. First, it was unfinishable. It was doomed by the weight of its portent, a monument to teenage folly. It was like painting the Forth Bridge; once you'd got to the end, the beginning needed repainting. The relationship that inspired it was long over by the time we got to the first of the many instrumental bridges.

More importantly though, 'Triangle' never got finished because right in the middle of its composition, the world was turned upside down. As we sat, grim of face and knotted of digit, in Prof's parlour on a leafy suburban lane where Wigan meets the Lancashire countryside, we could not have known that forces were at work that would bring forth a seismic change in postwar culture, that would change Britain for ever and that would, more to the point, really muck up Bill Grundy's chances of ever presenting *The Generation Game*.

9 Neat Neat Neat

No one knows who worked out that a sharpened flint tethered to a stick gave mankind the crucial advantage in early encounters with bears. Similarly, no one knows which enterprising soul first ventured that the resultant bear meat tasted even better if you held it over the fire for a while. And definitely no one knows which really smart cookie worked out, perhaps after a nice slow-cooked bear steak, that if you filed the edges of those big rocks till they were circular and strapped a few of them under a couple of logs, you had the beginnings of a Ford Mondeo. Nearer our own time, academics squabble like fractious children over who invented what and when. Take photography? Was it Daguerre? Or Fox Talbot? Or Friese Green? And where did they get their pictures developed?

So it is with punk rock. Americans will tell you that it all begins in the late Sixties with The Fugs or the Velvet Underground, rejecting the frilly, scented, beatific ethic of the times with anarchic noise and bilious sentiments. Others will say it begins when a whiny upstart London clothes designer called Malcolm McLaren met the New York Dolls in their home city and fell hopelessly, sarcastically in love with them. But I have my own version of history. And this, after all, is my story. So, exercise books out, write this down: punk begins on 10 December 1976 when John Peel aired his first live session with The Damned and my homework slid from my lap as I rose like an automaton and walked, stunned, across my bedroom to turn that awesome racket up.

'Neat Neat Neat' isn't the first punk record. It's not even The Damned's first punk record. That was 'New Rose', released two months before, two minutes of louche, drawling, garage love song that is, by common consent, now regarded as the first UK punk single. I don't know why, but I'd missed that. Peel must have played it, and like all teen bohemians I listened to Peel as often as my crowded social life would allow. It was the only place you could actually hear the records you read about in *Sounds* and *NME*. And I'd been reading about this punk thing for nigh on half a year now. So, I must have been out getting a love bite or round at Nigel's drinking home brew and listening to his *Aphrodite's Child* albums the night Peel played 'New Rose'. So I came to punk rock seven weeks late. I caught up fast though.

Till that fateful night when I heard 'Neat Neat Neat', I was unsure about punk. I wasn't entirely sure that punk rock wasn't just a scam perpetrated by the preening trendies of West 1. I was as keen on spitting, rioting, smashing things up as the next teenager. But I also fancied myself as an enigmatic intellectual, often found head buried in slim volume of difficult modern verse. Frankly, these Sex Pistols sounded like oiks. Even worse, Cockney oiks. I'd also got it hopelessly confused in my mind with pub rock – Roogalator, Dave Edmunds and Brinsley Schwarz. This I had heard and I didn't like it one little bit, horrible beery music for blokes with beards, the sort of music your chemistry teacher would like.

So there I was sitting in my bedroom, probably leafing idly though a music paper brushing up on the album charts when I should have been brushing up on the Chartists, listening to the pretty tired and ordinary selection of tunes Peel played that evening. If I remember correctly he played Poco's 'Rose Of Cimmaron' twice, which shows how desperate the times were. Then he played 'Neat Neat Neat' by The Damned and nothing was ever the same again.

Listening to it again – as I am right now – from the perspective of great age and wisdom, it's still apparent to me just what was so seismic about it. Since October 1976 there have been any number of new punks, acres of newsprint full of hyperbole about angry young men who are going to take the music business by the scruff of its bourgeois neck and shake it out of complacency. But in truth, you can only do this once. After Pandora has opened her box, opening it again will never have the same illicit and revolutionary thrill.

Put it this way. Do you know who Eugene Cernan and Harrison Schmitt are? If you do, go to the top of the class. They ought to be famous. They went to the moon. The problem is they went in 1972, three years after Armstrong and Aldrin. Just as the time for walking on the moon was July 1969, the time for punk rock was '76 when we needed it, not years later when the job was effectively done, wars fought, forces of evil – the Sutherland Brothers and Quiver – vanquished.

Punk rock, unlike the moon landings some would argue, really happened. I know. I was there. It all starts with a noise on the radio, a bass guitar low and growling, playing a two-note riff from right out of the primordial soup. After five seconds, with a crash of drums and a whoop of idiot glee, everyone joins in. Suddenly the racket subsides again and over the ghostly whoosh and clatter of that skeletal rhythm section, there's this bloke singing. Probably a bloke, but it's not certain from the sexy, lobotomised bleating. And what's that he's singing? Lean closer to the radio…

*BE A MAN, CAN A MYSTERY MAN / BE A DOLL, BE A BABY
    DOLL,
IT CAN'T BE FUN NOT ANY WAY / THERE CAN BE FOUND
    NO WAY AT ALL,
A DISTANT MAN CAN'T SYMPATHISE / CAN'T UPHOLD
    HIS DISTANT LAWS,
DUE TO FORM ON THAT TODAY / I GOT A FEELING THEN
    I HEAR THAT CALL,*

*I SAID NEAT NEAT NEAT, SHE CAN'T AFFORD A CANNON,
NEAT NEAT NEAT, SHE CAN'T AFFORD A GUN AT ALL,*

*NEAT NEAT NEAT !
NO CRIME IF THERE AINT NO LAW,
NO MORE COPS LEFT TO MESS YOU AROUND,
NO MORE DREAMS OF MYSTERY CHORDS,
NO MORE SIGHT TO BRING YOU DOWN.*

Half heard and hardly comprehended, it still had something that
Jon Anderson's and Pete Sinfield's would never have. It was
blank verse, in the sense that there was something nihilistic and
compelling about these elliptical phrases. Who was the distant
man? What were his distant laws? Why did the girl want a
cannon? And that final verse? What weird future world is this,
bereft of law, crime and policemen, and for that matter mystery
chords? You hadn't got time to ponder this though fully because
2.41 seconds later it was gone, taking society as I knew it with it.

If you go into a room that contains an opened paint can, you very
soon know about it. I think the same applies to music. The best
carries that unmistakable pungent whiff of greatness. Great pop
music – all great music, be it The Buzzcocks or Bartók, Thelonious

Monk or Johann Sebastian Bach – has a smell. Before your critical faculties have got out of bed, your subconscious is out of the shower, brewing up, opening the post, and telling you that this is the real deal. Punk records by the much more critically revered Buzzcocks, The Clash, and Wire would soon come to mean much much more. But The Damned had got my motor running. I knew that there was something in this punk rock thing after all.

I couldn't wait to go to school next day. Normally, there was little to look forward to on the average day at a Catholic grammar in the mid-1970s unless you really enjoyed playing shinty on tarmac in a hailstorm. This day there was something that needed to be discussed with my peers. I had seen the future and it worked. I needed to share my vision, we all needed to move forward, it was Big Bang 2, Year Zero, Lobster thermidor or whatever that first month of the French revolutionary calendar is. The past was a foreign country, they did things differently there. They bought Eagles records for one thing. It had been fun while it lasted, but now we must sell our records, buy some radically different trousers, put all of the Christian Brothers to the sword and march on Westminster where, after a brief and glorious struggle involving hand-to-hand fighting with Bruce Forsyth and Lenny Bennett, we would ask Jane Suck and Julie Burchill to form a government.

Back in 1976 John Rigby Roman Catholic School had a sort of semi-sheltered recess at the back of the art-room toilets that faced the tarmac football pitch. This was our water cooler, our Algonquin round table, our parish pump. All sorts of things got debated here, fully and frankly, sometimes with accompanying kicks, wedgies, and Chinese burns. This morning I was setting the agenda.

'Did you hear that Damned record on John Peel? "Neat Neat Neat". It's ace.'

'Bollocks! Churn on! It's shit. They can't play. They're all divs.'

'Punk. Fucking junk more like. You're just trying to be trendy, you queer.'

'Get listening to Richie Blackmore's "Rainbow", they're fucking lush, pal.'

A prophet without honour in my own land again, I fear. There was much hostility to punk rock. Young men for all their predilection for violence, mayhem and skiving are real sticklers for technique, ability, credentials and skill. 'Skill' was even a term of approbation, as in 'That new girl at the chippie is skill' or 'You've got tickets for the replay? Skill!' What the forces of conservatism, whatever their ages, didn't like about punk was that it made a virtue of lack of technique, of energy over certified ability. An early punk single by local act The Nosebleeds proudly proclaimed 'Aint Been To No Music School'; an unnecessary declaration to be honest, given how The Nosebleeds sounded. Similarly, the most famous cover of the *Sniffin Glue* fanzine, edited by Mark Perry and alma mater to one Danny Baker, showed a series of captioned fingering diagrams for aspiring guitarists: 'Here's one chord, here's two more, now form your own band.'

This was strong stuff to take after years of *Melody Maker* asking us to vote for best saxophonist and implicitly praising musicians for their flying fingers, paradiddles and 100 mph solos. Most were unwilling to expose themselves to ridicule by liking this childish, simplistic music played by goons in binliners. But on that fateful cold morning there were a few of us, stamping and breathing on our hands, who swore allegiance to this bold new music. My friend and Mammoth Frog colleague Nigel – by the way, this was clearly going to have dire implications for the Frog – had heard that The Ramones were good. Dylan, a former Slade bootboy with a compassionate streak, liked the sound of The Clash.

We were few but vocal and committed. Punk was still deeply underground, subterranean even. If I told my mum that I'd become a punk, she'd have assumed that I'd become a Jimmy

Cagney impersonator. How could we have known, we bijou breed of small town punks, that by the end of the month, everyone in Britain would have an opinion about this new youth movement, how punk rock would be on every snarling lip and every front page, of how we would have gone from being a curio to public enemy number one, a menace, the sick scourge of society. All thanks to the clothes, the records, some judicious swearing and Bill Grundy.

Quickly, the few nascent punks in school and in town coalesced into a knot of friendship, a social shift repeated in pretty much every town in Britain. The very bright and the very thuggish, the loners, the make-up wearers, the sexually confused, the outcasts, all of these kids saw in punk their salvation and were drawn together, huddling for security against the beery Brut splash-on football hooligan culture of the times. Here was music – raucous, electrifying music – that celebrated difference and dissent, that rejected the status quo, that thrived on mockery, jokes, anger, confusion. Music that sewed chaos and preached anarchy as recreation. After Leo Sayer and 'Hotel California', it was invigorating as an ice-cold shower or a headful of cheap biker speed, whichever you preferred. There could be no turning back now. The distant man couldn't sympathise, he couldn't uphold his distant laws. We'd got the feeling, and we'd heard that call.

10 White Riot!

Rick Wakeman once said of punk rock, 'People forget now just what a revolution it was. It put us old guard out of work almost overnight. It was like working in a factory or something, you turned up at the gates the next day and the record companies were saying, "Sorry guys, you're finished, here's your cards."'

It ought to be pointed out here that Rick didn't think this was a terrifically good thing. During the Eighties, whenever you saw a group of ashen-faced men leaving a car plant having been told by the management that, thanks for everything, guys, but their jobs could be done more cheaply in Laos and it was down to the dole office, very few ever said, 'Well, it's for the best. I'm sure British industry will emerge leaner and fitter, though for us personally there will inevitably be short-term pain.'

Similarly, very few of the prog dinosaurs, MOR mastodons and country rock stegosauri embraced the purgative spirit of punk. Let's not shed too many tears though. Unlike the miners, steel and textile workers and engineers who'd all be losing their jobs over the next bleak decade, rock stars generally had a little something put by. Rick could always sell a Rolls-Royce or two. Piqued by the Pistols joining his label A&M, it's said that Wakeman wrote to the board demanding that they cancel the Sex

Pistols contract. When we heard this, we punks, it just confirmed what we thought about yesterday's multi-millionaire rockers. If you weren't part of the punk solution, you were part of the boring old fart problem.

This was the real revolutionary impulse of punk. Even prog rock enthusiasts like me couldn't help but feel that this sort of well-placed kick up the velveteen loon pants was long overdue. In general, the rock aristocracy took it badly. They bleated every week in the music press – when they'd give them the space that is, as there were important Sham 69 articles to run – saying that this punk rubbish was a fad, that the punks looked terrible and couldn't play. This wheedling cut no ice with us young turks. They were like your dad, these geezers, or your granddad, as Glenn Matlock had said of Bill Grundy during *that* interview.

There were ritual bonfires of Greenslade and Yes albums on lowland hills. I kept my Gentle Giant albums but all the rest of my prog collection went into plastic bags under the stairs. Secrets hushed up, like burying a body. Some really cool people, who'd only ever bought albums by impenetrable and trendy Germans like Can and Faust or Nico records with their wheezing, bronchial harmonium, were OK. But I had all kinds of dark and gruesome things. Rather like someone who'd been burgled – in a nice way – I'd have to start again.

Punk meant new values, new records, new politics, a new aesthetic – but more important than any of this, it meant a new wardrobe. To put punk's fashion impact in context we must recall the prevailing couture of the mid-Seventies.

Everyone wore flares; only the degree, gradient and angle of flare differed according to age and subculture. Your dad's Man at C&A slacks would be just off the perpendicular, your French teacher wore purple bellbottoms whose colour matched his tinted aviator specs, you and all your peers wore Oxford or Birmingham bags so vast at the ankle that Scouts could do their Duke of

Edinburgh thingy sleeping beneath them. Of all the various bastions that punk demolished, flared trousers would be one of the toughest and most resilient, as we shall see.

Among the young, Wranglers, Levis, Lee Coopers and other denimiers of note were ubiquitous. Girls who wanted to stand out and look particularly ridiculous for a special occasion would wear culottes, a perfunctory, unfinished trouser that stopped at the knee. Collars were enormous, dwarfing the head so it looked like a grape. Fabrics were relentlessly and unapologetically man-made; wearing anything connected with an animal or plant would have been tantamount to living in a cave. Your shirts were designed by ICI scientists and produced in test tubes. In theory, they never needed ironing and possessed the half-life of uranium 360. Friction between the garments of courting couples would create a halo of sparks and a power surge that you could run a moped on.

Male and female alike wore unflattering rugby shirts or what we in Wigan called Simon shirts. Who Simon was I have no idea, but he must have been unreasonably keen on tight short-sleeved T-shirts with big collars and tiny breast pockets. Regular shirts were thought too boring and they had to be enlivened with motifs: cars, dogs, space hardware, the tackier the better frankly.

Everyone had long hair. Newsreaders, footballers, politicians, minor royals. Girls wore their hair flowing, flicked and fulsome after the fashion of Farrah Fawcett Majors. Blokes sought to emulate David Wilkie, pageboy haircuts curled slightly under, virile, verdant moustaches, the great smell of Brut hung heavy in every Berni Inn.

Let's return though to the vexed issue of the flared versus straight-leg trouser. You wouldn't believe the fuss, not to say, casual violence that this inspired. To recap, flared trousers were ubiquitous. Normal people would no more wear straight-legs than they would wear doublet and hose; it was the garb of a bygone era. 'Drainpipes' (or, worse, 'shit-stoppers') were what Teddy Boys wore and Teddy Boys were the most laughable subcult of all, men who would not admit to the passage of time. They drove buses generally, hair piled high with Brylcreem, hands decorated with tattoos and skull rings. Given that the punks brought their preferred trouser cuff back into fashion, Teds were notoriously ungrateful. Hell's Angels didn't much care for us, skins and mods mainly joined us, but Teds – once radical, now dreadfully conservative at heart, respectful of the Queen Mum and the rest – actively sought out our destruction. A gang of Teds once threw a table though the window of the Swan and Railway pub, on the occasion of one of Wigan's first punk nights. I was there, I'm proud to say, ever so slightly sorry not to have been a little bloodied by flying glass.

I can't remember where I bought my first pair of straight-leg trousers from; possibly Slaters in Makinsons Arcade, one of those curious traditional outfitters where you could buy Cash's woven nametags and PE kit as well as 32-hole Doc Marten boots for recreational violence when the day's studies were done. I wore them for the first time combined with a tartan shirt and baseball boots on a trip to Manchester's Free Trade Hall to see The Clash. Walking into Wigan town centre that night, the entire top deck of a 610 bus had turned to gawp and give me the fingers – that's 'fingers' as in *Kes* and Harvey Smith, not the 'finger' as in bratty Americans and those terrible bands with fat bassists, goatee beards and baggy shorts.

A couple of afternoons later, strolling through Mesnes Park, an urchin child of about ten had shouted, 'Look at fucking Johnny Rotten,' as I passed by. Once you put on your ripped T-shirt and straight-leg jeans, you ceased to be a local teenager, you became a folk devil, an agent of anarchy, an outlaw. The sort of person that ageing Bill Haley fans would throw furniture at. It was almost unbearably exciting.

In the first few heady months of punk, demand far outstripped supply as far as records were concerned. Whether by deliberate policy or sheer incompetence, few of Wigan's record shops stocked punk records. There was one exception to this: Javelin Records in the new precinct whose punk sympathies would later bring them into conflict with Wigan's notoriously dopey council. In 1938, when every other authority in Britain agreed to give Walt Disney's *Snow White* a 'U' or Unlimited certificate, Wigan cinemas were forced by the town's self-appointed commissars to award it an 'A' certificate (adults must accompany) in case some small children were frightened by a drawing of a witch.

Now the witch hunt had turned to punk. Up and down the county, pompous aldermen relished their moment of fame. In Derby, the council demanded that The Damned play a private show for them before loftily declaring that they couldn't appear in their town after all. It seems barely believable now but as '76 gave way to '77, battle lines were being drawn. As Julie Burchill put it in *NME*, 'The Sex Pistols are coming to your town. Are you going to support them? Are you going to rise up or are you going to sink back into your stupor for another decade?'

The Sex Pistols were actually coming to our town, to the Casino as part of the infamous SPOTS or Sex Pistols On Tour Secretly shows. On the evening of the gig the council and police summarily banned the show. The town centre swarmed with deflated punks from miles around, curious onlookers and bemused, slightly nervous policemen. Rumour had it that the Pistols had never had any intention of playing in Wigan and were currently somewhere between glamorous engagements in Doncaster and Wolverhampton.

As it turned out, they were indeed somewhere between Doncaster and Wolverhampton. They were in Wigan. At a loose end, we went into Mr M's bar next door to the Casino and there were the Sex Pistols, Britain's most feared social deviants, drinking gassy lager and playing pool. It was actually hard to distinguish them from the other safety-pinned and scrawny punks who had come to town that night. Steve Jones had a slightly worse haircut than most of his fans but that was about it.

Far too awestruck to even speak, we just hung around the environs of the table passing them chalk. After a few minutes they left. I feel certain, however, that at school that Monday, the incident had been embellished until, in the version we relayed to our peers, we had caroused with them till the small hours, enjoyed a fish and chip supper, exchanged phone numbers and arranged to go camping together. For other people, the night ended less amiably. The disappointed punks left the venue just as the Northern Soul crowds were arriving for the Allnighter. There was what the *Evening Post* described as 'a fracas', which makes it sound rather more amusing than it was. Two blokes were stabbed, one of them an old junior school mate of mine.

Meanwhile back at Javelin records, the search for punk rock kicks went on. Singles were a pot-pourri and a bit of a lottery; for every incendiary call to arms, every 'Neat Neat Neat', 'Anarchy In The UK' or 'White Riot', there was something terrible by Ed Banger and the Nosebleeds, the crap French band Stinky Toys or Birmingham's Killjoys. What few albums existed early on were played to death, debated, fetishised like artefacts of a primitive religion, which is what I guess they were. A big favourite of my circle was *Live at the Roxy*, a melange of punkish fellow travellers caught live one night at this famous venue. Johnny Moped was as bad as his name but also there was terrific and challenging stuff. X Ray Spex had a woman singer and a sax. Wire had strange dour cerebral lyrics and a song called 'Lowdown' which astonished simply by its loping, mid-pace time signature and the brazenly daring inclusion of a minor chord. A minor chord! It was the first I had ever heard in a punk record and it was as shocking as if they'd included a Mozart string trio or a choral section. When Wire made their own fully fledged album *Pink Flag*, I dashed down to Javelin Records to buy it. By the standards of the time, it was extraordinary. But I now realise that by the standards of any time, it's extraordinary.

But pride of place in my bijou punk album collection went to *The Clash* by The Clash. Siouxsie Sue once said that even in the tough camaraderie of punk, you were essentially either a Pistols or a Clash person. She's absolutely right. She and her famous Bromley contingent were Pistols people, drawn to the amoral nihilism of the band. I can see the appeal of that myself now but aged sixteen, full of splenetic righteous anger and outlaw romance, there was only one band for me.

By a conservative estimate I would say I played the first Clash album twice a day, every day for six months. It became ingrained on my psyche, from the terse 'bum titty, bum titty' drum intro to 'Janie Jones' to the ragged, glorious, anthemic close of 'Garageland' which mirrored closely my own music apprentice-ship in Mammoth Frog ('24 singers, one microphone, four guitar players, one guitar'). I loved how, in Joe Strummer and Mick Jones, The Clash had punk's very own Lennon and McCartney; Strummer, bilious and shouting through what seemed to be a mouthful of pebbles and rubbing alcohol, Jones, tuneful and slightly fey, with a voice as substantial as tissue paper.

The Clash were essentially romantics – while the Pistols sang about Belsen and girls from Birmingham called Pauline who had abortions and lived, implausibly, in trees, The Clash sang about the Spanish Civil War and Blackshirts and fighting the law, even if the law won. It's important to remember that the reptilian ur-nazis of the National Front were on the rise all across Britain, beating the Liberals into third place in terms of support in many constituencies. In this climate of fear and apprehension, The Clash's stirring evocations of Lorca, Victor Jara and the fight against fascism seemed like urgent and relevant social bulletins not the rhetorical gestures they might have done.

They also had relevance closer to home. By a real stroke of bad luck my mum caught me smoking outside the local off-licence and I was grounded for a few days. We hadn't embraced the language of *Neighbours* and *Buffy the Vampire Slayer* then though. We called it getting bollocked. The effect was the same. I sat at home in paroxysms of misery sustained only by playing 'White Riot' (the good version, with the sirens and the running feet) 26 times back to back. I'm not entirely sure what The Clash were on about when they wrote 'White Riot' or quite what they were trying to encourage. But I'd like to think that they'd be happy to know that it brought solace to a young lad who had been confined to his bedroom in generational conflict over a furtive Number 6. I fought my mum but my mum won.

To be a punk in South Lancashire in 1977 was to be pretty much a pariah. What few social ills couldn't be blamed on Harold Wilson or Denis Healey or trades union ogres like Scargill, Gormley and that post office bloke with the handlebar moustache were blamed on punks, whether or not there was clear evidence implicating them. The oil crisis, the Irish troubles, skyjacking. Punks were behind the lot of them. When not urinating on old ladies or spitting on the Queen, they were masterminding world evil from behind the scenes, like Moriarty or Dr No.

We had to stick together. And we did. We stuck together in a place called the Bier Keller on King Street, Wigan's most violent thoroughfare. In later years, my job has taken me to some hairy locales: not hairy in the Sandy Gall/John Pilger sense, as in the Gaza Strip or Grozhny. But certainly as hairy as the urban West gets, such as the Reeperbahn, the Chicago Housing project of Cabrini Green or Moss Side. But though I have walked, quite quickly it must be said, through the valley of the shadow of death, I have feared no evil; chiefly because I have walked down King

Street at 2 a.m. on a Friday night and that really is scary. On more than one occasion in my youth, the police, at a loss over how to contain the rucks and rolling mauls, simply cordoned off both ends of the street and went back to the station for a cuppa, leaving the fights to extinguish themselves naturally.

Beneath the pavements of King Street lay the Bier Keller, a subterranean temple to all that was outlawed, nasty and seductive. Pre '77, it had been a bikers and Hell's Angels pub. I'd attended the rock nights there as a small boy (Tommy the genial bouncer was marvellously vague about the finer points of licensing law) and found them intoxicating. I'd sit there, nursing a pint of mild that cost 23p on Tuesdays and Thursdays only, open-mouthed and vicariously high on patchouli oil and the earthy aroma of Red Leb, watching gorgeous unattainable hippy girls in their cheesecloths and faded Levis and blokes in bike leathers and military surplus gear idiot dancing and head-banging to Jethro Tull's 'Locomotive Breath' and Lynyrd Skynyrd's 'Free Bird'. I have never found a better nightclub. On the day of the Silver Jubilee, 1977, while the rest of the country ate jelly and drank fizzy bottled beer at trestle tables in the street in a bizarre throwback to the 1940s, I and my ilk lurked beneath the same pavements at the Keller's Stuff the Jubilee All Dayer where 'God Save The Queen' was played on the hour every hour, our unofficial anthem to sheer bloody-mindedness and 'not joining in'.

When punk broke out across the face of Britain like a disfiguring rash, it was natural and fitting that the Keller, the spiritual home of Wigan's outsider youth, should offer solace to the punks, rather like churches do with illegal immigrants.

There was me and Nigel and Stocky from our school gang. There was Mad Mick who looked like Jim Davidson with an experimental Afro and who, as his name implies, was more drawn to the opportunities for mayhem and casual violence of punk than its aesthetic qualities. There was his girlfriend Louise, the most sour-faced girl I have ever seen. She made Siouxsie Sue look like Moira Stewart and had a face, as the local adage had it, like a bulldog licking piss off a nettle.

There was Sue and Lynne who dressed in binliners and lived in the high-rise flats behind my house on the Worsley Mesnes council estate. Sometimes we'd go there after the Keller closed and listen to Suicide's 'Ghost Rider' or Television's 'Little Johnnie Jewel'. Sitting there on their moth-eaten settee on the sixteenth floor, drinking Breaker Malt Liquor and listening to New York No Wave with a blonde girl in a PVC skirt, I thought life had nothing more decadent, modern and glamorous to offer. I think I may have been right.

There was Steve Coyle, who was hard as rock, wore demob suits and looked like Bryan Ferry would have if he'd forgotten about all that art school nonsense, stayed in Newcastle and got a job in a scrapyard: a lustrous coal-black quiff, a handsome jaw, an armful of homemade tattoos and a broken nose.

There was 'Jem' (this the ages-old Lancastrian factory and colliery diminutive for James) and his mate Pete. Pete was a nice, if none too bright lad. Jem was a nutter who worked in Rathbones bakery; 'Rathbones Gold Medal Bread, it'll make you shit like lead, and no effing wonder, you fart like thunder after Rathbones gold medal bread' as local kids sang. This wasn't their official advertising slogan by the way. He wore boiler suits, cut his own hair with scissors and liked The Stooges. It was once said of Humphrey Bogart, 'He's a hell of a nice guy until 11.30. After that he thinks he's Humphrey Bogart.' This very much applied to Jem. Before last orders, you could have a really very thought-provoking discussion with him about Metallic KO or whether 999 really were just a poor man's Clash. But after that, he was unpredictable to say the least, liable to punch you in the throat or steal a car radio. Mad, bad and quite taxing to know. But he was fun.

And he had a drumkit.

It was, frankly, only a matter of time.

11 Anything Goes

Mammoth Frog's days were numbered from the first moment I heard 'Neat Neat Neat'. Prof didn't share my enthusiasm for punk rock; indeed, mischievously, he tried to convince me that The Clash were using, whisper it, a synthesiser on 'Garageland'. Synthesisers were indissolubly associated with progressive rock. For The Clash to have been caught twiddling the knobs of a Moog would have been tantamount to them wearing silver capes or writing songs about *The Hobbit*. Thankfully it wasn't true.

As Nigel and I had gone over to the punk camp with all the vigour of the recent, shining-eyed convert, it was plain that Mammoth Frog, with its unconventional instruments and songs that made T.S. Eliot's *Waste Land* seem like 'Shang A Lang', was doomed. I don't recall there being much fuss; there was no tearful final session, certainly no farewell tour. We had never ventured further than Prof's cosy suburban parlour. That was part of the problem. Progressive rock was predicated on the notion of great technical accomplishment. You couldn't just get up and play; you had to have paid your dues.

Punk scorned such tardiness and cowardice. Both Nigel and I were raring to go. And this time, the cheap gear and Winfield amps would be a positive advantage in the DIY, ragged-trousered ethos of punk. It was said, in fact, that all of The Buzzcocks' equipment had come from Woolworth's. So we'd be in very good company. What had previously been attributable to mere poverty was now a moral and aesthetic statement.

One night at the Keller, Jem, the unhinged baker, turned up in a works overall on which he'd spray-painted the legend 'Dennis Lethal' across the back. A wry, Northern take on punk's proliferation of daft, cod-threatening pseudonyms, it made me laugh and showed that behind the casual violence and law-breaking, Jem was a smart cookie. 'You need a pseudonym if you're in a punk band. Terry Chimes was Tory Crimes,' he explained with reference to The Clash's enigmatic drummer, soon to be replaced by Topper Headon. 'I'm a drummer. I'm Dennis Lethal. It's written on my kit.'

A drummer. This was very interesting news. Nigel and I repaired to a corner with pints of mild while Penetration's 'Don't Dictate' wailed over the disco. We weighed up the pros and cons. Jem was an unstable if entertaining nutter. He could turn nasty and he was prone to emotional outbursts: tears, rage, hysteria, black depressions, destruction of furniture. But he did have that drumkit.

As anyone who's ever tried to form a teenage band will know, drummers are gold-dust. Tone-deaf, troglodytic gold-dust maybe but gold-dust. Drumkits cost a lot of money, especially when compared to a guitar from the Grattans catalogue. They are a bugger to transport, taking up the entire back seat and obscuring all the rear window of the average Seventies saloon car. Assembly and dismantling the kit takes hours. If you rush home from MFI salivating at the prospect of spending a weekend putting together a flatpack bookshelf with poorly translated instructions and a tiny Allen key, then the drums are your instrument.

Worst of all, you can never practise. Not unless you possess your own small Scottish island or underground silo anyway. No one in their right mind wants to listen to a trainee drummer. Let's face it, no one in their right mind wants to listen to an accomplished drummer if he's playing solo. As for amateurs, well, a struggling guitarist in an upstairs bedroom can still sound vaguely like music. A fledgling drummer in an upstairs bedroom sounds like domestic violence in suits of armour. Jem, though, had apparently been playing for years. We reasoned he wouldn't need to practise much. And if he did, we wouldn't be there. If we were, we could drown him out with our own electrical devices.

Nigel and I had wanted to try our hand as punk musicians for months. After the complexities of Mammoth Frog, it would feel like liberation, like being let out of musicians' prison. But the age-old problem of drummer scarcity had so far stymied us. Now we had one in our clutches, almost. There had to be a catch though, and so there was.

Jem was as keen as us to get Wigan's first punk combo off the ground. So keen that he had already done much of the ground-work. He already had a band, albeit a largely theoretical one. It was/would be called The Idiots and comprised Jem on drums, his chum Paul Collis on vocals and two as yet unconfirmed musicians on guitar and bass. On the surface, it seemed as if our aspirations and abilities would dovetail sweetly. But there were clouds on the horizon, as you may have guessed.

First, there was the name. Even by the standards of punk's first lurid summer, The Idiots struck me as crap. It was dumb; it didn't have any of the menacing cool of the Sex Pistols, The Clash or The Damned. It didn't even have any of the menacing cool of determinedly second division punk acts like Slaughter and the Dogs or The Vibrators. It sounded like a punk band in a bad Grumbleweeds routine.

The other problem was more serious though. While I entertained no 'lead singer' fantasies à la Robert Plant-style chestbaring or Johnny Rotten gurning, I had generally assumed I'd sing in any band I was in. I wrote lyrics, and, as any fule kno, you had to sing your own words. I had things to say, and I was the man to say them. Plus I could sing a little, certainly by the standards of punk. Paul Collis looked the part, I had to admit. He had a really cool black mohair jumper, a savage, asymmetric crop and some ripped jeans and 'bumper' boots just like Dee Dee Ramone. 'Maybe he can sing,' offered Nigel brightly. To be honest, even if he'd sung like a combination of Frank Sinatra, Marvin Gaye and Joe Strummer, I'd have been loathe to relinquish the microphone. I said nothing.

After some discussions in the Keller, we decided to hold a preliminary rehearsal at Nigel's house in Shevington. For some weeks I had been amassing material in the new punk idiom, strumming into the small hours on my unamplified, weighty Zenta and making hurried jottings in an A4 refill pad. As these songs would form the kernel of our early set, I should perhaps take you through them.

First, there was 'Who Needs Karl Marx?'. I'd started studying sociology and had become slightly obsessed with it. There was a lot of overlap between punk rock and sociology, the former borrowed much of the latter's language and terms of reference. Anarchy, deviance, social control – you could hear it discussed every day in class and hear it bellowed about every night in clubs by people with only the slenderest grasp of what it all meant.

My first year Sociology A level provided much grist to my punk songwriting mill. 'Who Needs Karl Marx?' was not so much a diatribe against socialism as an unreasonably sneering attack on left-wing demagogues, bearded Open University lecturers in peardrop collars and their ilk. It wasn't so much a song as Chad Valley Maoist dialectical faction fighting set to a simple three-chord riff. I say simple, but even the presence of that third chord meant that it was already enormously more advanced than the work of Chelsea or The Lurkers. Only one line sticks in my mind now: 'Karl is the opium of sociology teachers'. Perhaps it's as well that I've forgotten the rest.

By song two, I was already getting dissatisfied with the constraints of the format. 'New Society' (named after the now defunct sociological journal of course) was daringly littered with minor chords and obscure philosophical references. Completing a trio of early compositions was 'Prague', based on, or more properly I should say stolen brazenly from, the gorgeous descending chord sequence from Bob Dylan's 'Lay Lady Lady', thus straying even further from the punk template. It was another diatribe against an irrelevant chimera only I cared about; in this case the growing glamorisation of Cold War conflict, the Soviet Bloc and dictatorship in general. David Bowie's brilliant *Low* had been around for a year or two and had encouraged lesser talents/ pillocks to don the long overcoat and affect mitteleuropean alienated sang froid. This trend, of course, would reach its apotheosis in Ultravox's terrifically silly 'Vienna'. 'Prague' had no fixed political targets, containing irate and wide-ranging broadsides and references to gas chambers, Torremolinos and petrol bombers.

These were the three original songs that I brought along to the very first rehearsal of The Idiots. They were supplemented by what I thought was a witty and thought-provoking choice of cover versions. A few weeks previously, I'd spent an evening in Springfield babysitting my little twin nephew and niece while Auntie Maureen, Uncle Brian and my mum and dad had gone out for a few pints. While there and bored with *Charlie's Angels*, even though it was an episode in which Cheryl Ladd rarely changed out of a swimsuit, I had leafed through my auntie and uncle's record collection. Along with the *South Pacific* soundtrack and a *Mario Lanza Collection* – Uncle Brian had remained impervious to successive waves of hairy youths with guitars – there I came across, resplendent in its iconic sleeve portrait of old Blue Eyes looking carefree in a trilby – a copy of Frank Sinatra's *Songs for Swingin' Lovers*.

Listening to Nelson Riddle's opulent arrangements and Frank's laconic offhand delivery, a thought occurred to me. A thought that would only occur to a real grammar school smart-alec. These would make great punk songs. It would show not only a certain sense of humour but it would be one less song I'd have to write in order to get a set together. Speed, you see, was of the essence. Things happened so fast in the early days of punk that everything might have been turned on its head again by next Thursday. Punk was broadening into new wave, power pop and reggae already; next week it might be banjos or synthesisers. It was imperative that The Idiots became a touring live act as soon as was humanly possible. In this endeavour Frank Sinatra and Cole Porter were about to lend an unwitting hand.

I thought for a while about reworking 'You Make Me Feel So Young' as 'Youngers Makes Me Feel You So', a punk paean to the amorous properties of Tartan Extra. In the end though I chose 'Anything Goes'. It was simple and catchy; moreover, Porter's elegant lyric was neatly applicable to the whole punk revolution. 'In olden days a glimpse of stocking was looked on as something shocking, now, heaven knows, anything goes' would, I felt sure, sound great when snarled over our full sonic arsenal.

The first Idiots rehearsal was convened one Saturday afternoon in mid-1977 in Nigel's bedroom in Shevington, where Wigan turns unexpectedly leafy. I had my Zenta Stratocaster copy purchased in instalments from the GUS catalogue and my Winfield amplifier, whose colossal weight was in inverse proportion to its amplification powers. Nigel had an electric bass of obscure provenance and lineage plus 'Fred' the battered Vox AC30 so individual and characterful that we had given it a name. Fred was capricious and had a grouchy temperament; often mid-song he would emit a terrifying, high-pitched buzz that could only be cured by striking him. A comically large wooden mallet was kept in the cable store at the amp's rear for this purpose. Jem arrived with an ancient but roadworthy Premier drumkit and began the lengthy process of setting up, which involved him strewing the ground with metal rods and swearing. In many ways, it was like an ancient tribal rite.

'New Society' became the default opener by virtue of its big power chord intro and swishing hi hat. Swishing hi hats were more likely to be found in the works of the Bee Gees than The Clash but we were soon to learn that Jem's style was a rich and eclectic mix of all the pop music of the past fifty years played with gusto and at varying tempos. This was fine. He could play, even if he was very much his own man in the time-honoured tradition of rock drummers.

No, the problem was Paul. A certain 'couldn't give a toss' spirit was de rigueur among punk singers. Jimmy Pursey sang like a costermonger at closing time; many another stuck to the basic sneered Johnny Rotten sprechtssang. Paul though was something else. He had, its fair to say, a high voice. Dizzyingly high. Sometimes he would lapse into inaudibility and we would notice neighbourhood mongrels lined up on the lawn outside panting expectantly. But unlike Neil Young or Aled Jones, Pete's vocalising was not just at the upper end of the male range, it was scarily random. John Cage himself would have thought Pete's avant-garde approach to melody had gone too far. It was tough on the nerves and tough on the ears even by punk's standards. Plus he was singing my lyrics; overly complicated pun-laden missives on a series of topics only I cared about and then only half understood. Within ten minutes it was apparent that it was never going to work.

At the end of our first session, we had a five-song set: 'Prague', 'New Society', 'Who Needs Karl Marx?' and two covers, 'Anything

Goes', which had worked rather well in a silly way and 'Satellite Of Love', from Lou Reed's *Transformer* album. While Jem, Nigel and I had got to grips with these quite well, Paul's vocal on 'Satellite Of Love' was more reminiscent of Beryl Reed than Lou.

The next week we arranged a band meeting at the John Bull pub in the town centre; a former bikers pub, now – like the Keller – offering refuge to punks and with a great jukebox spanning Cream, The Stranglers, Jethro Tull, Mink Deville and Hawkwind. Nigel, Jem and I arrived first. Jem looked morose and haunted. It didn't take him long to expound on his depressed mental state.

'He can't bollocking sing, can he? He said he could but he can't. He couldn't carry a tune in a bucket. He'll have to go. Besides, you've written all these rum lyrics. You should sing 'em.'

All of this was music to my ears, unlike Paul's singing. As Jem pointed out, he would have to go. But how did we do it? We decided we would have to sack him. Or rather we decided Jem would have to sack him while Nigel and I would hang around in the background shrugging and looking sheepish. We did it, for some reason, in the pub toilets. Paul took it well. I think at heart even he had been shocked and horrified at what had come forth when he opened his mouth. I would often bump into Paul around town afterwards (he was a top bloke when not singing) and, if he'd a couple of pints, he'd often say, slightly slurred and melancholy, 'I was a shit singer … I know that … but I might have improved. I needed a bit of encouragement. And I know it was them two bastards who wanted me out. I know it wasn't you Stu. You're on the level.' I would listen to this in a hot, sticky mix of guilt and embarrassment. But I would do nothing to disabuse him of the idea. It has haunted me, ever so slightly, ever since. So in the unlikely event that you're reading this, Paul, I apologise. I wanted you out every bit as much as them other two bastards I'm afraid to say. It was a sordid business. But let us now move on unburdened.

Without Paul things moved on apace. In a heavily ironic gesture, we picked deliberately ludicrous Lancastrian punk alter-egos. Jem, as mentioned, was Dennis Lethal, Nigel became Harry Maniac, I rejoiced in Bert Dangerous. I also took over, as Jem proposed, what the sleeve notes of Sixties records always called the vocal chores. This at least speeded up the learning procedure. We became quite a tight little three-piece, certainly as good as Eater and, by virtue of our speed out of the blocks, the best punk group in Wigan. Indeed, the only punk group in Wigan. You would sometimes hear rumours of Clash-soundalikes in Bryn or television wannabes in Whelley but there was no proof of their existence. We had little competition, though what little we had we were soon to share a stage with.

Emboldened by our new-found compactness and verve, we felt we were ready to make our live debut. To pad out the short set we acquired another cover version, a track from Elvis Costello's *My Aim Is True* record called 'Mystery Dance' which was short, rancorous, light on chords and therefore ideal. Nigel was a fan of this funny, geeky guy with the glasses, the poor man's Buddy Holly, as Cannon and Ball called him with the usual lack of chortles. I wasn't so sure about him since he set off my pub rock radar. This was ironic considering the despotic, beady-eyed influence that Costello would cast over me for the next year or so.

Right now though, the addition of 'Mystery Dance' meant that The Idiots were go. We had been booked to appear at Wigan's second punk club, Trucks on Station Road.

We had the songs – seven, count 'em – we had the clothes, we had the ridiculous pseudonyms. All we needed, though we didn't know it yet, was the crash helmets and the riot shields.

12 Keep On Truckin'

As King Street, Wigan's Most Violent Thoroughfare, passed Wigan Wallgate station on the right, it became King Street West, slightly more sophisticated but with a taxi rank that would run red with blood most Saturday nights. At the bottom of King Street West were two squat brick buildings that must have once fulfilled some obscure function pertaining to the nearby railway.

Implausibly, they were now adjoining nightclubs. One was called Sleepers. Non-members were welcome but membership was restricted to those who could carry a railway sleeper a mile along the railway line. Next door was the less forbidding Sloopies which, at some point in the mid-Seventies, became Trucks. Trucks' gimmick, and it was a good one thought most, was that it contained a full-sized flatbed truck, the sort that carried Corona pop door to door or took sheep to slaughter. The DJ sat in the cab and the flatbed served as a small raised dance floor-cum-stage. Trucks was also famed locally as a death trap. The electrician who'd done the wiring was the brother of Kathy Hollingsworth, raven-haired, pint-sized sex siren of the lower sixth. Neither Kathy nor her brother nor any of their clan would set foot inside the building. I was made of sterner stuff though. As a band, we had to be. For Trucks soon became Wigan's second new wave disco and it was to be the venue for the first live appearance of Les Flirts.

Les what? Having ousted Pete in that bloodless coup in the toilets of the John Bull, Nigel and I moved on to our next objective – to find a better monicker than The Idiots. Les Flirts would never ring down the decades like Led Zeppelin or The Who. In truth, it couldn't even muster the tinkle of Paper Lace or the 1910 Fruitgum Company but it was an improvement on its predecessor.

Punk was sweetening into new wave and power pop. New wave loosely meant angular, arty and catchy like The Buzzcocks and Wire; power pop was much vaunted in the pages of the inkies and reached me as The Records, a jangly group of longhairs in skinny ties somewhere between The Hollies and Thin Lizzy whose *Shades in Bed* album I wore down to a sliver of black vinyl. And of course there was Elvis Costello. All these heady new influences were assimilated hungrily into Les Flirts' style.

We had an ambitious new song called Little Flirts, very much in this new vein and something of a new wave epic at four and half minutes, plus we had a backdrop designed by an artistic mate which featured a tricolour and the silhouette of a poster girl. Hence Les Flirts as stopgap name. It was essentially meaningless but it would do. We needed something to put on the flyers pronto.

How we got the gig I have no idea. I imagine it was something to do with Jem. Nigel and I were the intellectuals of the set-up. Jem was the sturdy proletarian muscle. I would have thought it was he who nagged and cajoled Trucks owner, a squat rhomboid of a man with a gold earring and a shaggy perm, the missing link between Kevin Keegan and Eddie Large. Les Flirts were booked to play at Trucks one Saturday night in the spring of 1978.

I'd been to Trucks many times as a punter. It was here that I first heard 'Bingo Masters Break Out' by The Fall and 'I'm Bored' by Iggy Pop and James Williamson. I had found its darkened chilly rear section behind the parked truck an ideal spot for canoodling during Eddie and the Hot Rods tracks. But it was only on entering early that Saturday evening with a motley ragbag of cheap, often faulty electrical equipment that Kathy Hollingsworth's fears began to make sense.

The place buzzed. Not in the sense of being lively but in the sense of being not properly earthed. Every metal surface gave off a faint but disturbing crackle and hum.[1] Everything you laid a hand on – rails, tables, the bar – gave you a small but memorable shock. It was not the sort of place to take a 1960 vintage Vox AC30 that shorted at certain volumes and had to be struck with a hammer to persuade it back to life. But we didn't care. We cared for naught except rock 'n' roll and our first faltering steps on the ladder to fame, riches and kidney-shaped swimming pools in the grounds of Surrey mansions.

We shared the bill with an outfit from Scholes of whom I remember nothing except the singer's mournful bleat and a rather good song whose chorus went 'London London, capital of the world'. This was geographically inaccurate, worse it was treasonous to our own North West, but it had a catchy hook that I could still sing you. The crowd was boisterous during their short set but reasonably good-natured. This was crucial since some earlier punk gigs at Trucks had been marred by violence, some of it directed at bands. All punk bands expected a shower of gob; as long as you weren't performing a benefit in a TB ward you didn't mind terribly. But a couple of the bands at Trucks had had a beer mug or two heaved at them. In fairness, this could have been due to involuntary spasms brought on by sitting on a live bar stool. Like gobbing, it may have been intended as a compliment, a

---

1 Had we made a live album of our appearance, *Crackle and Hum* would have been a good title for it.

display of exuberance. But we, or rather Jem, were having none of it. 'Just let the fuckers try,' he muttered through the froth of a pint of chestnut mild.

I don't remember very much of our set. The crowd were enthusiastic, every now and then I'd catch a rather off-putting glimpse of Nigel's mum and dad, a retired post-office worker and a teacher in the middle of a throng of pogoing youths in eyeliner and ripped T-shirts. We were getting near the end of the set – 'Little Flirts' or our faithful cover of Wire's 'Mannequin' maybe – when it happened. As I moved towards the mike for a chorus I saw something flash across the periphery of my vision. There was an ominous, sudden clang from the gantry above us followed by a splintering crash and then, like being caught in a hailstorm, we were showered in broken glass.

We all knew in that split second that some bonehead, embracing the peripheral loutishness of punk but missing the real point, had lobbed a pint pot. I shouted some obscenity, chucked down my guitar and turned to go. Nigel was doing likewise. Turning to Jem though, I was shocked to see that his drum stool was empty. A cold feeling ran though my stomach. He must have been hit. Where was he? I turned back to survey the dance floor.

A small space had formed and was surrounded by onlookers. In the centre of this was Jem, feverishly and methodically punching a member of the audience in the head. Soon a bouncer appeared and separated them, dragging the other fellow away, leaving Jem cursing, calling for strong drink and bellowing like a wounded elk.

Reconvening in the darkened canoodling space behind the stage, we felt like The Stooges – battle-hardened veterans of the mean streets of rock. The set had been curtailed but not by much, we had only got our new, faintly experimental, number 'True Teen Romance' to go. Then the owner appeared. 'What's up, aren't you going' back on?' he asked, toying with the gold ingot that nestled in his chest hair.

I can't remember exactly what Jem's verbatim response was. It went loosely along the lines of, 'The fusillades of pint glasses have somewhat dampened our enthusiasm for tonight's performance. Perhaps we might conclude proceedings a tad early.' Mr Trucks was having none of this reticence though. I should point out here that we had been promised a fee for our performance. It was, and I remember this vividly, nine pounds. Three pounds each. We were delighted. It would pay for several chestnuts milds, a packet of fags and a celebratory chips and gravy from Greasy Lil's, the local chippy on Warrington Road that once inspired the following exchange with Stocky's kid brother Jeff:

Jeff: Chip, Stu?
Me: Ta, where are they from?
Jeff: Greasy Lil's.
Me: Oh no, Greasy Lil's are horrible. Why didn't you go to Benthams?
Jeff: Well, you see, Greasy Lil's are horrible. But you get more chips there.

But our chips and gravy were now under threat. The Trucks proprietor, a man with all the relaxed, generous spirit of Sir Bernard Ingram or Van Morrison, spelt it out. Go back on or you don't get paid. No more songs, no nine quid. So we went back on and did the whole set again.

By all accounts it was great. Inhumanly fast, white knuckled, delivered through clenched teeth. People came up afterwards and bought us beer, slapped us on the backs, asked when we were playing again. Some of them were girls. It was ace.

The owner counted out nine quid in the old 'green drinking voucher' folding money. As he did, there emerged a hitherto well-hidden friendly side to his reptilian character: 'Not so sure about this punk stuff myself but that were a pretty fair little set. You've got some good songs. What you need is a good manager. Now I've had some experience in the live music game myself and I know raw talent when I see it. What I'm saying is' – and here he paused for dramatic effect – 'I could make you boys bigger than the Dooleys.'[2]

To round off a memorable evening, the bouncer came over and beckoned us into a corner conspiratorially.

'Now, lads, I obviously couldn't let you loose on that bloke who threw the glass. That would have been irresponsible and a dereliction of my duty. But what I can offer you is ten minutes each with him near the beer crates behind the club. I've locked him in the office. Up to you.'

There was something so coldly pre-meditated about this that Nigel and I felt uneasy about it. In the first heat of rage, yes, not an hour later with the help of a bouncer. We said no. Jem, though, had no such scruples. He went round the back and punched him a bit more.

---

2 The Dooleys were a big-haired family from Manchester then enjoying a brief dalliance in the limelight. Perhaps you remember their hit 'Love Patrol' with its accompanying dance that involved giving a little salute thus: 'We're on love – salute – patrol'. It was intended to suggest Glenn Miller but unintentionally evoked Benny Hill's Fred Scuttle. We said we'd get back to him.

13 Elvis and his Dad

That summer we became a regular attraction, if that's the word, around the pubs and clubs of New Wave Wigan. For bits of kids, we weren't bad. A little rough around the edges, saddled with my gauche, daft songs about girls and the Iron Curtain but good fun if you'd had a few. As punk broadened and matured, we started to play around with the format and the image. Some gigs stick in my memory. We dressed in black Oxfam suits and ties for a gig at the Keller and played 'All My Loving' by The Beatles to the horror of the Sex Pistols fans and the delight of the power pop crowd. We played at Cassinellis in Standish, an ice-cream parlour by day and a chic restaurant and supper club by night, and a girl ran on the stage during Little Flirts and kissed us each in turn to our utter shock and, naturally, delight. We played the school disco and the young English teacher Mr May wrote a review for the school magazine that I can still quote: 'raw, urgent and pounding, their music demands to be heard'. Whatever happened to Mr May? With that kind of cultured appreciation of great music he should at be least head of Sony or editing *Rolling Stone*. Mr May and his long-suffering wife once put us up after an out-of-town gig and I found a copy of David Bowie's *Heroes* and the *Collected Poems of Baudelaire* in the bin in his spare room. It was the same night that the economics teacher Mr Fleet drove his orange Volkswagen into the canal. Happy days.

We became a fixture at benefit gigs for Rock Against Racism. I'd like to think that the NF's humiliation and defeat in the late Seventies was in no small part due to the mobilisation of a broad fun-living opposition and perhaps directly attributable to the many Les Flirts gigs in and around Wigan.

It took me a while to realise that the Anti-Nazi League had strong links with Wigan's Socialist Worker Party, a gang of humourless fellow travellers that I had no time for whatsoever. When I did suss this, I began taking things much less than seriously. We played one benefit gig dressed in cricket whites and Bertie Wooster weekend casuals. At another I made gentle fun of the Tom Robinson Band, which was a bit like putting your fag out on Lenin's tomb. Finally, I announced from the stage at another benefit that every penny spent on mild that night was going straight into the coffers of the Kremlin. After that we stopped getting asked to play.

I still went on the marches, demos and gigs though. There was one in particular that I would not have missed for all the vodka and cabbage in Russia. It was to take place in Brixton and would be headlined by a man who had started to obsess me to an alarming degree.

I first saw Elvis Costello perform on our early evening news magazine show *Granada Reports*. This was the coolest show on TV, chiefly by virtue of the presence as presenter of a local lad made good who'd gone off to Cambridge and returned to make his mark. His name was Tony Wilson. To a generation, Wilson is the man behind Factory Records and the Hacienda, the shadowy though mouthy *eminence grise* behind Madchester. To my dad, he is the bloke from *Granada Reports*. To have combined two such disparate careers – scintillating, cool, situationist alternative music guru on the one hand, bloke in raincoat doing item on new bus station in Bury on the other – is worth saluting. Wilson made *Granada Reports* unmissable fare. He would routinely slip a short set by This Heat or The Slits in after a piece on rates increases in Warrington. He was little less than a god to us; a really smart-alecky one but a god nonetheless.

Two things in particular stand out in my mind from the host of great stuff Wilson engineered into the show's What's On feature, hitherto a showcase for amateur dramatics and light operetta. One was the early, truly amazing Human League performing their astonishing cover of 'You've Lost That Lovin' Feelin'.' Three blokes harmonising behind Korg keyboards, one of them with a fringe as long as the M62 and one standing at the back showing slides of *Land of the Giants* and *Joe 90*. My dad almost choked on his meat and potato pie.

The other was the first time I saw Elvis Costello – which instantly etched him indelibly into my youthful consciousness.

That night he wore a pastel blue 1950s suit and his trademark owlish specs. On the cover of *My Aim Is True*, he sported a demob jacket and drainpipe jeans with huge comedy turn-ups. He looked like a camp farmhand on flood alert. In many ways, it was an even more extraordinary image than Johnny Rotten's. It was Buddy Holly without the urbane suavity, Syd Little without the existential menace and glamour. He looked like someone who would be relieved of his dinner money every playtime without fail.

He also *sounded* like someone who was relieved of his dinner money every playtime without fail. That night, he played 'Welcome To The Working Week' and 'Red Shoes', two of the more easy-going songs from the debut album but still shot through with a murderous, in-growing self-doubt and rage that made most punk acts look positively genial. A highlight of that patchy first album is a song called 'I'm Not Angry', the most untruthfully titled song in rock history. 'I'm Not Angry' is so biliously, vituperatively, seethingly angry it should be kept chained to a post in the yard. Lyrically it starts with a man listening to the girl he wants having sex with someone else and gets cheerier from there on in. Perfect fodder for the late adolescent. Romance is rarely benign but usually predicated on lust, wantonness, pride, avarice, forged in violence and secrecy and flecked with blood and tears. 'I'm Not Angry' was truly a drop of the hard stuff.

The Gas Showrooms in Wigan is famous for one thing. Not for its excellent displays of argon or nitrogen – actually it's a place that sells cookers – but for being the pick-up point where all coaches left for distant exotic locales and special trips. This is where you got the charabanc when Wigan Rugby made their almost yearly trips to Wembley for the Challenge Cup final, this is where you set off for your holiday to Devon or Scotland if you were the adventurous globetrotting sort, this is where you departed, draped in tinsel and sporting deeleyboppers, for your works Christmas do at Rotters nitespot, Manchester.

   This is where we assembled, early one Saturday morning in May to set off for Brixton and the Anti-Nazi Carnival of 1978. Stocky and I were in Leo Connolly's sociology class at the time. Leo – a tiny, bearded, voluble Irishman whose early years in England were spent 'on the wrong end of a spade' – had no time for the value-free, politically neutral academic sociology that you read about in books. He was a fervent communist who made sure that the *Morning Star* was delivered to the school library every morning to counter the imperialist propaganda of *The Times* or the faux-socialist sop that was the *Daily Mirror*. When he learned we where going on the Anti-Nazi League march he encouraged us to break a few fascist heads. Actually we were more concerned about not getting our own broken, if not by actual NF members then their representatives in the establishment, the SPG or Special

Patrol Group: folk devil baton-wielding paramilitary cops generally thought to be no stranger to the goosestep themselves.

The journey was a fraught one. The coach comprised bearded lefties from the tech, trade union types, the more politically committed new wave intellectual such as myself and a small cadre of cartoon punks. These were the kind of oik who had come to the movement late, when it was essentially safe. They'd acquired fancy-dress bondage trousers, studded leather jackets, bad tattoos and generally made an exhibition of themselves. You can still find them leering comedy fashion from those postcards you can buy at Euston station that say 'Greetings from London'.

One of these cartoon punks made Sid Vicious look like Noel Coward. He belched and swore and farted throughout the five-hour journey to London. Many on that coach entertained authoritarian fantasies towards him of a highly dubious right-wing variety involving truncheons, electric cattle prods and stocks. On arrival at London, he found a stick – he was the kind of person who would always find a stick, even if you were at Stockholm airport or in an isolation hospital – and he rattled it along every iron railing in London as we marched through the streets towards Hyde Park.

There was a rally, a speech by Tony Benn and we lay on the grass and snoozed through various dignitaries. The cartoon punk tried out various new vocal effects; honking like a goose, bellowing like a caribou. Tony Benn must have felt like bringing back the birch and wielding it himself. Bathed in righteous glory we marched to Brixton where we had a splendid day; Jimmy Pursey made several heartfelt not entirely comprehensible addresses; Elvis, in a maroon drape jacket, and his Attractions played a tremendous set. There was a spot of first-hand political violence with the SPG in Brick Lane (how we would elaborate on this on Monday morning) and on the way back we skilfully conspired to lose the cartoon punk at Newport Pagnell services. Add this to the defeat of fascism and it was not a bad day's work.

Such was my enthusiasm for Elvis that it seemed only natural that I should start stalking his dad. Stalking is putting it a bit strong actually. But that's what it must have seemed like. It began when my mum mentioned in an idle moment between *The Cuckoo Waltz* and *In Loving Memory* that Ross MacManus was playing at Worsley Mesnes Labour Club that week. 'You know, he used to sing with Joe Loss and his son's a punk rocker.' It became apparent that his son was in fact Elvis Costello. My mum had mentioned it because even she had noticed the album sleeves lying around and the sudden predilection for dressing like Buddy Holly. It was a date.

Wednesday evening found myself and pals John and Josh sitting at a Formica table in a large room drinking the cheapest, gassiest beer available in Lancashire and playing bingo with novelty pens. We were the only people in the room under forty. As such we cut something of a dash. We certainly attracted some stares even though there were several other patrons of the club wearing thick glasses and prewar tailoring, albeit for different reasons.

At half past eight, a small bespectacled man who looked a bit like, well, Elvis Costello took the stage. Backed by a the club's resident organist and drummer who sported lank quiffs and played with minuscule effort, he ran through some old standards from his Joe Loss days plus a few Seventies chart hits like The Strawbs' 'Part Of The Union' during which he did a jerky dance in a strobe light and finished his first 'spot' by playing a rather good trumpet version of 'Georgia On My Mind'. Then off he went, followed slowly by that resident organist and drummer, already reaching into coat pockets for their Embassy Regal.

When he returned some half an hour later, it was clear that my mum's high standing with the committee had helped in getting a message through to Mr MacManus. As he returned to the stage, he made a little speech.

'Now it's come to my notice that there are some fans of my son's in the audience. In case you don't know, my son Declan metamorphosised into the rock and roll phenomenon we call Elvis Costello.' Purple-haired septuagenarian ladies looked at each other in bafflement. We shone with delight and disbelief. 'So for them I'd like to do a few of his songs.' He handed out some sheet music to the club's backing duo. They looked at it as if it were scrolls of ancient cuneiform.

Fair play, the lads took a pretty respectable stab at it: 'Oliver's Army' and 'Alison'. Ross even sounded a little like Elvis, evidently something in the DNA. Later we had a drink with him. Over the next few months we had lots of drinks with him as we followed him from club to club. He drank those little bottles of barley wine and would always say, 'Oh, go on then, just a barley wine' as if it were a soft drink when, as any self-respecting boozer knows, they have the kick of a bad-tempered donkey. We'd stand him barley wines and he'd tell us stories of Elvis's recent purchases ('His accountant told him he wasn't spending enough so he's bought a grand piano. Tax deductible, you see') or of Steve Naïve, EC's keyboard player ('Chockful of tunes, that lad') or of the infamous bar-room row between Elvis and some American musicians where he had allegedly called Ray Charles 'a blind, ignorant nigger'. Elvis Senior, Mr MacManus reserved his greatest animation for this: 'There's no way he's a racist. If he was, his mother and me would have knocked the tar out of him years ago.' He was a lovely man and we had a wonderful summer, carrying his little amp from club to club, car parks in the dusk, barley wines and hot pies and two fat ladies, 88. Then we drifted apart, he to the North Pier, Blackpool. Us to the rest of our lives, which a great deal of the time meant a nightclub named, for no good reason, after the unshaven bad guy in the Popeye cartoons.

Bluto's stood on the site of the old UCP café in Market Street. On quiet midweek nights, the upstairs disco was free, played

fabulous music and closed at 2 a.m. Even on Thursdays – tradi-
tionally the wage packet payday of the factories and a lively old
night in the industrial North – you could hire Bluto's for a private
party and have the place to yourself if you guaranteed 200 people
would fetch up. We could manage this with ease, my extended
peer group and I, and thus every Thursday it was someone's
birthday. I myself had four birthdays in 1978. Why we even bothered with the subterfuge I don't know. Bluto's management surely
couldn't have cared if we'd put 'Flimsy Pretext for Frankly
Inexcusable Midweek Piss-Up and Wing-Ding' on the tickets. Not
as long as they ran out of Breaker and Colt 45 by half ten and sold
150 quid's worth of cider for 'the ladies'.

Wigan's poor A level results in '78 and '79 correlate directly
with the excellence and conviviality of Bluto's as a watering hole.
The DJ, perched above the floor in a kind of crow's nest reached
by a kind of ladder, was very much a creature of his time; blond
highlights, canvas baggies and elasticated belt, espadrilles. Every
night he finished up by saying, 'That's all from me, kids. Be good.
And if you can't be good, be careful. And if you can't be careful,
get a good doctor.'

But he played music that would have made a dead man
dance. High marque disco, top-end US funk; Commodores of
'Brick House' and 'Flying High' vintage, Stanley Clarke, Foxy's
'Get Off', Peter Brown's 'Do You Wanna Get Funky With Me',
Ohio Players, Earth Wind & Fire at their bonkers Eygptological
best, Funkadelic, Bootsy's Rubber Band and, best of all, Chic.

Chic's music is a dream pop music is having about itself; all
hedonism and aspiration, all fantasy and impossible glamour.
Disco is too small a word for it. Nile Rodgers and Bernard
Edwards's music, if heard in the right conditions, the dance floor
of Bluto's at 1 a.m., say, is religious music. 'My Feet Keep
Dancing', 'I Want Your Love'; these were truly adventures in the
land of the good groove, as Nile's solo album had it. Trance music,

ecstasy music, before those terms came to mean something entirely different.

Then, suddenly, it's time for 'Love Don't Live Here Anymore' by Rose Royce (pow, pow-po-pow, po-po pow). The plug of the evening is pulled and the sudden undertow of the last song smooch drags everyone centrifugally from the darkened corners to the dance floor, and as they come they cling together in the swirl; some together already, some fetching up together like flotsam, some looking around for the one they mean to go down with.

Then it's the wisecrack about being careful and finding a good doctor. The lights are on and the party's over. And it's cold outside. It's 1979.

14 Simply Thrilled, Honey

As the strikebound, candlelit, tank-topped Seventies gave way to the brightly lit, upwardly mobile, red braces and Christopher Biggins glasses of the Eighties, nobody quite thought to tell the North of England. Margaret Thatcher was newly installed as Prime Minister and I had a sticker on my guitar that read 'Don't Blame Me I Voted Labour'. It wasn't quite Woodie Guthrie's famous guitar logo 'This Machine Kills Fascists' but it was well meant. Thatcher's project, her concerted effort to destroy the Northern working class, was about to begin but still, as far as pop music went – and that was about as far as I went – we were as fertile and teeming with life as a particularly industrious anthill. Essentially there were three hives of activity, Manchester, Liverpool and Sheffield.

Manchester had Factory Records. This was run by Tony Wilson still holding down the day job alongside Richard Madeley and Judy Finegan, still doing those 'Accrington man builds model of the Kremlin from beer cans' tales by day but by night nurturing the gloomy, imperious Joy Division; the bearded indie folkies of James; the completely inexplicable Stockholm Monsters and Crispy Ambulance; the knotty, funky A Certain Ratio and the gorgeous Durutti Column, whose first album had been described as the post-punk *Tubular Bells* and which came in a sandpaper sleeve designed to ruin the sleeves of the albums you stored it next to. Very Guy Debord. Very Factory.

Sheffield had a clutch of rather dour intellectual youths in long overcoats and black T-shirts, namely Cabaret Voltaire, Prag Vec (still the worst live act I have ever seen by some distance) and Clock DVA. But they did have the Human League whose early releases I was besotted with. 'The Dignity Of Labour' was typical, an austere four-part electronic instrumental meditation. A 12-inch single (a recent, sexy innovation), it came in a sleeve with a great picture of Yuri Gagarin and had a free flex-disc on which the band argued for five minutes about the piece's underlying concept ('it's not simple, it's not complex, it's multiplex; it's about human frailty and however big you are, you're gonna be dead pretty soon') before, apropos of nothing, one of them picks up a magazine and says, in broadest Yorkshire, 'Kid here wants to swap a fishing rod for a Doctor Feelgood album.' Top stuff.

Liverpool was better yet. They had the legendary band Crucial Three. These were Ian McCulloch, Julian Cope and Pete Wylie. Each had their own very distinct personality and persona which they imprinted upon their new ventures.

McCulloch was gorgeous, pouting, sarky and pseudy, a cross between Sinatra and Jim Morrison and the lead singer in Echo and the Bunnymen. Pete Wylie was bolshy, cheeky and bombastic and outlined his mad philosophies on the liner notes of the magnificent early Wah records. He wore leather trousers intended to make him look like a rock god, but which actually made him look like a freak hybrid of man and black pudding.

Julian Cope and his Teardrop Explodes were my favourites though. Cope was dizzy, bravura, silly, romantic, grandiloquent, not characteristics you normally associate with someone from Leicester. He had a mop of Old English sheepdog hair and wore a flying jacket. He namechecked AAP cartoons (the people who made Mister Magoo) and sang 'You can watch Rafferty turn into a serial' which could only be a reference to the rubbish daytime thriller featuring Patrick 'The Prisoner' McGoohan. Years before *Teletubbies* and TV nostalgia shows, Cope was raking the detritus of the dopey, dole-ite, student culture and turning them into pop litanies.

I had seen a lot of *Rafferty* recently. I was signing on waiting for the signally tepid A level results that would nevertheless get me to college ... just. When it came to choosing a city then, it was Manchester, Liverpool or Sheffield. As you've probably gathered, the dice were loaded. Manchester was too near and too like Wigan. Sheffield was a bit too, well, Yorkshire frankly. Liverpool was sufficiently alien to feel like leaving home but near enough to come back and get my washing done and keep the band – now called the Salvation Air Force – functioning reasonably well. Also, it boasted the club of the moment, Erics. Here I felt sure was where I would spend my evenings drinking hard liquor and swapping yarns of Camus and Joe 90 with Julian Cope while making gentle fun of Pete Wylie and Ian McCulloch's leather trousers.

Edge Hill College turned out to be nowhere near the centre of Liverpool.[1] It was actually in a satellite market suburb called Ormskirk. It was a teacher training college of the University of Lancaster that had outgrown its original purpose and now offered sundry other degrees. It also had the best Eng Lit course I could find, all twentieth-century British stuff in year one: Larkin, Gunn and Ted Hughes, Pinter, Wesker and John Osborne. Liverpool was twenty minutes away by bus too, so my nocturnal revels with Ian and Pete and Julian were still a possibility

So committed were we at this point to the band's future – and also maybe for mutual support in those uncertain days –

---

1 I soon learned that 'getting off at Edge Hill', i.e. some way before the delights of Liverpool, was traditional Scouse for coitus interruptus.

Nigel and I both fetched up at Edge Hill. We roomed on the same floor in Lancs Hall and I remember arriving the same afternoon, lugging Fred the amp and guitars and boxes of records into the lift, both dressed in Oxfam finery, me in a blue knitted tie and my dad's Fifties tweed overcoat. The oldest member of our hall was Dewi, a Welsh rugger bugger too cocooned in the cosiness of hall of residence life to move out even though he was a fourth-year. Someone told us that they had sneaked a surreptitious glance at a letter he was writing to a friend back home during that first week of term. One part read 'I was hoping we'd get some good lads in hall this year who could bolster the second row. All we've got though are bloody punk rockers with electric guitars.' Punk rockers with electric guitars. That was us. My chest swelled with pride.

Dewi apart, I made friends quickly on my corridor. There was a genial Geordie called Stod who liked The Stooges and Neil Young. There was a gentle, fey Buddhist from Fallowfield called Spav who meditated for an hour a day and at all other times played the Human League records he'd borrowed from me. There was a short, hyperactive bloke from Blackburn called Daly, a kind of human centrifuge around which bizarre and hilarious things happened unbidden. Daly told me that he and a friend had once got drunk on home brew and decided, for a laugh, to give themselves a tan with his mum's sun lamp ahead of a big night out in the town that night. Inevitably they had fallen asleep beneath its hot and soothing rays and awoken some time later to find their faces on fire and late for the pub. They dashed for a bus and made it to the city centre pub where the gang was gathering. When they entered the bar, their friends erupted in laughter. 'You've been under a sun lamp, haven't you?' they cried.

'Don't tell me,' said Daly as he realised what must be amusing them. 'We're red as lobsters.'

'No. You've still got the little black glasses on.'

Daly's real name was Charles. For a spell though he had another nickname. Never the keenest academic, he began a film studies essay with the opening flourish 'The Cabinet Of Doctor Caligari burst onto the European film scene like a rocket from Venus.' The rest he filched from critical texts: rather too well-known ones it would seem as when the essay came back it was marked tersely 'Plagiarism. 10%' After this he was known as Bo Derek.

Daly was obsessed with Paul McCartney. Or rather McCartney was one of his obsessions. Still burdened with his virginity, he was desperate to be rid of the thing but constrained by (a) his vague but seemingly resolute Christian beliefs and (b) the absence in his life of any girls. When he did get a girlfriend that first term, and when she turned out to be just as corseted in good old-fashioned Catholic guilt as he, well, he became even more agonised and repressed. You could find him wandering the corridors bent double and blue-faced, like a man with a permanent hernia.

I fell into a relationship with Chloe, a tall, shy, willowy girl from Manchester. Fear not, I won't be going all Barbara Cartland on you; this is a musical memoir and I mention this because it does impinge on my musical development. She had painstakingly taped all her favourite albums on a stack of C90s and would play them on her ghettoblaster[2] late at night in her room, where we drank Gold Blend and Martini by candlelight under a poster of a deer bearing the legend, 'If you love someone set them free, if they do not return it was not meant to be.' One of the many prejudices I have against Sting is that he had the gall to pass this guff off as a thoughtful lyric imbuing a personal philosophy. Mind you, compared to de-do-do-do, de-dah-dah, it is pretty bloody thoughtful. Even so, I have since then always expected him to release a single called 'Today Is The First Day Of The Rest

---

2 The first I'd ever seen and the size of a washing machine.

Of Your Life' or 'I'd Rather Have A Bottle In Front Of Me Than A Frontal Lobotomy'.

Let's break the habit of a lifetime and be fair to Sting. He was in the charts with The Police and 'Walking On The Moon' during the first few months of that particular love affair and its words rang true to my own elevated, light-headed state as I crept across the girls hall quad at dawn on a frosty morning before climbing into my own bed, falling fast asleep and missing a nine o'clock lecture on John Donne.

Daly and Sting are linked in my mind for another reason. I have never believed for a moment Sting's (or rather Gordon Sumner's) tale of how he got his nickname. Sting says it's because he used to wear a yellow and black striped jumper in his formative muso days in Newcastle. Yeah, right. Sting, to my mind, is called Sting because he quite fancied being called Sting. Rest assured, his Geordie compadres would have called him Bumble Bee or Waspy or something equally dismissive and crap and not the enigmatic, slightly racy Sting. On leaving the 'toon, I'm sure Sting gave himself the identity he'd always fancied.

College affords ample opportunity for this kind of reinvention. Daly was called Bruce but he told us that, being a fine amateur athlete, he'd been christened Daly by schoolmates after the then triumphant decathlete Daly Thompson. Years afterwards, someone who had been at school with Bruce told me that this was complete bunkum. We should have guessed anyway. Schoolboys would never give you an admiring soubriquet based on something you excelled at. They hone in on your weaknesses and flaws. Zitty, Big Ears, Spazzo yes; Daly and Sting, never.

Because Edge Hill had been until quite recently exclusively a teacher training college and was still one of the country's first-choice venues for would-be teachers, it was generally quite a conservative place. Nigel and I stood out as mavericks. That's not to say that there weren't cool people in college but you had to be

Sherlock Holmes to find them among the jocks and geog teachers in waiting. We reserved our greatest antipathy for the PE students. These were the hated 'human groovers', a distortion of their course title Human Movement. All week they would come into the union bar in tracksuits and drink pints of orange juice. Then on Friday they would pull on a sweater with a college rugby crest, spray some Brut onto their moustaches, have three pints of weak beer and embark on a pickled-egg-eating contest before vomiting into an empty crisp packet.

Some of them seem to have been there for ever – portly blokes around the age of thirty-five, it seemed, clinging to their student days via a succession of union positions and mature student courses. Worst of all, many of them had inveigled their way into positions of power on the Entertainment Committee. Because of this, I encountered some desperate live entertainment that first year at Edge Hill. Richard Digance and his uniquely unfunny comedy folk songs, Gordon Giltrap playing the theme from the *Holiday* programme and several million variants thereof, Europe of 'Final Countdown' infamy. Edge Hill's cretinous Ents Committee was once offered as potential bookings, on the same night, Echo and the Bunnymen, The Cure and Liquid Gold of 'Dance Yourself Dizzy' fame. They chose Liquid Gold.

That was the final straw. Music-loving peasantry stormed the bastille, or union office at least, and carted the ancien regime off to the scaffold. After that the live entertainment improved. The most immediate manifestation of this is we got Orchestral Manoeuvres in the Dark for freshers week. Appropriate really, since Andy McLuskey's jerky, leg-snapping dance became the dance-floor routine of choice for all trainee teachers until 1987.

But let's go back to that bedroom in the girls' hall, the candles, the posters, the smell of patchouli, the Nescafé and Martini – the music. Chloe's tastes in this department were very different from mine. But, softened and mellowed by the boudoir ambience and the cheap booze, I grew to love some of those albums.

I would never have thought that Rush's '2112' was an appropriate soundtrack to such tender moments. Rush were and indeed are a Canadian power trio who make muscular, Byzantine prog metal based on the right-wing philosophies of Ayn Rand. The late Barry White never feared them as competition vis-à-vis providers of late-night bedroom sounds. Geddy Lee and his shrill delivery of all those lyrics about free will, economic libertarianism and 'By-Tor And The Snow Dog' can take the heat of the steamiest moment if you let him. Plus he looked disconcertingly like a parrot.

Marginally more suitable was Fleetwood Mac's eponymous 1975 album, the one that paved the way for the globe-dominating *Rumours*. Frugality itself, Chloe had squeezed both onto one TDK C90 that tantalisingly missed off the last couple of minutes of each. For a post-punk intellectual, they were forbidden pleasures. But I loved them both, guiltily but lustily, as Raymond Blanc might enjoy a furtive Pot Noodle.

I have Chloe to thank for introducing me to Steely Dan, still a contender for my favourite band. Again, maybe it was the mood, the thrill of embarking on my first really grown-up romance, the Martini. But I thought I'd never heard a song as sweetly, darkly beautiful as 'Here At The Western World' or 'Doctor Wu'. I still haven't. I returned the favour by introducing her to my new favourites the Diagram Brothers whose repertoire of bleakly downbeat observational songs included 'There Is No Shower', 'My Bad Cough's A Lot Better Now', 'I Would Like To Live In Prison', 'I Don't Care About Nuclear Weapons As Long As It Doesn't Affect My Holidays'. I like to think she's eternally grateful.

The Diagram Brothers were funny, slightly scary and like no one else in the world. For this I loved them. I also had a more prosaic reason. I was about to embark on life outside hall of residence, my first footling, nervous steps into rented accommodation. 'There Is No Shower' rang all too plaintively true. To be truer still, it ought to have been called 'There Is No Shower, The Beds Are Propped Up On Bricks And The Kitchen Is A Deathtrap Frankly'.

In theory it looked like the last word in glamour and sophistication. Four young bucks in the first flush of youth full of vim, cheap drink, the Teardrop Explodes and the poetry of Thom Gunn and Ted Hughes sharing a beachfront 'pad' if you will, overlooking the sea at Southport. Looking back, neither myself, Nigel, Daly or Vitty (a third-year we had fallen in with) can have been well established with our various new girlfriends. Otherwise, why would we have countenanced bunking up together with the much more attractive prospect of cosying up to pretty young women in nice flats full of feminine touches like loo roll, milk and clean towels?

The conductor Thomas Beecham said that you should try everything once except incest and morris dancing. Maybe we just felt that shared bachelor dissolution in a seaside hovel was another one of those things. In our minds, we felt sure that 10 Booth Street would become both a heady pleasure palace and a place where great things would be achieved in the fields of music, writing and the arts; a cross between Kubla Khan's Xanadu, Heffner's Playboy Mansion, the Great Library at Alexandria, with a nod to David Niven and Errol Flynn's famous house Sirrhosis By The Sea and a dash of Andy Warhol's Factory thrown in.

We found the flat via the good offices of the colleges accommodation officer. He was a man thwarted in the pursuit of his real vocation, the clergy, and tried to make up for this by quoting scripture, nodding and smiling a lot and wearing long black coats and black shirts buttoned very high at the throat but exposing a section of white rollneck vest beneath. Unless you looked hard, you assumed he was wearing a dog collar. Exactly the effect he wanted. For this reason, he was known to us all as the Bogus Vicar. When he wasn't attending – unqualified – to his flock, the Bogus Vicar found flats for you. Other colleges did things differently. There was also a huge countrywide organisation that you yourself may indeed have made use of called Unipol which did the same thing on a much larger scale. Stocky and Paul Moran, two friends of mine who had gone to college in Leeds, were once sent by Unipol to look at a prospective flat-share in the Leeds suburb of Horsforth. They arrived at the front door of a dilapidated rambling Victorian terrace, attired in the de rigueur Joy Division/Bunnymen look of 1979: long overcoats, ties, muted colours.

They knocked and after some interval, the door was opened by a dishevelled barefoot hippie, releasing a thick fug of aromatic smoke.

'Good morning, we're from Interpol,' they announced mistakenly.

'What!' gulped the hapless resident faced with two tall over-coated men from Europe's leading law enforcement agency. 'Christ! Well, you'd better come in then I suppose,' he stammered, ashen-faced. 'It's Interpol' he wailed, disappearing inside, as all through the house was heard the sound of slamming doors and flushing toilets, followed by Stocky and Paul trying to gabble a retraction. 'No, sorry, not Interpol … sorry … Unipol.'

Over in Southport, we should have realised that one large four-bedded dormitory was not an ideal sleeping arrangement for any grouping other than a very small, elite Scout unit who got on terrifically well, never mind sexually active young men. Also, one of the beds had no legs and was supported, precariously, by four teetering columns of house bricks. This became known, wittily, as the brick bed. In theory you should have been able to see the sea from the high, angled windows were it not for a geographical quirk known to all Lancastrians. The sea at Southport is a shy, coy, flirtatious creature. Not for her the brazen exposure of her charms as at Blackpool or, for that matter, any other seaside resort. No. Southport is 'the seaside' in a purely theoretical sense. The sea is out there somewhere. But few have ever seen it. You just have to take it on trust.

Aside from this cheerless dorm with its view of a bleak ribbed expanse of sand, the flat consisted of a bathroom (soon to become the stuff of nightmares and arcane fungal experiments obviously), an oblong lounge dotted with dark olive furniture that the Bucharest housewife of the 1950s would have rejected as too dismal. And, finally, a kitchen. The kitchen was really a corridor lined with faulty electrical equipment that culminated in a floor-to-ceiling, wall-to-wall window that overlooked the street from five storeys up. Young men think themselves immortal, they laugh at danger. But on seeing it for the first time, we all let out an immediate chorus of 'That's a bastard deathtrap.' Despite what Jona Lewie had said in his hit song of the day, you would find no one in this kitchen at parties. Step back from the fridge too energetically and you would instead find yourself falling through air, haloed in broken glass, clutching a can of Stones Bitter.

For a day or two we were happy there. We fell into an odd kind of domesticity. For our first meal, Daly made a bowl of something called piperade from a dog-eared Italian cookbook. We ate it, having no idea what the Italians accompanied it with, with sliced buttered white bread. We asked each other nicely to pass the salt. We made dinner-table conversation about issues of the day – education cuts, the Russian incursion into Afghanistan, the early novels of Martin Amis – under a poster of a chimpanzee on the toilet that Vitty thought was really funny.

It started to fall down around the third day. Daly began to query the allocation of food, counting the fish fingers, mentally sizing up the portions of mushy peas, saying we had it in for him. We made a vile Madras with offcuts of cold meat, crabsticks and ancient curry powder found in the back of a cupboard. Daly was explosively sick and Nigel's nose bled. Even though he had been almost poisoned, Daly still claimed from his sickbed that we had deliberately given him the smallest portion.

In the way known to all students, tiny, meaningless aspects of domestic routine became heated issues that would require ACAS intervention to placate the parties. Who had eaten whose Dairylea? Whose turn was it to empty the bin? Who should nip out for sugar? Tea was only made via a complex routine called 'making it in stages'. One person would fill the kettle and switch it on, another would put the teabags in, a third would pour on the water, a fourth would add milk. Certain elements would become hotly disputed: who should put the teabags in the bin, who should put the milk away? These became our Kashmirs, our Gaza Strips. At night we would get drunk, bang on guitars, play our favourite records and throw things at one another.

Daly remained utterly impervious to the charms of alternative music. Like Josh, he was a traditionalist. Songwriting was his thing, Paul McCartney was his god. Everything Nigel and I liked he dismissed as 'trendy shit'. Another friend Jolly John, a rotund, jocular fellow, was obsessed by Mike Oldfield. I liked *Tubular Bells* as much as the next closet revisionist prog adolescent but John's devotion went much further than this. He would attempt to introduce Oldfield into unconnected conversations about football, Leon Brittain or the meals in the refec. He even tried, optimistically, to use *Tubular Bells* as a lure with the ladies. One day I was chatting to a girl from Salford who I knew Jolly John had 'set his cap at' as people once curiously put it.

'He's lent me an album he thought I might like,' she began.

'Oh yes,' I replied, warily, 'it wouldn't be *Tubular Bells* by Mike Oldfield by any chance, would it?'

'Yes it is,' she answered. 'It's quite nice really … though I prefer UB40. But—' and here she drew closer and her voice fell to a whisper '—he's done a really strange thing on the tape. He's recorded himself coming in over the instruments telling me exactly what they are. You know "two saxophones", "electric banjo" that kind of thing. Weird.'

Jolly John was odd but he wasn't that odd. She had assumed that the famous MC role taken by Viv Stanshall was JJ himself. And so whenever I hear *Tubular Bells* today, I can't help but see Jolly John, leaning over the turntable helpfully announcing the instruments into a Dixons handheld mic.

When we went to watch the Human League in Manchester, the tickets read No Dress Restrictions.

'What does that mean?' asked JJ and a few of his compatriots on the B.Ed Primary course.

'It means you have to wear a jacket and tie,' I said as a joke.

So at the gig that night, most of the audience including me affected huge Phil Oakey fringes, long overcoats, leather flying jackets and the like. But there were four blokes in moustaches wearing houndstooth sports coats, white nylon M&S shirts and polyester ties with crests. They looked like young Des Lynams on a Friday night at the Bauhaus.

Most of the gigs I saw at this time were at Erics club on Liverpool's Mathew Street, the site of the old Cavern Club, lunchtime haunt of The Beatles, Cilla Black and, if you believe them, everyone who lived in Liverpool between 1945 and 1970. I saw Wire and The Selecter. I saw, as was only fitting, the Bunnymen, Wah Heat and the Teardrop Explodes and drunkenly invited Julian Cope to a party back at the flat. He didn't come. I saw Clock DVA, the Glaxo Babies, Pink Military, Stand Alone, Girls At Our Best and a whole host of then iconic but now utterly forgotten groups. Every week I read about them voraciously – their views on nuclear disarmament, Derek Hatton and rate-capping – in the pages of the *NME* and I would have listened too to their sessions on John Peel were I not normally lying under a snooker table in the Union Bar or wrestling with recalcitrant undergarments or climbing up the lift shaft to the roof of the hall of residence. All of these I considered natural counterbalancing measures to days spent teasing out the metrical nuances of Ezra Pound's *Cantos*, struggling with Chaucer's alien spellings and wondering whether Pinter's Caretaker would ever get those bloody papers from Sidcup. By day I was Byronic, by night I was moronic. Yin and yang.

One other gig stays emblazoned on the mind. Southport's wonderfully named Floral Hall was a few brisk steps along the promenade from our rapidly disintegrating bachelor pad. It was here that Chloe and I had, by accident, gone to see the Nolan Sisters thinking that it was the movie *Airplane* ('Go on, call it a quid, get in sharpish, it's only just started,' the woman on the ticket desk had said). And it was here that I first met Elvis Costello. He and the Attractions played there on 18 March 1980: we had tickets of course. Vourneen, an Irish girl of my acquaintance, had for some time claimed to be working alongside Elvis Costello's mum at the United Biscuits factory in Huyton. Vourneen was sweet but she was known to be 'terrible fond of the romancing' so I gave little thought to it. Vourneen phoned me and said she'd be coming to the show and might see me there.

It was a great show by the way; Elvis did the pigeon-toed dance and played two great new songs 'Watch Your Step' and 'Shot With His Own Gun'. When it was over, we sat in the bar, nursing the cheapest pint the bar could offer, smoking and chewing over the concert. A man about seven feet tall passed by. Instantly I recognised him as the Attractions drummer Pete Thomas. On a whim, leaving my pint, I followed him. I followed him through a fire door and down some red velour steps. I followed him through another fire door. I followed him along a passageway and into another room. And there was Elvis Costello in a long overcoat, fiddling absently with a guitar case, sipping from a glass of wine and reading the *NME*.

The security man's loss was my gain. I had, flukily, entered the inner sanctum of a man who, if I was no longer certifiably obsessed with John Hinkley-style, then certainly was a man I was still unhealthily keen on. To his lasting credit, he did not have me forcibly ejected but merely said, 'Hello. Can we help you?'

I burbled an explanation that became an embarrassing eulogy and eventually a request for an autograph. The only signable thing I had to hand was, it turned out, a packet of Benson & Hedges.

'I'll sign this but only if you promise me you'll give up smoking.'

'Of course,' I lied and returned to the throng. When I got back to the bar, Vourneen was there. She was on her way to the after-show party. Mrs MacManus had given her a pass. I didn't believe her right until the moment that I saw her leave with a middle-aged woman and get onto the tourbus that was parked in the street outside.

I contented myself by showing off my cigarette packet – faux gold but now priceless – to Vitty and Nigel. We mooched about outside for a while in the rain. Then we climbed on each other's shoulders and stole, methodically, the giant blue letters advertising the show on the Floral Hall's illuminated white cinema-style hoarding. For weeks afterwards, we ate our chips and crispy pancake nightly beneath the words Elvis Costello And The Attractions Sold Out. That's when we were there at all. Elvis Costello was my first real live rock star. 10 Booth Street was my first real live home of my own. There would be more of both. But our brief time in our very own Sirrhosis by the Sea was coming to an end. We had never even seen the sea.

Girlfriends, simmering arguments and the funny smell from the fridge were driving us away from the flat. I was there least, preferring to spend my time in the female-only John Dalton Hall with its convivial company and free heating. To help with bills, we took in a new flatmate. His name was Al White, a baby-faced lad from

Accrington with a perm and a tash who resembled a cross between Bobby Ball and David Cassidy, a combination the ladies found irresistible. Al was two or three years older than us and had left our college the year previously having failed to cover himself in glory academically. In his final Biology paper, Al had scanned in dismay the questions on zygotes and photosynthesis before his eye had lighted on the final question. It read 'Write an essay about a flatfish.'

Al did just this, rather well he thought, bringing in the flounder's under-appreciated aesthetic qualities and the like. Leaving the examination hall, he bumped into his tutor in the corridor.

'So, White, which essay did you attempt?'

'The one about the flatfish,' Al replied.

'The one about the flatfish? That was just a joke to cheer people up.'

Al failed his degree. But by now, he had grown to love his shabby bohemian life on the Lancashire coast and took a job in Southport as a minicab driver. He introduced me to Chick Corea and King Crimson's *Starless and Bible Black,* I introduced him to the Teardrop Explodes. Best of all, Al provided me with one of the enduring memories of my time at Booth Street.

I had a pair of shoes that Al was keen on. The design of this shoe now eludes me but I remember that I had bought them on a trip home to Wigan. So keen was Al that he worked a couple of extra hours to make the necessary funds and then drove the not inconsiderable distance to Wigan in the early morning to be there when the shop opened and purchase another pair. He returned with them and they became a prized possession.

A few nights later, we threw an impromptu party at the flat after a Salvation Air Force gig. The partygoers were mainly students but there was one odd-looking guy who no one seem to know. Just as we were about to challenge him, it seemed he'd left so we resumed the boozing and frugging.

Cut now to the darkened streets of Southport. Al White, the lonely cabbie, is smoking an Embassy Regal and listening to his Chick Corea tapes. He gets a fare headed for Ainsdale, a scruffy-looking fellow but a fare nonetheless, and they strike up a desultory conversation. The passenger it seems is every inch the scallie. He'd fallen in with a group of 'fucken' students' and gatecrashed a party at one of their flats. While the students had disported, he'd gone stealthily from room to room looking for items to steal. Nice guy, thought Al, but kept his counsel. And had he nicked anything? asked Al. Not much, came the reply, I nearly got a chequebook and a pair of jeans but I got disturbed by some twat going into his room. I did get these though.

With this, he reached into his coat, and pulled out a pair of shoes.

And with that, Al White slammed down on the brakes, jolting his passenger onto the dashboard and said, 'Those are my fucking shoes, you thieving Scouse bastard.'

There was a brief moment of calm and silence during which the passenger looked at Al in fear and bewilderment. Then he leapt from the car. Al gave pursuit along Lord Street, kicking out at him as he ran, landing a few choice ones, causing him to drop the shoes; Al picked them up and carried on running, until he lost him somewhere by Scarisbrick roundabout when the scallie jumped over the railway embankment, landed heavily far below, screamed in pain and dragged himself into the darkened gardens that backed onto the track. Al returned to his cab deep in thought, came home and, finding us still blithely grooving and snogging to the sound of XTC, lifted the stylus from the record and delivered a lecture about domestic security that I, for one, will never forget.

It's a pity that he didn't give us a lecture about domestic electricity while he was about it. Since Daly had found out that the lock on the cash tray of the electricity meter didn't work, we had used the same 50 pence piece for all our power-related needs: placing it in the slot, winding the little device, hearing it clunk satisfyingly into the tray, watching the dial ratchet up another few hours precious heat and light ... and then taking out the 50p and placing it on top of the meter for use the next time. At heart, we knew this was wrong and we decided after a week or two to make a clean breast of it with the landlord, a local builder. It was our first meeting, we wore the smartest clothes we had, sat on his settee in his vast chintzy living room in suburban Maghull and threw ourselves on his mercy. Sadly, he was looking to get out of the student housing market and seized on this as a first-rate reason to evict us. He gave us a week to move out. The Bogus Vicar merely wrung his mottled hands and looked heavenward like Derek Nimmo. We kept the 50p.

On our last Sunday night in the flat, we ate caviar and Stilton that Nigel had brought back from a visit to his sister's in London and drank a bottle of illegal Irish poteen that Vourneen had given me for my birthday. Thanks largely to this, Daly temporarily lost the sight in one eye and we sat on the carpet in front of the three-bar fire and sang along to our favourite records.

'Hey, I bought a great single in Camden today,' said Nigel, surely mindful of the effect this casual cosmopolitanism would have. He reached into his bag and pulled out a seven-inch single in a funny homemade sleeve with line drawings of a man and a woman and a little cat. It was called Blue Boy by Orange Juice and it was love at first sight and sound.

Orange Juice began life as the punkish Nu-Sonics in late 1976 around a nucleus of sparky Glaswegians Edwyn Collins, Steven Daly and James Kirk. They soon tired of punk's lumpen machismo and nastiness though and affected an air of fey insouciance. They met a young botany student called Alan Horne and between them Postcard Records was born, soon home to a whole clutch of engaging mavericks such as Aztec Camera, a vehicle for the songs of boy genius Roddy Frame and the wiry, clanking Josef K.

Horne said he wanted Postcard to be a 'punk rock version of

the Chic Organisation'. Each release bore the legend The Sound of Young Scotland, a wry reference to Motown's famous The Sound of Young America slogan. Everything about the label made me love them more. Postcard releases also came with actual picture postcards. 'Blue Boy' came with a charming illustration of a cat drumming such as you'd find on a tin of shortbread. Aztec Camera's 'Just Like Gold' included a postcard of the group – they were eleven years old apparently – standing around a drainage culvert in a muddy field.[3] It was so un-rock 'n' roll that it made me chortle. And the music inside, as with all the Postcard releases, was simply thrilling, honey.

Orange Juice sounded like the Velvet Underground would if they'd made music for pre-school children's TV. They sounded like The Byrds from Bearsden. They were louche but engaging, jangly but tuneful, their tinny, skeletal songs were always on the verge of collapse but never did and instead blossomed into things of great beauty and even grandeur: 'Simply Thrilled Honey', 'Poor Old Soul', 'Felicity', every one a masterpiece. Aztec Camera were similarly not of their time. They were led by a teenage boy, a few years my junior gallingly, who wrote beautiful elliptical acoustic ballads that made my stuff look like junk. The only consolation I could draw was that it made pretty much everyone's stuff look like junk.

What I really loved about the music, the fashion, the ethos surrounding Postcard Records was that it was cute. Cute but not wimpy. I had grown rather tired of the overweening self-regard of Ian McCulloch, the not terribly convincing existential intellectualism of The Cure or the grand-standing chest-beating bluster of new bands like U2 from Ireland (I knew they'd never get anywhere with their stupid back-combed hair and awful studenty

---

3 The phrase 'drainage culvert' now occurs twice in this book which, outside technical works on sewerage, must make it unique in publishing history.

noms de plume). Postcard Records and their clan were the best possible antidote to all this; they were smart, funny, knowing, ebullient, charming: yes, cute. They wore tartan shirts, bootlace ties, fringed buckskin, shades, kilts and Davy Crockett Hats. In interviews, they made silly jokes and referred to the Simple Minds-loving herds of the day as 'poser neds' which I loved. Edge Hill was full of poser neds.

I rapidly became obsessed. In this I was joined by my old friend John from the school bus days, now studying Chemistry in Bangor. We scoured Oxfam shops for buckskin jackets and racoon hats. Unsurprisingly, we didn't find any. Back in the early Eighties, Oxfam shops were great places to pick up a copy of the *Battlestar Galactica* annual or a cerise trouser suit but American frontiersman garb was at a premium. But we tried. I affected every nuance that I could of Roddy Frame's sartorial style: boot-lace ties and plaid shirts. I would have done the accent if I could have gotten away with it.

Around this time, a film called *Gregory's Girl* was released; a delightful, lemon-sharp comedy about growing up on an estate in Cumbernauld. You could say I liked it. Barring some minor exposition in the middle, I can easily recite every line of dialogue. Even now, twenty years on, I am still prone to throw choice nuggets from the script into appropriate situations even though no one ever knows what I'm talking about. When an irksome individual leaves the room I will mutter – in bad Caledonian brogue – 'Arriverderci Gordon, hurry back'. On being given a tasty-looking drink or meal, I often comment 'The nicest bit is just before you taste it,' the remark Gregory's sister makes before consuming her huge pink milkshake. When counting in seconds, I always, always, do it thus: 'one elephant, two elephant, three elephant' because, as the young photographer says, 'You don't get real seconds unless you put the elephants in.'

Gregory's Girl deepened my obsession with Glasgie's new

towns, their music, their culture, their girls. Tragic, isn't it? Like those little Japanese girls who move to Whalley Range just because they heard about it in a Smiths' song, back in 1981 I would happily have moved to Cumbernauld or East Kilbride. That must seem truly bizarre if you actually lived there. I just wanted to hang out in that park where John Gordon Sinclair and Claire Grogan lie down and dance on that endless, luminous summer evening at the film's close. Maybe Roddy Frame and Edwyn Collins would come by on their way to the 'Dip'; the Diplomat pub featured in the Aztec Camera song 'Down The Dip'.

To be honest I needed something to cheer me up. The air of tousled, mischievous fun exuded by the Postcard Records groups offered an escape, however illusory, from the drab realities of everyday life. After the heady, liberating bliss of the first year, college life had become something of a drudge; an endless round of bad plumbing, penury, arguments over gas bills and essays on Beowulf.

After leaving Booth Street, a semi-nomadic spell followed. I'd bunked up with Chloe (against all rules of course) in her college rooms. Then six of us – myself Chloe, Stod, his girlfriend Pauline, Daly, Nigel and a girl called Sue who had red hair and wore feather boas – moved into a sprawling, dilapidated Victorian end terrace on Linaker Street where ice formed on the inside of the windows in winter and we lived off huge tureens of soup flavoured with HP sauce and chicken bones. Eventually, when the chill and tension of that arrangement had grown too much, Chloe and I shacked up with some postgraduate radical feminists from Hull who taught me how to cook. Every time I make a kedgeree, which is not often, I think fondly of them. I don't think fondly of much else from this time of chilly, penniless, peripatetic seaside life though. My relationship with Chloe was limping along, joyless and threadbare and familiar as an old carpet slipper. Maybe it's something about student life, but the process of evolution in one's emotional life seems wildly accelerated, like a silent movie comedy; all arms and legs, chases, love affairs, scrapes and alarms and, just like Chaplin movies, sometimes funny, more often not. Chloe and I had reached, in three years, the stage some couples get to after thirty. Add to this the fact that I was a self-obsessed, opinionated, unworldly but bolshy quasi-intellectual – poor girl – and it was doomed. Like an old dog, it would have been better to give the affair a lethal injection in the back of the neck, even hitting it with a spade would have been kinder. Instead, out of misguided loyalty, we let it die of hunger.

College was nearly over, my first real relationship was nearly over. It was a time of endings, in my corner of Lancashire at least. Thirty miles east though in Stretford, Manchester, a part-time clothes shop assistant and amateur guitarist named Johnny Maher was ringing the doorbell of 384 Kings Road. Their world, and mine, was about to be turned upside down.

15 *This Charming Man*

'This is how Lieber and Stoller met.' Thus spake John Maher to
Steven Patrick Morrissey on that doorstep in Stretford that May
morning.[1] Actually it was probably nearer afternoon. Morrissey
was on the dole and not known for being an early riser. I imagine
he was in his dressing gown watching Selina Scott, and Johnny
Marr may have put in a morning selling jeans at X Clothes or
Crazy Face in the city centre. From this meeting came forth The
Smiths, a group who, over a decade after their messy dissolution,
still inspire fervid, unhinged devotion, still act as shorthand for a
particular aesthetic and sensibility, still haunt the canals and railway sidings of Lancashire. To get an idea of why The Smiths
meant so much, why they were on first hearing the most important group in the world, why they stopped you in your tracks,
why they did not emerge but rather explode on to the British pop
scene you have to remember just what the state of Britain and
British pop was in 1983.

---

1 Morrissey himself has claimed that he and Johnny Marr actually met 'at a Patti Smith
concert in 1979 and not, as most pop historians record, in 1982'. If true, this would
rather put the kibosh on Marr's cracking opening line. Of course, it's more than possible
that Morrissey, the scamp, is embroidering again.

The Falklands War may have been 'two bald men fighting over a comb' in Borges memorable phrase but it was a comb-over that spared the blushes and hid the inadequacies of the Conservative Party. Just before this war, Margaret Thatcher was the most unpopular Prime Minister of the century. She had set about destroying British industry and social life with zeal. Her apologists were full of thin blather about 'tightening belts' and 'emerging leaner and fitter' but this was verbiage. She detested the working class and their political representatives, and she was out to get them. Perhaps they wouldn't buy her dad's over-priced cabbages.

Whatever, the feeling was mutual. Before those scrap metal workers planted an Argentine flag on South Georgia, Thatcher was loathed by anyone with a shred of compassion or common sense. But the Falklands saved her skin. Suddenly, and you could understand why, she was Boudicca, Churchill and Britannia all rolled into one, the living embodiment of British pluck and inde-fatigable will. She could do as she liked now.

Life in Britain got significantly uglier and began to divide and become fissile. To us in the jobless blighted Labour-voting North, London and the South East seemed another world, a world of crowing tabloids, Jim Davidson and men in eyeliner wearing tablecloths to nightclubs.

Yes, it was the fag-end of the New Romanticism, another reason why The Smiths shone like a beacon; something genuinely true as opposed to, say, Spandau Ballet's 'True'. Spandau Ballet were the worst of a bad lot. Each week you read in the *NME* or *The Face* – a magazine predicated on vacuousness, the *Hello!* of the New Romantic movement – that Spandau were the acme of style. And I would look at the pictures of these men, grinning Romford hod-carriers in jodhpurs and stupid ponchos, and wonder if this could really be the group touted as the saviours of British music with their dull lyrics, bellowed by a man with all the subtle nuanced delivery of the public address tannoy at a Third Division football ground.

Even to one as agnostic as I, it was obvious that this was the ultimate Thatcherite music and that was why it stank. It was obsessed with aspiration and acquisition, padded-shouldered, ostensibly classy but underneath cheap and shallow and heartless. The soundtrack to a life where nothing mattered but empty vanity, accessories and schmoozing your way behind the velvet rope at some Soho nightclub. In the North, we brooded under lowering skies with our Fall albums and waited. It wasn't Mark E though but another Smith who saved us.

It would be so cool and arresting to say that I first heard 'This Charming Man' in the boot of Geoff Stokes's car. But it would be a lie. That was the second time I heard it. On the first occasion, I was indebted once again to John Peel for another life-changing moment with a pop record. But how did I come to be in the boot of a car in Wigan listening to The Smiths for the second time. How did we get here?

I graduated in the worst year ever for graduate employment. That's the worst year … ever. I call that bad luck. Armed with a 2:1 in English, an unbeatable line in quips about Auden, an overdraft and a shrivelling relationship, I emerged blinking from the unreality of student life. It wasn't a pleasant experience.

The only thing that made it generally more palatable was that pretty much everyone I knew was in the same boat. The day I went to cash my first benefit cheque, the woman at the post office said, 'Have you any identification? Driver's licence? Birth certificate. Or could you tell us what honours degree you have just graduated with?'

Some enrolled on arcane MAs or went to train as teachers; I'd had enough though of academia and decided, foolishly, to take my chances in the world outside. The world outside had quite enough on its plate to give me much of a chance. My friends returned home to Wigan – from Leeds, Manchester, Bristol, Sheffield, Newcastle – jobless, penniless and desperately planning their next move. We skulked around in pubs, the Pear Tree mainly, bought the *Times Ed* for the non-existent jobs and bought the *NME* for the latest on the bands that helped give some focus to our becalmed lives. If it was a bad time for bookish, wry, romantic young men who'd just left college, it was a good time for bookish, wry, romantic young men in bands.

There was the former Postcard boys, Roddy and Edwyn. There was Prefab Sprout from County Durham whose first single 'Lions In My Own Garden (Exit Someone)' was enigmatic, melancholy, tuneful and therefore perfect for a jobless literature graduate with girlfriend trouble. Very soon, there would be Lloyd Cole and his Commotions who namechecked Norman Mailer and Truman Capote and played Dylanish country music in the Caledonian style. Without these records, 1983 and 1984 would have been a very bleak place indeed. Instead, I carried them around in my head daily. Daily and literally, thanks to a fantastic new piece of Japanese technology called a Walkman. I would listen to Aztec Camera's 'We Could Send Letters' or 'Stroll On' by Prefab Sprout as I walked though thin drizzle to the pub, pulling my long overcoat tighter around me, dragging on a soggy B&H and hoping that Paddy's words – 'Winter takes a while to pass but soon it will be May' – were true.

Early one evening, we bored of the taproom banter in the Pear Tree[2] and chauffeur for the evening Geoff Stokes decided we should drive out to another pub, anywhere, just for the change of

---

2 It was in the Pear Tree that I overheard my favourite fragment of pub conversation. In the middle of one of those sudden inexplicable silences that sometimes occur in noisy rooms, a lone, broadly accented, middle-aged woman's voice rang out, 'How's the pork pie situation, Jean?' Some time later, Geoff Stokes, who appears above, went on holiday to Israel. His postcard back to us read, in its entirety, 'Pork Pie Situation Not Good.'

scene. There were six of us and strong drink had already been taken, not wisely but too well, which is why I offered to travel in the boot. This is the kind of thing young blokes at a loose end with no sense of purpose in life and a skinful of booze do; it's not big or clever, it contravenes the laws of the road and common sense. But they do it.

Have you ever travelled in the boot of a car? It's really unpleasant. Claustrophobic, dark, uncomfortable, noisy, disorientating and a bit scary. If you have to travel in the boot of a car, it kind of helps if you've put away three pints of Burtonwood Top Hat and a couple of ginger wines first. This at least gives you a relaxed perspective on the journey.

Probably because I was in the boot, Geoff and my so-called mates decided to drive a hell of a way out of town; to the Farmers Arms in Parbold, a rural inn on a sprawling low hill ten miles distant from Wigan. I felt every camber, cat's eye and bump of the road, cursing the tardy ratepayers of Wigan as I went. One thing made this ordeal more palatable. Geoff's car radio speakers were casually mounted on the rear window shelf of his car and I heard Janice Long's evening show in perfect stereo reproduction. As I lay with my head on the spare tyre, staring at an empty banana milk carton and *The AA Book of the Road*, I heard a sound that transported me far from my current, fairly tawdry situation to somewhere far more magical. It was the sound of a guitar, a chiming, luminous frill that darted around in your head. It sounded, like 'Neat Neat Neat' had years before, like nothing I'd heard previously; thrilling and new, a sense compounded when the singer entered with a plaintive, lovelorn refrain:

'Punctured bicycle on a hillside desolate … will nature make a man of me yet.'

I banged hard on the bulkhead between boot and back seat. 'Stop!' I yelled, and then again, and then again until eventually the car was pulled over to the side of the road. The boot opened and mildly concerned faces peered in, behind them raggedy clouds and high stars

'Had enough then?' came the enquiry.

'No, listen!' I cried, unfolding myself painfully and leaping from the car. 'It's that record I told you about. The Smiths.' And so we listened and we loved. It is a rather sweet, odd tableau, don't you think? A small knot of tipsy young men in long overcoats, standing by a car on a high, deserted country lane listening to The Smiths in the chill November night.

'Punctured bicycle on a hillside desolate'. It was some opening gambit. Six words, four of which I don't think I'd ever heard in a pop song before; a hell of a strike rate. It fitted the moment perfectly of course. The template for the next year was set: of The Smiths getting into every corner of life, illuminating the everyday, celebrating the streets and hills and canals of the North of England. It's no exaggeration to say that for the first time pop music spoke directly to me. It said something to me about my life. Joblessness, glamour and charm in the face of sullen circumstance, lovelorn musings, lust, furtive encounters, politics, the landscape of the North – The Smiths took all these things and elevated them into poetry, made them radiant, made them worth something. Morrissey himself caught this perfectly when, speaking of his muse and his fascinations, he said, 'I am forever chained to a disused railway clearing in Wigan.' I wish he'd meant it literally. I could have gone round and taken him a Thermos.

A month or two later, compassion fever gripped the land. Paul Young, Bono and Bananarama emoting 'Do They Know It's Christmas' was inescapable in every pub, shop and leisure centre, Morrissey was one of the few voices in pop, in the nation as a whole come to that, that dared raise itself in dissent.

'I detest it all,' he said of Band Aid and Live Aid. 'It says that the responsibility for solving hunger and world poverty lies with an eleven-year-old girl in Wigan.' This struck me as the last word in sound analysis and common sense. And he mentioned Wigan again. Who was this great man?

Steven Patrick Morrissey was but one-quarter of The Smiths; without the contribution of them all, notably Johnny Marr's coruscating guitar work, The Smiths would never have stolen the hearts of a generation the way they did. But Morrissey was The Smiths in excelsis – mouthpiece, style icon, spokesman, public face. A blousy, camp, square-jawed Mancunian who claimed to be celibate, quoted Oscar Wilde and said things like, 'Anyone not wishing to be excessively charming should be shot.' With Tony Hadley and Howard Jones as competition, it was no surprise that he became, almost immediately, pop music's greatest frontman.

Rather like my romper-suited experience with The Beatles two decades before, I was soon to get my chance to see these new idols of mine in the flesh. It would be in a matter of days, 18 November 1983. The venue, curiously enough, was the old alma mater that I had only recently left, Edge Hill College, whose entertainments secretary, in a rare paroxysm of taste, had actually booked the best band in Britain, a band who, within weeks, would have left the college circuit behind for good.

Chloe, my just-about girlfriend, was still at the college and I was still paying visits there in a desultory, unsatisfactory way. I have to confess, though, and I take no pride in this, that there was a spring in my step as I boarded the train at Wigan Wallgate that weekend. I had tickets for The Smiths, and if you had to endure the death throes of a love affair, you might as well do it to a brilliant soundtrack.

The Smiths played the 'refec', the same large, depersonalised glass and metal hall where I had watched, half cut on Autumn Gold cider, acts as diverse as Orchestral Manoeuvres in the Dark and Liquid Gold. It was here that I had got involved in a mass brawl with Ormskirk townies during a set by Girls At Our Best and here that I had shouted disparaging remarks at Richard Digance. Long years of partly washed students availing themselves of chicken curry, oven chips and jam roly poly had imbued it with an unmistakable odour of demoralising institutionalised domesticity. I imagine maximum security prisons are the same. Nothing in its dull life had prepared it for the coming of The Smiths, that was for sure.

For ten minutes before the show began, gladioli showered down upon the audience from behind the amps and curtains. It was the perfect gesture of flamboyance and defiance of the stultifying rock norms. It was also, I later learned, a tactic that blew gaping holes in The Smiths' take-home pay most nights. But Morrissey wanted it, and so loyal roadies crouched behind amps hurling flowers at amazed students every night.

When they took the stage, I don't think I've ever seen a band look and sound so completely ineffably right. In Morrissey and Marr, they had a Jagger and Richard for different times. Morrissey wore a billowing violet chemise, a hearing aid, a gladioli in his back pocket and draped the back of his hand across his forehead like a distressed damsel in a silent movie. But this was a melodrama that somehow rang truer than any amount of gritty realism.

Every song seemed better than the last: 'This Night Has Opened My Eyes', 'Wonderful Woman', 'These Things Take Time'; rainlashed, smoky tales of young marriages failing in flats by the gasworks and illicit meetings under viaducts, a world populated by Albert Finney and Rita Tushingham, The Shangri-Las and Ena Sharples. At this point The Smiths were more than just a group, they were a whole, fully realised world. Drunk with infatuation that night, I even think they played a brief snatch of The Velvelettes' 'Needle In A Haystack, a Motown tune from my Northern Soul days. I could have been wrong though. The details are sketchy now, seen through a haze of longing and misty memory. Afterwards, we took a late train back in silence to an unheated furnished room in the back streets of Southport. It was in itself an almost comical Smiths tableau.

Weary of the daily humiliations of the dole, and of the daily round of news about record unemployment figures, video nasties like *I Spit On Your Grave* and Greenham Common protests, I decided I needed a break. My friend John had enrolled on an MA in Chemistry in Bangor and one weekend I took the 'Bangor Banger', the notoriously slow, ramshackle train from the North West to the North Wales coast. I met him in the lab and we tried for a while to locate some amyl nitrate in the cupboards (science labs often carry it for its properties as a cyanide antidote. Don't say I told you though). We drew a blank, decided the evening would have to be fuelled by nothing stronger than Brains bitter and went back to his shared house detouring via the Menai Vaults pub across the road; a classic North Wales boozer where everyone, but everyone, would switch into Welsh the minute you walked in and the air would be thick with phlegm and gurgling. Good luck to them, I thought. Who wanted anything to do with the country that closed your pits and gave you Cecil Parkinson? I'd have joined in if I could. Instead we nodded and smiled and they tolerated us while taking our money. We sat and drank mild and put Scritti Politti, the Rock Steady Crew and Aztec Camera's 'Mattress Of Wire' on the remarkably eclectic jukebox.

John's house had once been owned by a man from Beaumaris who was obsessed with fire safety. Every room in the house – every single one from the downstairs toilet to the space under the stairs where you keep the hoover – had a fire alarm of the 'In case of fire, smash glass' variety mounted on the wall. Later that night, during an impromptu party, I mentioned to John that I'd always wanted to smash the glass of a fire alarm.

'Be my guest. They used to be on a direct line to the fire station but they were all disconnected two years ago.'

So I put down my can, took off my Doc Marten shoe and whacked the glass with it. The glass shattered satisfyingly, and then a shrill, insanely loud ringing rent the air and within seconds three fire engines had arrived. I think we said that the chip pan had caught fire but we'd heaved it into the Menai Straits. They went away looking suspicious.

I mention Bangor because it became a kind of second home and, in truth, a kind of salvation briefly. There was pop music here and girls, the two best things in the world for raising the spirits and picking you up when you're a little down. And I was down, probably more so than I'm willing to admit now. The pop music was The Smiths, Josef K, Edwyn and Roddy of course, Lloyd Cole and Prefab Sprout. The girls I won't even name pseudonymously. They may not want to appear in this odd little tale. But I can never hear 'Reel Around The Fountain' without being transported to an upstairs room in a steep, slanting street that led down from the college past the Union Garth pub with its nets and anchors to the little harbour and pier. Outside, it's snowing a little and the lights on the shoreline are coming on. Inside it's warm, there's Nescafé Gold Blend with a jigger of brandy in it and Morrissey is singing 'Fifteen minutes with you, well, I wouldn't say no.'

I came back from that first trip and disembarked in Southport where I'd arranged to visit Chloe. She'd got used to me moping about, all tortured and agonised and D.H. Lawrence-like and, understandably, she was getting a little sick of it. She wanted to hang out with the fun crowd on her course, and was saddled with a boyfriend whose outlook on life was based on Ian Curtis in his lighter moments. That night, though, I walked in wearing shades – in winter at night – a scarlet and russet cowboy shirt, a skull tie and a leather cap like Donovan used to wear. I was carrying a copy of Aztec Camera's *High Land Hard Rain* and the first Smiths album. And whistling. She took one look at me and smiled. 'I knew that another girl would be good for you.' Women's intuition is a cliché but clichés don't get that way without being true a lot of the time.

Chloe went away to teach in Chadwell Heath, Essex, just down the road from the West Ham training ground, the sort of place where no 'r' is knowingly sounded and everyone goes to the pub on Sunday lunchtime in polyester short-sleeved shirts worn outside the trousers and gold sovereign rings. It was no place for a jobless Wiganer who thought he was Roddy Frame.

My memories of East London are uniformly grim. One day, Chloe and I were walking in the park, doubtless agonising over where we were going and what we were doing, when Chloe's flatmate came running across by the swings to catch us up. There was bad news from home. She told me, almost casually, that a friend had committed suicide. Take it from me, this is no way to break news like that. I ran, sweating coldly, past the kebab shops and dingy minicab offices of Chadwell Heath High Street, back to the flat, and made a phone call with my heart hammering in my ear.

It was Jem, our drummer. He'd lost his job at the bakery some time before, had married in haste and repented at leisure, was drinking too much and trying to become a photographer. Crushed by the endless small defeats of life in the middle Eighties, he had hung himself in his shabby flat on Gidlow Lane. At the funeral, the raddled old Irish priest made some tactless remarks about whether suicides still went to purgatory and several of us walked out. We repaired in silence to the beer garden of the Pear Tree and drank the sweltering afternoon away as Jem would have wanted.

It was a season of endings. Chloe and mine's last outing together was to *My Beautiful Launderette* (or was it *Absolute Beginners*) at the Odeon Marble Arch. Afterwards, we walked gloomily down to Tottenham Court Road tube station, knowing that the end was pretty much here. But into this miasma of self-pity and regret, an angry defiant thought asserted itself. I looked around at the bustle of life on Oxford Street, the tourists and girls in white stilettos out on the town, the rank, greasy, yet alluring smell of the hot dog vans and I thought – and believe me I don't often have embarrassing thoughts like this straight out of early drafts of bad Mel Gibson movies – but I thought, 'I'll be back. You haven't seen the last of me. You haven't beaten me, London. I may be slinking off back to the frozen North and the dole, defeated, demoralised and now a fantastically ineligible bachelor to boot but I'll be back on this street in better times. You just watch. And next time I'll have the money for a hot dog and I might even buy a fake Rolex from that shouty red-faced man over there. That's a promise.'

It's your prerogative, dear reader, not to believe this. But believe me, I did stand, just by John Lewis on the corner of Regent Street, a few strides from Broadcasting House, and think all of this and maybe even mutter it under my breath. And then I see Chloe eyeing me curiously, and I pretend to have spotted something in the John Lewis window, and I turn and walk towards her and we head down to the Central Line to travel to Chadwell Heath and kiss for the last time and then to never see each other again.

16 *Young Guns Go For It!*

It is the middle of the 1980s. I am standing in the vast winding shed of a cotton mill in Oldham, shouting to make myself heard above the deafening clack of the machines, wondering if I will ever learn to love or even understand the processes by which bobbins of silver-grey yarn are taken to mills in Leicester and turned by young Asian women into Umbro tracksuits to be worn by Scousers.

The ageing Teddy boy overlooker, the man who rules the winding machines and the teams of winders with absolute power, is telling me, at the top of his voice why 'we can't stop all this effing production of magenta now' and furthermore that if us effing pricks upstairs had known we'd wanted effing silver effing grey, why hadn't we told him before he put 48 effing bobbins of effing magenta on, for eff's sake. It was a question to which I had no adequate response. And frankly, I couldn't give an eff anyway.

Cotton ran in my family. We were as steeped in it as any downtrodden Negro picker in a Louisiana cottonfield. They had Mint Juleps and Iced Tea, we had Burtonwood Mild and Cherry B. My mum had worked in cotton mills all her adult life, like most of her female antecedents. Words like 'bobbin', 'loom', 'weave', 'yarn', 'slub' and 'weft' had rung like incantations all through my childhood. Then they had sounded faintly magical, like Norse gods. Now I knew that they belonged to a world of noise, of premature deafness, of draining physical labour, and shadows on the lung from a lifetime of breathing in microscopic fibres. It was no place for anyone. It was no place for me certainly. So what was I doing here?

My mum had risen rung by rung over the years from the actual winding room floor with all its din and crashing metal to the relative serenity of an office. She'd become a personnel officer and a minor perk of this was alerting her underemployed, moping son of a job coming up with Courtaulds, the textiles giant who'd once employed great swathes of the North West. Cheap foreign imports were slowly strangling the Lancashire textile industry but there were still mills in Bolton, Oldham and Manchester and as long as there were football kits and walking socks to be made, these mills would stay in production. They had, of course, got along fine without me for years and I'd have been happy to let this arrangement continue. But by now I was desperate. The demagogues of the day were full of vicious sneering about spongers and the workshy but from my slight acquaintance with it, no one would choose to be out of work. All the clichés are right; it undermines the foundations of your sense of self-worth so that no matter how bullish you are, the dole will suck the joie de vivre out of you. On *Life's A Riot With Spy Versus Spy* (a new favourite of mine heard once again on Peel) the bard of Barking, Billy Bragg, sang passionately 'The system has failed, don't fail yourself.' You knew this to be true; none of this was your fault. In fact, you knew just whose fault it was. But that didn't dispel the sapping sensation. Life on the dole was not so much freedom as a different insidious kind of drudgery. And I was lucky; I had no kids to support, no mortgage, just a pressing need for the new Prince album.

So I took the job at a Courtaulds mill in Bolton. It hadn't been a complete shoe-in. There had been a couple of other candidates, evidently even less enthusiastic about modern commercial textiles than I. The job was Sales Planner. What this meant essentially is that you were the hapless stooge who liaised between the clients and the shop floor of the mill. The former wanted yarn yesterday, changed their mind about colours incessantly and complained if they were a bobbin short on a consignment of 30,000; the latter not unreasonably wanted a quiet, orderly life, steadily producing one colour of yarn at a relaxed pace. Their desires were fundamentally irreconcilable. But sales planners, a fraternity I had just joined, had to try to bridge this yawning chasm. On a daily basis, it involved complicated maths and being sworn at on the phone by strangers in Derby.

For a month or so, I 'went through the mill', that is worked, or pretended to, on every stage of the production. This was dirty and exhausting but it was fun compared to what was to follow. The women, young and old, joked with you and made improper suggestions, the old Asian guys gave you chapattis and bhajis, delighted and amused to find a 'suit' who was so keen on their native food. But all too soon, it was time for the office.

I didn't really fit in in the office, in the same way that Larry Grayson wouldn't have really fitted in on an oil rig. For a start, I didn't have a moustache. There were four other men in the office and every one apart from me had a moustache, a percentage rate that I doubt could have been bettered at the Baghdad branch. And then, there was … well, then there was everything else. Everything else in the world really. So, let's concentrate on one particular stumbling block and what is after all, the kernel of our little narrative.

In the office was a transistor radio permanently tuned to Radio 1. If memory serves, the day began with Mike Smith, later to woo the fragrant Sarah Greene, fly helicopters a little too casually and make a fortune via Carphone Warehouse. I had no real quarrel with Mike Smith. It was just that, like Noel Edmonds who was rumoured not to even have any records in his own home/farm, Mike never really convinced me that here was a man whose heart beat faster at the thought of an unreleased Nick Drake rarity or a Captain Beefheart live album. Mid-morning would pass in the company of Simon Bates, whose almost biblical authority and mahogany tones would later make him the natural choice as the man who explained what PG meant at the beginning of rental videos. Simon's whole show revolved around the twin pillars of its two main features: the Golden Hour ('it was the year we lost Sir Ralph Richardson and gained this from Kajagoogoo!!') and Our Tune. Our Tune halted the nation at eleven o'clockish. Daily it came, a mawkish tale of terrifying ill-fortune culminating in 'If You Leave Me Now' by Chicago. Or Nilsson's 'Without You' if wet. An endless parade of meningitis, stillbirths, brain tumours, alcoholism and freak hang-gliding accidents, Our Tune could severely dent your faith in the notion of a loving and benevolent God. If not, Steve Wright In The Afternoon was next.[1]

The same records were played in what would later be termed 'heavy rotation'. All of them are still emblazoned on my mind; Matt Bianco, Nick Kershaw, Cyndi Lauper and Wham. Wham I really liked. Wham's records were funky and danceable and they didn't sound like they were taking themselves entirely seriously. I loved 'Young Guns Go For It'. Paul Weller had sneered at it in the *NME* ('Go for fucking what') and that actually made me like it even more. I thought 'Wham Rap' was more gloriously defiant about the unemployment experience than any amount of turgid boy rock. Admittedly, though, I was perturbed to hear of George Michael stuffing shuttlecocks down his shorts and then whacking them into the throng of hyperventilating girls at a London gig.

---

1 Sorry Steve. I just couldn't resist it.

At lunchtime, everyone went to the pub, I stayed at my desk, warmed up a Pot Noodle and if it was Wednesday – please God make it Wednesday – fell on that *NME* like a parched man on a desert oasis. This was my sole contact with the notion of another world out there. Unlike everyone else in the office, I didn't care what the *Sun* said. But I did care what the *NME* said. I trusted it implicitly. It was flippant, enigmatic, adolescent, sexy, glamorous, all the things that were being leeched out of me every day. It was a place where I could read about The Housemartins, whose single 'Happy Hour' captured perfectly the bullying blokeiness of this new world.

I stood stoically alone in the office on other matters apart from facial hair. Everyone else in the office bar me loved Queen. I hated them.[2] 'Well, who do you like then?' the fat little accountant would ask. Whenever I told him, he would reply, 'The Smiths?! The Smiths!!' and would do a little dance, waving his arms around, pirouetting and warbling in a bad impression of Morrissey's vocal style. 'Oh I want my mummy, I need the toilet, and I'm really unhappy.'

Apart from Mike, who'd once done the hippy trail to Marrakesh, whose moustache was a little more verdant than the rest and who, bless him, would sometimes try to strike up a sympathetic conversation about magic mushrooms or the Bunnymen, everyone else in that office hated me. Some of it was my fault; my lack of enthusiasm for the work coupled with my residual student gaucheness must have galled and irritated them. But a lot of it was their fault. I was scared, lonely, unsure of what I was doing. No one offered to help, the general feeling being 'let the student tosser sink'. I learned a true lesson here. Always show

---

2 In recent years, Queen have undergone something of a rehabilitation and reassessment. They are now regarded as brash, grandiloquent, larger than life. I still think of them as a pantomime version of Led Zeppelin; horrible boot-clicking music for torchlit rallies.

a little kindness to the funny little guy or girl who isn't fitting in very well and is eating a sandwich alone by the photocopier. Not only is it your duty as a human being but otherwise one day he might write a book and tell the world that you, fat little accountant from Bolton, are the most self-important twerp he has ever met.[3] Apart from Mick Hucknall, of course.

I stuck it a year, mainly out of loyalty to my mum. I didn't want the whole of Courtaulds thinking her only son was a hopeless, derailed misfit with only the vaguest idea of what he wanted to do in life beyond, ha, writing for a music paper. My friend Vitty from college had gone to teach English in Greece and he would write me letters telling me about his taxing routine of sitting for an hour in a lecture room each evening chatting about 'Wembley' and 'fish and chips' to pretty Greek girls, then spending his other waking hours drinking ouzo and Amstel at the harbour café eating fresh swordfish chargrilled before him in lemon juice and coriander by a smiling toothless man in a jaunty hat. I would read these letters at the bus stop in Bolton in the twilight, rain running down the neck of my trenchcoat. Via him, I applied for a job out there and, demand far outstripping supply, got it. Alain De Botton has written 'teaching English as a foreign language is what respectable people do when their life has come apart'. And he's absolutely right. My life had come apart. Vitty got me an application form. I filled it in. And I got a job.

I didn't exactly tell Courtaulds where they could shove their sales planning. I think I just said, 'Thessalonika here I come, here's your slide rule back.' Liberated, I skipped along the streets of Bolton. That the Greece job didn't start for another year didn't unduly trouble me. I would pass the time somehow. There was the band for one thing.

---

3 This real name I would use. But it has gone.

After Jem's suicide, the Salvation Air Force (at that point, a curious agglomerate with two keyboard players, mates of Jem's who rejoiced in the splendid nicknames Cosmic Joe and Mr Asia) petered out. Purely for fun, which was in short supply, my Bangor friend John and I began to make odd, funny tapes heavily influenced by our old shared love of the Diagram Brothers, Burt Bacharach, easy listening, country and western, punk, John Barry soundtracks, the Human League and Brian Eno. Our resources were meagre: a couple of second-hand guitars, my dad's home organ, the newly invented Casio VL Tone keyboard, a Roland drum box. But armed with these, we spent enjoyable afternoons making oblique concept pieces which, like The Residents whom we also worshipped, referred to a whole hidden world of private mythology. There was 'Death At Barclays', an instrumental suite about a bungled bank robbery, there was 'Dream House For Fun Family' based upon a forlorn second-hand toy we'd seen languishing in a local Sue Ryder shop. There was 'Man At The Outdoor', a concept drama about a back street off-licence failing due to its owner's obsession with Tommy Cooper. Another of our sidelines were impassioned songs about everyday events, our intention being to celebrate life as it was lived. Most of these elude me now but I think with fondness of 'What Time Does The Take-Away Shut?', 'Can't Give Up Smoking' and 'Where Are My Clean Socks?'.

From the back of the *NME* we got the address of Cherry Red records and sent them a demo of what we laughingly thought were our most commercial moments. In our covering letter, we said that it was 'about time they shed their Walter Softy image and started playing with the big boys such as Billy Ocean'. They sent back a letter politely explaining that we weren't what they were looking for right now, the subtext being 'and never will be'. As a duo we did play a gig though; a party thrown by Bangor Rowing Society, where we premiered some new proper songs that we were quite proud of. We dressed in what we thought was our best rock finery. Afterwards, someone asked whether we were going for a deliberately daft image.

Out of these proper songs grew a proper group, though, the Young Mark Twains, a five-piece combining our new-found love of what would now be called Americana (The Band, The Byrds, Neil Young, Gram Parsons), the Postcard bands and, oddly, a dash of funk. The other members of the band were Shrub, a keyboard player we'd met during a brief foray with Amateur Dramatics; Neil, a drummer who was obsessed with Frank Zappa; and Lydia, a university friend of John's whom we press-ganged into joining and taught to play the bass simply because we fancied the idea of having a girl bass player. We were adopted by a well-heeled, computer whiz kid Welshman called Dave who lived high up on the Pennine moors. We would practise in his huge house on Sunday mornings, then retire to the pub and eat disgusting game soup. That's a soup made with pheasants by the way, not a shop in Tokyo.

The Young Mark Twains were fun but at heart I don't think any of us really thought it was our ticket out of the depressed North West of the 1980s. Slowly, despite Nigel Lawson's best efforts, my generation were falling into regular employment. While waiting to take up the job in Greece I did some work at a drop-in centre teaching schizophrenics about Philip Larkin. Out of this came a job at a community college in Skelmersdale, a vast, concrete, economically blighted Lancashire new town. I taught A level English and Sociology to redundant car workers, dopehead scallies and feisty eighteen-year-old girls. And I loved it, so much so that I quietly forgot all about Greece and became rooted in 'Skem' for the next few years.

Skem had been built in 1961 to house the exodus from Liverpool's slum clearances. By the mid-Eighties, there were 45,000 people there but considerably fewer jobs. Thus the college was a bulwark of community life. Another was the

Transcendental Meditation Village, a world centre for folks of that particular religious bent. They had a factory which made ionisers and provided Skemmites with some of the few employment opportunities that existed. For this reason, the 'trannies' were regarded with affection if no little amusement. The college stood between the Nye Bevan Leisure Pool and the Concourse or 'Connie'. This was a massive shopping precinct-cum-bus station patrolled by gangs of kids in Fila leisurewear and packs of feral dogs, the descendants of generations of abandoned canine Xmas presents.[4]

Built into the foot of the Connie's sheer concrete cliff face was a pub called the Viking, simultaneously the roughest and yet most invigorating drinking establishment I'd ever visited. In my first week at the college, I booked the TV and video system to show a documentary on health policy or some such. On the day of the lesson I was dismayed to learn that the college had been broken into over the weekend and the TV and video stolen.

'Never mind,' said the principal. 'We'll go over to the Viking at lunchtime and buy it back.' And this we did, for twenty quid if memory serves. Once, playing in a five-a-side tournament, police burst onto the pitch and arrested the opposition for stealing the calor gas heaters from the dressing rooms at half-time.

If all this sounds like the most deplorable stereotyping, then I'm sorry. Skem was a cowboy town in some ways but I loved it. I made good, true friends and had wild times there and helped some bright, undervalued kids to university. It was a siege mentality, us against the world. It was also my first experience of what we have come to call retro-scally. It was quite a shock. By and large, Skem's young people, particularly the lads, had no interest in the chart music of the day. They would hang around in

---

4 In the shops of the Connie, you could buy a car sticker that read, 'I've seen the wild dogs of Skem', a brilliant parody of the ones you can buy at Longleat and safari parks.

the Connie or the lounges of council high-rises, wreathed in aromatic smoke from huge joints of Lebanese Scarlet or Pakistani Black, listening to Pink Floyd's *Meddle* or Genesis's *Foxtrot* or, way further out, to Captain Beefheart's *Trout Mask Replica* with its growls, discordant riffing and broken-backed time signatures. To them, Stock, Aitken and Waterman were the spawn of the devil. These crazy tunes found in older brothers' record collections were the real deal.

I liked the staff too. There was my buddy Steve who accompanied me to wild parties in Tanhouse and the rougher edges of town and whom I tried to wean off Phil Collins and Cat Stevens. There was Keith, a raffish French teacher who could be found most days reading racing-form books. There was June, a young sociology teacher who let slip one day that her boyfriend wrote for *Sounds*. At first, I thought I'd misheard her. But apparently not. We met him in the pub after work one night. I was shocked. He was after all a rock journalist, the ultimate apotheosis of cool, my dream job. I expected someone a little like Jim Morrison, Iggy Pop or at least Nick Kent; a saturnine creature in leather pants and a Byronic frock coat. He was an amiable plump bloke who looked a bit like David Jason. He got the job he said by bombarding them with unsolicited reviews; eventually they'd relented and he now did a bit of Liverpool reviewing on a slow week.

Ah but that's *Sounds*, I thought but didn't say. *Sounds* had changed rather since it had been my journal of choice at the age of twelve. It had nailed its colours to the heavy-metal mast in the early Eighties when it championed Def Leppard, Tygers of Pan Tang and Iron Maiden, giving them the unpronounceable acronym NWOBHM or New Wave Of British Heavy Metal. Since then it had maintained a certain greasy-bikerish demeanour. *NME* – my paper – was much more likely to feature pieces on the films of Fassbinder, or the depressing rise in youth suicide or Neil Kinnock or rhythmic innovation in the works of Can. That citadel couldn't be broached by a dashed para or two about Bogshed or the Macc Lads sent first class.

Or could it? Around this time, I saw an interview with the *NME*'s editor Neil Spencer on the Oxford Roadshow or some other yoof TV outlet. Filmed in a fashionably untidy office, his elegantly louche drawl rising above the clatter of poor typing, he said that the *NME* did, in fact, cast an appraising eye over unsolicited reviews. Sadly though, and here he sighed, 99.99 per cent of them were dreadful. The remainder were so so. The message could not have been clearer; don't bother.

I had in fact made an abortive, humiliating foray into rock journalism already. Just before I'd left Edge Hill, some enterprising college type launched a fanzine called *The Only Fun in Town*, named after a Josef K album. I offered casually to do 'some stuff for them' and was delighted when they asked me to interview The Bluebells, the jangly Scottish pop group who were coming to college soon. I saw the gig and pretty fair it was too, marred only by the wretched posturing arthouse combo who supported them. After the gig, I sought out the band in the smelly, cramped, cabbagey bit of the refectory kitchen that served as a dressing room, explained that I was from the college fanzine and wondered if I could 'grab a quick chat'. They agreed, surprisingly readily I thought, and we convened around a table, me with a borrowed Dictaphone and a clutch of thoughtful questions about art, the vampiric relationship between performer and audience and whither rock culture in the Thatcherite maelstrom. They engaged with these readily and volubly. After twenty minutes or so, I figured I should let them do whatever jangly pop/rock bands do after gigs and I decided to wrap up.

'So,' I ventured in conclusion, 'things seem to be going pretty well for The Bluebells right now. I guess it vindicates that notion that classic pop never really dates.'

I will never forget their answer.

'We're not The Bluebells.'

I had interviewed the support band. No wonder they'd seemed so keen, so bloody keen, to talk Roland Barthes and Jacques Derrida. I'd like to say that I kept my cool, laughed it off as a situationist prank and extricated myself with aplomb. I didn't though. I said, 'Oh. I see. Shit. Sorry,' clicked off the tape and walked away with as much dignity as I could muster, which wasn't much. That, as far as I was convinced, was the beginning and the end of my career as a rock journalist.

But hearing Neil Spencer had made me think again. Yes, he was disparaging. But he said that they read everything. Everything. He was lying of course. But fortunately I didn't know that at the time.

When the Young Mark Twains weren't playing gigs, or rehearsing in Dave's freezing pile on the low Pennine moors (which left a lot of free time, I have to say), I took in gigs around the local area, assisted by mates who could drive and had transport. We saw The Housemartins at a tiny club in Farnworth and they were wonderful; doo wop harmonies, jokes, a selection of great dance routines and we shared a battered sausage with them in the chippy afterwards. We saw New Order in Blackburn in an atmosphere of simmering violence thanks to the presence of the local NF. Loyal as ever, we went to the International in Manchester to see Edwyn Collins, then trying to get his solo career off the ground and promoting his single 'Don't Shilly Shally'. He was terrific as always; dry, debonair, daft. You felt that his time may have gone but you hoped not and we drove home with a couple of girlfriends in John's Morris Minor van, cold, wistful, happy.

The next morning I had an hour or two to kill before setting out for college and an afternoon of lecturing on embourgeoisiment theory. Embourgeoisiment theory was a leftover 1960s sociological doctrine which propounded that we were all now

middle class and it always went down hilariously well with a
clutch of embittered, redundant middle-aged factory workers and
a class of kids staring twenty years of unemployment in the face.
To kill that fateful hour I could have done many things. I could
have watched the Open University, or listened to the Golden
Hour with Simon Bates ('It was the year we lost IRA hunger
striker Bobby Sands and gained this from Tight Fit!).

Instead I took down from the top of the wardrobe the
battered Olivetti manual typewriter that my mum had brought
home after an office clearout. I fed in a piece of A4 torn from a
refill pad, twiddled with the ribbon till a nice unused dark patch
came along, and started to write a review of Edwyn Collins at the
Manchester International.

I know that I mentioned 'racoon hats' and I made a brief,
sneering allusion to 'failed boxers' meaning Terence Trent D'Arby
(then all over the pop media like a rash and certainly on *The Tube*
more often than Paula Yates). I remember nothing else of the
review except that I tried to keep it pretty short like the ones I read
in the back section of the *NME* and that the print came out slightly
reddish, as it is wont to do when you've needed a new ribbon for
two years. I put it in an envelope, addressed it to 'The NME,
Commonwealth House, New Oxford St, London, W1' and posted
it. Then I went to college and taught some sociology and after that
doubtless went to the pub with Steve and our favourite students
and discussed Everton and Phil Collins, both subjects Steve was
unnaturally keen on. The next week *NME* came out and my heart
fluttered for a moment when I saw a review of Edwyn Collins. But
it was from The Click Club in Birmingham and written by live
section regular DJ Fontana. Sniffily, and a little wounded, I didn't
think it was as good as mine so I forgot all about it. Pretty soon
after that term ended and I went to Andalucia for three weeks to
drink gin y tonica at 50p a half-pint.

When I came back, brown and a stone lighter after a diet of

gin and cherries, there was the usual daunting snowdrift of mail behind the door; Wigan Leisure Services demanding the return of overdue Thomas Mann books and Steely Dan albums, letters informing me that I may already have won £67,000 in a *Reader's Digest* lottery, leaflets from the government asking me nicely not to catch AIDS or take heroin. At the bottom of the pile was one postmarked London. I opened it and read it. Then I put it back in the envelope and walked around for a while. Then I sat down on the stairs and took it out and read it again. It went something like this:

> *Dear Howling Studs Macoines,*
>
> *I liked your review! Are you interested in doing more for the NME? If so, give me a ring.*
>
> *Yours truly,*
>
> *James Brown*
> *Live Editor*
> *NME*

So they read them after all. James Brown obviously had. He had even noted the stupid pseudonym I had given myself, a nickname I'd briefly been given following a misprint on a plane ticket and my temporary but disturbing habit of shouting in my sleep. James Brown was a name I knew well from the pages of the paper; a bolshy new acquisition whose style was in lively counterpoint to the *NME*'s beardstroking demeanour of the period. He'd read my review. He liked my review! Give him a ring!

I put the letter in my inside pocket and went about my daily business. Occasionally I would pat it, take it out and check it as one would a winning lottery ticket but strangely I did nothing else till nearly six that evening. Then I rang the number, asked for James Brown and announced myself, a little embarrassed naturally, as Howling Studs Macoines. James Brown (Live Editor *NME*) was clearly finishing up for the day. He yelled out to someone across the office (David Quantick? Paul Morley? Julie Burchill? Tony Parsons? Nick Kent come back for some Tippex he'd forgotten?), 'Which pub are you going to? I'll be across in a sec. I just need to talk to our new Northern freelancer.'

That night I went to Gems, a bar on Wigan's Dicconson Terrace and met my friends Eleanor and Mike. We chatted about this and that but I have to confess I wasn't really concentrating, which was odd because I had a huge and desperate crush on Eleanor. But in truth, my conversation with James Brown was endlessly replaying itself in my head; in particular the phrase 'our new Northern freelancer'.

'So what's happened with you today?' asked Eleanor, smiling. Normally I'd have answered quickly, snappily, with a choice bon mot or enigmatic witticism. But I just floundered around, stalled, muttered, until after a while I said, 'Well, errm, the usual, I should say, apart from, well, that is. Well actually, I've started writing for the *NME*.'

And I took a sip of my beer and waited to see what happened next.

17 Hit the North!

Stunned and delighted though my friends and I were at this new job, daily life carried on much the same at first, but I didn't go and move into a squat with Shane MacGowan or live on a tourbus with Metallica. I carried on hanging out with Skem scallies, passing on to them all I knew about Emil Durkheim and Alienation Theory, and waiting for my rock 'n' roll lifestyle to begin.

It began about a week later, not at the Madison Square Gardens or the Concertgebouw, Amsterdam, but at the Busman's Social Club by Seven Stars Bridge, Wigan. Most nights of the week, this squat, drab building behind the bakery and the Kwikfit Tyre Fitters was where bus drivers and conductors went to play snooker and drink subsidised bitter. Once a week, though, it was utterly transformed. Transformed at least. Changed anyway. Slightly.

Russ and Richard's Northern Soul Shop on Hurst Street had long since gone. It had become a shop selling baby clothes and then, in keeping with its proud history, reverted to a record shop known as Alan's after its shaven-headed, genial owner. I called in there a lot and spent a chunk of my wages on – a few items at random from that year – the 12-inch of the Sugarcubes' 'Birthday'; My Bloody Valentine's 'Strawberry Wine'; the first House Of Love album; and anything I could find on the On-U label that was played all the time on Radio Lancashire's terrific *On the Wire* programme. Alan sold the gamut of indie rock but, at heart, he was a skate punk. He would much have preferred that I picked up a Stupids album, an Extreme Noise Terror single or an Anti-Vivisection T-shirt. Alan and a few like-minded souls put on a special night at the Busman's club at Seven Stars Bridge. It was the cheapest venue they could find and once a week it became the Den rather as, under Tony Wilson's tutelage, the Russell/PSV club became The Factory. Except, obviously, without changing the whole face of British music.

No, the Den just changed the face of a few hundred Wiganers' weekends. Hardcore and skate punk were enjoying a purple patch, the bands were getting a lot of press in the *NME* and *Sounds*, and the Den nights were usually well attended. The bar staff were the same middle-aged ladies who worked the pumps the rest of the week and they would look on in amused bewilderment and mock horror as twenty or so skinheads would slamdance to Black Flag records.

One of Wigan's hardcore bands, The Electro-Hippies, were making quite a name for themselves. They had had a John Peel session, an accolade not be taken lightly even considering some of the bands who've had Peel sessions down the years. Mindful of the ease with which it could be accomplished on public transport (on foot even), I suggested The Electro-Hippies as my first professional gig review for the *NME*. James Brown concurred. He's heard of them and it promised just the kind of raucous provincial snottiness he was keen on bringing to the paper which had become ever more effete and esoteric during the late Eighties.

Let me give you an example. Here's the opening of a piece by Don Watson from April 1987.

ITEM: Report on case 154, an autonomous cell placed in suspended animation by its 4 constituent members. AIM: To

discern whether Wire is an anachronism in the modern age
which should be left to its inevitable extinction or whether it's
capable of addressing itself to the current climate thus posing a
direct threat to Operation Pleasure Drone.

The piece is an interview with my old favourites Wire. The intro
is essentially asking whether Wire should knock it on the head or
not. But it's typical of the *NME* of the time that this fairly straightforward notion is buried beneath a screed of cod-futuristic depersonalised sci-fi babble and ends with a swipe at chart pop which,
in case you hadn't guessed, is the point of that clunking Operation
Pleasure Drone reference. It's easy to sneer from this vantage
point. I had no real problem with this rarefied style at the time,
though I preferred jokes. I didn't mind that the *NME* put politicians and film directors on the cover either. I thought it elevated
the paper into something more that a music magazine; what I
didn't realise was what a disaster it was for the paper itself.
Unbeknown to me, the *NME* was haemorrhaging readers and
riven with internal squabbles. I was to find all this out. Before
that, though, I had to take my first steps on the hack ladder by
getting my first piece published.

I told the punkish lad on the door of the Busman's club that I
was from the *NME*. He didn't believe me, which was perfectly
reasonable. After all, he did see me in the pub, at the bus stop, and
in Alan's records. Wigan is a big town, but it's still a town and
sooner or later everyone who shares your tastes and enthusiasms
– be it carp fishing, traction engines, coprophilia or Megadeth –
will swim into your ken.

'Ah, well, you see, I wasn't from the *NME* then. But I am
now.' Explaining it this way made it sound even less plausible,
like Peter Parker being bitten by the radioactive spider. I was
bitten by a radioactive typewriter and now I'm *NME*-man. In the
end I just paid him my fiver and went in. I am ashamed to say

that I probably flourished a notebook along with my Marlboro Lights and I'm equally ashamed to say that this must be one of the last occasions I paid to get into a gig.

The Den paled quite quickly back then, to be truthful. There weren't enough girls around for my liking. I say this not lecherously but sociologically; single-sex gatherings always make me vaguely uneasy. I'd make a terrible Freemason, even if I could stand the aprons, compasses and rolled trouser legs. The music was nasty, brutish and short, as were a lot of the clientele. Years later, I was to see the very particular appeal of hardcore, those microscopic bursts of pure ugly bile made by vegans and peaceniks. I even grew to quite enjoy it, at least until I went on the road with Napalm Death. But back then, it made me queasy; music by pimply boys for pimply boys, I thought.

So I hung around by the bar with some mates. Unknowingly, I had already adopted classic music hack traits. I don't think you learn it, I think it's in your DNA, predisposing you to a career in music journalism, just as stubby fingers mark you down for the violin. If you're the sort of person who dashes on ahead through the foyer at gigs saying, 'I'll grab a drink later, I really want to check out the support band first,' then there may well be many outlets for you in the music business (personal trainer perhaps) but rock journalist isn't one of them.

Beneath my suave, slightly dissolute exterior (at these prices, I may have ordered a chaser) I was quivering with excitement. Yes I was in a dilapidated bus drivers' social club in one of Wigan's shabbier industrial districts. But I was on assignment! Oh how I longed for someone, anyone – attractive young woman, balding no-necked beer monster, anyone – to say 'What brings you here then?', thus affording me the opportunity to toss back the dregs of the second cheapest whisky on the optics saying, 'I'm covering it for the *NME*. Another Scotch and make it a large one, Tony.'

I did get asked actually, this very night and many times in the months ahead. I soon learned that people can sense when you haven't paid good money of your own to see the band. It's something in your unconcerned but secretly over-alert demeanour, the way you smile knowingly at the between-song banter, or maybe the way you shout, 'Testing Testing, *NME* reporter on assignment, testing testing,' into your brand new extra large Dixons Dictaphone.

The Electro-Hippies possessed the kind of name that bands were called on *Two Ronnies'* skits on pop music; Barker in an Afghan coat and a headband, Corbett in a thick black centre-parted wig, Nazi helmet and shades, saying 'man' a lot. When The Electro-Hippies took the stage, it soon became clear that they played the kind of pop music that only existed in the most fevered nightmares of *Two Ronnies* viewers. The songs were thunderously loud, stupidly fast and prehistorically simple. A singer flailed around and yelled incomprehensibly, presumably about a whole range of social injustices. From the bijou but attractive review that appeared in the *NME* the following week, the 26 Sept. 1987 to be precise, it seems I wasn't impressed.

Oblivious to the single-sex apartheid on the dance floor, The Electro-Hippies doubtless want to change the world. But how? With some old Uriah Heep riffs played at escape velocity? Much vaunted Peel session notwithstanding, The Electro-Hippies are stuck in fanzine flexi-ghetto land.

That's how it ended. Not that I know that from memory by the way. I had to go and find it in the dusty bound volumes of *NME* that lurk in the bowels of the BBC. I ended with a curious reference to a Stevie Wonder song and, as you can see, was desperate to make my rather minor point abut the lack of women. Earlier in the review, among other clangers, there was an entirely uncalled for and modish slur on Deep Purple whom I can now happily admit to loving. But everyone's got to start somewhere.

I bought the *NME* on the way to college the next Wednesday as always. But this time there was a crucial difference to the normal routine. There on page 36, alongside Sisters Of Mercy at ULU and the Bad Seeds in Camden was 'The Electro-Hippies. The Den. Wigan'. I could be wrong but I think this the first and only time Wigan has graced the *NME* live pages. My heart leapt. Or it did the thing that I assume people mean when they say their heart leapt; it skipped. Like a dirty CD. Like it does when you drive over an inadequately signposted cattle grid.

Since then I must have had thousands of pieces printed in various publications, millions of words, some well chosen, some grabbed at in haste, some phrases elegant and finely turned, some botched and bolted like a Friday afternoon Skoda. But I have never quite lost the thrill that comes with opening a paper or magazine and seeing your words and your name glance coyly back at you. I hope I'm not alone in this. You take the paper down from the shelf in Menzies or WH Smith and, making sure no one's watching, read it all again, furtively, greedily, at speed. You tell yourself that it's just to check that 'the subs haven't mangled it'. But really it's just to get that jolt of pure warming pleasure in your chest, like a pricey Armagnac going down. It's pride in your work, I suppose, and nothing wrong with that. Besides back on 26 Sept. 1987, I had no idea what a sub was.

I had become what we might call 'a stringer' – the local guy who covers local stories and feeds ideas and pieces to the paper's HQ in London. In the regional TV world, stringers are the people who alert ITN to skateboarding ducks in Frome or the man from Barrow-in-Furness who can whistle though his ears. In the music paper milieu, they cover the waterfront, or at least that part of it that includes the polytechnic bars, the refecs and downtown clubs. For me, in essence, this meant Manchester.

That was a problem. The last train from Manchester Victoria to Wigan left tantalisingly too early, just as headlining bands would be hitting their stride. The bus journey was long and circuitous. I had no car. And even had I a car I couldn't drive. Via the protocol of the guest list, I arrived at a happy solution.

Journalists, friends of the band and other assorted 'liggers', as they are known, gained access to the venue via the guest list. This, as the name implies, is a list of guests left at the box office or ticket desk. If you're pushy, you can normally squeeze what's known as a 'plus one' out of the record company PR. This isn't, as you might think, a forgotten variant of the plus four golfing trouser. It's basically a free pass for a friend. On the list, you're down as 'Stuart Maconie Plus One'. That means you can take someone with you.

The system I arrived at is that I'd confer my 'plus one' on any mate who fancied a free night out and was willing to give me a lift. By and large this worked, at least when the band concerned presented an attractive proposition; someone who you'd heard of at least and who were reasonable timekeepers. Sometimes it didn't. My poor mate Mike nursed his one pint of bitter for hours, waiting with me for the appearance of famously tardy Jamaican reggae legend Dennis Brown. When he eventually appeared at midnight, he was stalk-eyed on ganja, unsteady on his feet, rambling incoherently and, unsurprisingly, turned in a truly terrible set. When we got back to the car in the small hours, someone had smashed the side window and had the car radio away. It was a long, draughty, quiet ride back to Wigan.

Then again, Mike was with me at the same venue when we saw The Triffids, an evening to remember. I knew little about them, except they were from Australia. Within seconds of their taking the stage, though, it was clear that we were in the presence of the real deal; huge music written under huge skies for long road trips through empty deserts. I later found out they were from Perth, the most isolated major city on earth, a settlement of a million people a thousand miles distant from their nearest neighbour. You could hear that in the music; vast, yearning, frontier songs that even sounded goose-pimpling in a back street in Chorlton. I finished my review by saying, 'This is Saul on the road to Damascus signing off.'

There were other memorable nights. Microdisney at the Hacienda, Aztec Camera at the International. I saw a band from London called The Godfathers at the poly who so annoyed me with their faux Kray Twins chic and their awful whining political anthem 'Birth School Work Death' that I absolutely went for them. 'Birth School Work Death? Plenty of vacancies down the pit, lads.' Not only is this savage, it's not true. Pretty much every pit in the country was under five hundred feet of water but I wasn't going to let the truth get in the way of a slagging. The Godfathers were livid apparently. James Brown told me on the phone that, wounded and furious, they'd pulled out of an interview that week. I apologised sheepishly.

'No problem,' he laughed. 'We can always run an ad on that page instead.' He even seemed a little proud of me.

I was mildly keener on New Model Army, the crusty Yorkshire anarchists who remind me once again that there's nothing as malevolently violent as a pacifist vegan animal lover in clogs. I ended this one by asking of the fans, not entirely seriously I fancy, 'Hey, why can't we mobilise these kids into a revolutionary proletarian army?'

There was The Fall, John Cooper Clarke and Pete Shelley at Manchester Uni, three of the city's finest sons in a positively back-slapping orgy of civic pop pride, culminating in a set by The Fall at the height of their powers. 'Hit The North', 'Mr Pharmacist' and 'Victoria' were all yapping worryingly at the trouser leg of the chart. They were sexy, literally. Brix and Marcia providing the visual counterpoint to the preponderance of pasty-faced blokes in pullovers on stage. I described them as 'the sniper in the trees of independent music', I'm embarrassed to say.

But there were worse faux pas I could have made. A month or

two after I'd joined the paper, I read with interest a report in the news pages at the front of the *NME* about a serious disturbance at a Primal Scream gig at the University of London union. Halfway through the show, a nutter who'd somehow got hold of a tear gas canister set it off at the front of the stage, provoking in the hall a near riot and eventually the panicky incursion of police with dogs. At the back of the paper, in the live pages, was a review of the show. In it were observations about Primal Scream's leather trousers and mild reservations about their new material. But there was not a word about tear gas or snarling Alsatians. I fancy the reviewer (who shall be nameless) must have been impressing young ladies with his rock 'n' roll war stories in a nearby inn while, weeping and retching, Primal Scream had played 'Velocity Girl' though a noxious fog above the sounds of barking. You can't help thinking that if *NME* had reviewed plays, Lincoln's assassination would have been overlooked in favour of a moan about the price of the little opera glasses.

Rudyard Kipling, an old hack himself, wrote a poem about his journalistic maxims. In it he famously declared, 'I keep six honest serving-men / (They taught me all I knew); Their names are 'What and Why and When / And How and Where and Who.' I can now add to this my own version, specifically for music journalists, 'I keep four dodgy serving men, they do all right by me / Hyperbole, lies and insults and the daft analogy.'

Snipers in the trees, revolutionary proletarian armies, Saul on route to Damascus. It seemed I was well on the way to becoming a proper rock journalist.

18 Martha's Harbour

There are certain people that everyone knows one thing about. Everyone knows that Sarah Miles drinks her own urine. Everyone knows that Geoff Capes kept budgies. In the world of pop music, everyone knows that woolly-hatted Monkee Mike Nesmith's mum invented Tippex and that Delia Smith baked that lovely-looking cake on the front of *Let It Bleed*.

The one thing that everyone knows about ethereal goth rockers All About Eve is that their one and only *Top of the Pops* appearance was one of the great farragos in that programme's history. As they performed their modest hit 'Martha's Harbour', some bright spark on the show's crew – perhaps the same one who put a picture of darts legend Jocky Wilson rather than soul legend Jackie Wilson up during a Dexy's Midnight Runners' appearance – piped the backing track through to everyone but the band. The result was that the song was plainly audible to all but singer Julianne Regan who, though plaintively warbling according to our ears, was, according to our eyes, sitting on a stool absently looking around the studio. Guitarist Tim Brichenko strummed in the background, shoulders heaving with laughter.

So, to the public at large, All About Eve are a bit of a joke. I think of them with great affection though. For All About Eve were, if you don't count the group who turned out not to be The Bluebells, the first group I ever interviewed. They will forever have a place in my heart.

'What do you know about All About Eve?' asked James Brown on the phone one day.

'Goths,' I replied.

Drive up the M6 motorway and, once you're some way past Lancaster, pull off west into the Lake District fringe or east into the Pennines. Find a reasonable-sized market town and drive through it, at twilight, past the war memorial. Sitting on it, sharing a bottle of cider, will be a boy and girl in their late teens dressed in black with mauve hair. These are goths.

'All About Eve. Do you like them?' asked James.

'Not really. They're OK. Why?'

'I thought you might like to interview them.'

Naturally, I then reconsidered and realised that I loved them. Well, not quite. No one's that disingenuous. But I certainly drew on hitherto unexpected reservoirs of interest and enthusiasm.

Looking back I don't recall how I got the day off work. Maybe it was a Saturday. Maybe I indulged in some nefarious timetable juggling. Whatever, the day in question found me wandering down the Caledonian Road in North London carrying, I'm embarrassed to say, a huge Panasonic ghettoblaster.

I had no idea how journalists conducted interviews. Did they scribble shorthand down in notebooks with a pencil plucked from behind their ear, like in Ealing comedies? They obviously taped them. But what with? Were there products specially designed for this? Whatever, I didn't have the money or time to acquire one. I was still hammering out my reviews two-fingered, like a caveman hacking down a tree with a flint axe, on a child's portable typewriter. So it seemed somehow fitting that I had to take the train to London with an Adidas bag and a 'portable' cassette player the size of a small car.

If All About Eve found this excruciatingly funny, they were far too gracious to let their mirth show. They smiled, shook hands, said hello, made tea. It was all rather a shock. This was my first proper experience of a rock band in their natural habitat and thus far they had shown no inclination to snort huge lines of cocaine from the bald pates of dwarf Filippino manservants or to pleasure groupies with fresh fish.[1]

Instead, they ushered me into a little room in the North London studios and, with great tact, Tim Bricheno offered to tape the interview using the studio's whopping and very much 'state-of-the-art' mixing desk. This has happened twice in my journalistic career: once here and once, a few years later, with novelty popsters Jive Bunny (if anyone wants a superbly mixed, panned, stereo balanced and EQ'd conversation with Jive Bunny, by the way, I'm open to offers).

The interview was chatty and cordial; much more so than All About Eve expected. It was their first proper feature with the *NME* and you knew – because they said so – that they expected an altogether less genial encounter. The *NME*'s reputation went before it, I soon learned. Bands were often suspicious, even hostile. They expected a 'stitch-up', a smiling assassin who'd be offhandedly pleasant to their faces but then mock their trousers and new concept album as soon as he was back in the *NME* office. They were often right. As an *NME* cub reporter I had a lot of history and foreground to get over before a word was spoken.

Mostly, I did though. I wasn't a typical *NME* writer. Really, there isn't, or rather wasn't, a typical *NME* writer. The accepted stereotypes, established largely by those luminaries Kent, Shaar Murray, Parsons, Burchill and Morley, ran thus: lanky smackhead who lives on *Rolling Stones* tourbus, drawling hippy with Afro and

---

1 Readers intrigued and salivating are referred to the infamous red snapper episode of the Led Zeppelin biog, *The Hammer of the Gods* by Stephen Davis.

shades, chippy punk, vitriolic glamorous communist harpy or Mancunian intellectual with situationist fixation. I didn't really fit into any of these, much as I loved these writers. Danny Baker had that very month been lured back to the paper and turned in one of the funniest selections of single reviews I'd ever read. In one of these, he described an exchange on Tom Robinson's tourbus some years earlier where Tom had been shocked to learn that Nat King Cole was dead. 'Old Blue Eyes, eh? Gone.' Spluttering as only he could, Baker wailed against the narrow musical range of the average touring rock star. Baker never became a stereotype, which is a pity as he was in some ways the best role model of all; a very funny working-class bloke who loved pop music in all its forms.

I'd never entertained any fantasies about being a nasty, vulpine, confrontational interviewer. Now I realised, disappointingly, that it was true; I was a bit of a wuss. I make absolutely no apologies for this. The vast majority of musicians are charming sorts and great company. Many are among the nicest people I have ever met (we shall come on to the exceptions). I had no desire to spend an uncomfortable hour or two squabbling with them in a hotel suite or restaurant just to bolster my self-image. As I learned from my little chat with All About Eve, I was destined to be a nice cop pretty much all the time.

I like to think I got good interviews in my own sweet way. As Sir Jimmy Young once said when defending his chummy interviewing technique, you catch more flies with honey than vinegar. I was never going to make nice Julianne Regan cry.

The NME of 30 January 1988 duly appeared with, on page 7, a large colour picture of All About Eve and an accompanying feature headlined 'We're Nice People'. In it I said that All About Eve were hugely unfashionable and to be honest not really that good but via some convoluted rhetoric only I understood, they were far far better than the obscure tripe that was in the paper most weeks.

This kind of battle for the soul of the paper was going on in smoke-filled rooms behind closed doors in New Oxford Street – although there was no way I could have known this: I had yet to even glimpse the *NME* office, even from afar with field glasses. Having completed my jolly, convivial chat with All About Eve, I had made my way into the West End and tried in vain to find the fabled New Oxford Street home of the *NME*. I imagined it to be something like the Cloudbase HQ of Spectrum in the *Captain Scarlet* series: an enormous citadel in the sky resplendent with the letters 'NME' picked out in eight-foot neon. There'd be a terrace bar, like the House of Commons, and in it you'd find Julie Burchill, David Quantick, David Bowie and Bono sharing a packet of pork scratchings and a pitcher of margarita.

The truth was that actually I couldn't work out where Oxford Street ended and New Oxford Street began. There was nothing round there that looked like the headquarters of the world's biggest-selling rock weekly either. Just a big branch of Argos, a greasy spoon and, I thought with a shudder, what could easily have been the office block of a cotton mill.

I shouldered my huge tape recorder, pushed my way through damp commuters and made my way through the dusk to Euston and home.

19 London

Very soon though, I was coming back on the southbound train beloved of blues singers. Regularly and often in fact, if slowly and erratically due to failure of line-side equipment near Crewe. I'd listen on my Walkman as Morrissey sang on 'London' by The Smiths, 'Train moves onto Euston, and do you think you've made the right decision this time?' The coming year was to be full of decisions, some of them personal, some of them professional, daunting and exciting.

I was still working at Skelmersdale College, just. On a weekly basis, though, I would now have sizeable screeds of stuff in the *NME*. Seeing 'my byline' was now a regular though undimmed pleasure. Whenever I could – weekends, afternoons off, the odd half-term – I'd take on *NME* assignments. I went to Manchester to meet two men who ran a small independent record label called Playhard. They were Nathan McGough and Dave Haslam, two men who I'd see a lot more of in the next few years as the eyes of the pop world turned to Manchester. I interviewed the Go Betweens who told me that Sigmund Freud's theories of personal motivation and behaviour were the curse of the twentieth century. I interviewed Green Gartside of Scritti Politti who told me he'd got an *NME* subscription when he was eight and joined the

Cwmbran Young Communist League at twelve. I interviewed Wigan's only half-famous pop stars, the Railway Children, over a pint of Burtonwood's bitter in the Cherry Gardens hotel by Haigh Hall. I didn't interview The Smiths – they had split up by now – but I moved nearer to their orbit; interviewing a Manchester hairdresser called Andrew Berry, coiffeur to the stars and immortalised in Morrissey's 'Hairdresser On Fire' and also a quintet from Blackburn called, confusingly, Bradford who were Morrissey's current favourite band.

On one of these London trips though, the Go Betweens or Scritti Politti I assume, I finally broached the portals of the *NME* – which turned out not to be particularly hallowed, but a rather tawdry office block a tramp's spit from Centre Point which I had dismissed as unlikely on that previous visit. This was New Commonwealth House.

There was a dismal, carpeted reception area with a couple of piles of unsold *NME*s and a pair of lifts. Via these, five floors up, were the offices of the *NME*. It was a large open-plan area, hazy with the fug of cigarettes and swearing. Dotted around the room at various overflowing desks were numerous young men and even a couple of women typing in my own two-fingered style, squinting at the page through one half-closed eye and a wisp of blue smoke from a fag clamped between their lips. This was gratifying. It was exactly what I'd hoped and imagined a newspaper office to look like – dirty, crowded, seedy – and sound like: the clatter of typewriters, the muffled thud of the office stereo, the occasional hacking cough.

The staff individually were less striking. Many of the blokes preferred the same mode of dress: black Levis and a T-shirt proclaiming the wares of a different band, some of whom I'd actually heard of. It was some time before I realised that these were not genuine purchases proclaiming loyalty to a much loved artist but items that arrived through the post daily and, importantly, gratis; promotional freebies from the PR offices of record companies. If the band involved were half decent or actually the hack's favourites, all to the good. The item might then become saved 'for best' as it were. But to the less sartorially scrupulous, the band displayed were an irrelevance. What counted was that the shirt stood between you and nakedness – never an attractive proposition with music hacks – on a day when everything else was in the wash. On such a day, the less stylish staffer would have worn a Living In A Box or Chris De Burgh T-shirt, even before the days of widespread irony.

Elsewhere in the room, there was a large man in incongruous Christopher Biggins glasses and a Fred Perry shirt. This was Danny Kelly, the deputy editor. The actual editor, the legendary Alan Lewis, was elsewhere, perhaps lunching not wisely but too well in the Falkland Arms across the road. Another mainstay, David Quantick, wore a paisley waistcoat and was sitting, smoking furiously, at a typewriter, quietly slaughtering the new album by the King of Luxembourg. Not the real monarch but the foppish indie act of the same name. There were a couple of rake-thin young women – Helen Mead and Barbara Ellen (or the new Julie Burchill as she hated being called). There were lots of fashionably retro spectacles and polo necks around and the overall feel was not so much a thrusting rock weekly as the Film Studies department of a provincial university.

At first glance, from what I could make out through the indigo mist of Benson & Hedges smoke anyway, only one person in the room looked remotely as I imagined a rock journalist would. He was perched, languidly, on a desk in the corner. He wore a black beret on his shaved head, had an elaborate Mephistophelean goatee and sported a black tunic that seemed to comprise the top half of the full dress uniform of the Egyptian navy. That was how a rock journalist should look, I thought admiringly. When I learned that this gentleman was the raffishly named Jack Barron, I was even more impressed. It was only a year or so later that I found out that his real name was Nigel Parker and he was a PhD Sociology student from Oxford. As I soon discovered, for every rough-hewn proletarian firebrand in the music press, there are two or three sons of archdeacons who attended minor public schools.

Finally there was my benefactor James Brown, the office's undisputed live wire whose teenage fanzine *Attack on Bzag* had propelled him to samizdat stardom and who had been poached from *Sounds* with the explicit intent of rousing the slumbering beast of *NME* from its torpor. James wore regulation black Levis and a 'Touched By The Hand Of God' New Order T-shirt that I was rather jealous of. He buzzed from desk to desk, cajoling, baiting, antagonising, complimenting. In the actual office pecking order, he was two or three rungs down from the top, only recently promoted to features editor. But you would not have guessed this. This, clearly, was James Brown's magazine.

I soon found out that not everybody welcomed this incandescent Jimmy-come-lately who had moved through the paper's hierarchy with such alacrity. There was a feeling among the older guard that there was something crass and anti-intellectual about him. For one thing, he was at this point defiantly and unashamedly championing a style of music that he had invented and then christened 'Grebo'. The very name – Midlands slang for unwashed biker types – appalled some of the paper's ancien regime. Then there were the bands. Essentially, they were unwashed biker types from the Midlands: Pop Will Eat Itself, the Wonder Stuff, Crazyhead, Gaye Bykers on Acid. They made lairy dance pop and greaser rock for provincial tykes and James was keen on putting one or all of them on the cover at every opportunity. This disturbed those sections of the paper that wished things to continue as they had done for most of the middle Eighties, where ideally each week's cover would feature

Nick Cave and his new soundtrack to a Werner Herzog movie set in Berlin. Certainly, this gave the paper more gravitas. Unfortunately, it was scaring the readers away in their thousands. This fact had even permeated the long, liquid lunches and boardroom buffets of the top brass. The *NME* was disappearing up its own immaculate fundament.

Hence, after a few mildly indifferent editors, IPC had appointed as top man Alan Lewis. Lewis had once run a pub and had steered *Sounds* through its major successes of the last decade. He'd pretty much invented, in cohort with the hated Garry Bushell, *bête noire* of the *NME* liberal left, the New Wave of British Heavy Metal and Oi. Both were as far from Herzog and Nick Cave as you could conceive of. The former saw the resurgence of blokey, tight-trousered hard rock and had given the world Def Leppard and Iron Maiden. The latter was less amiable, more problematic – punk's stunted idiot half-brother, musically primitive and politically unsavoury with its close links to far-right groups.

Alan Lewis was a smart, funny man. Left to his own devices, I doubt if he'd have any sooner spent the evening listening to Screwdriver or the Four Skins than he would have gone to Glyndebourne to hear some shrieking woman in a horned helmet. But he had newsprint for blood. He knew what made papers tick and he knew that the *NME* was in desperate straits. A fixation with film and politics, with semiotic theory and self-consciously literary style, the absence of humour – all of these had alienated sizeable swathes of the paper's core audience: ordinary, bright, broadminded music fans with a sense of fun. Before Lewis and Brown and Kelly's stewardship, the paper had become *Sight and Sound* with record reviews, the *New Statesman* in a Cramps T-shirt. Many people liked this, some of the time I was one of them, but many more didn't. Alan Lewis had charged his young protégé James Brown, along with deputy Danny Kelly, a former railway complaints clerk with a passion for The Clash and roots reggae, with the business of shaking *NME* out of its complacency. It was, at heart, a rock 'n' roll paper and it needed to re-engage with this motherlode.

Sporadic war was part of the body politic of the paper it seemed. Danny Kelly was a survivor of what was known as the Hip-Hop Wars of the middle Eighties, when the paper's intellectual Maoist wing led by Stuart Cosgrove had demanded more black faces on the cover and more black music coverage throughout. In itself, this was surely admirable but its downside was that guitar rock, the paper's lifeblood since the early Sixties, was regarded as trivial and beneath serious consideration when compared to Marvin Gaye or Public Enemy.

The new men then were, by instinct if not design, keen to put some pep and life back into the effete office culture. Later, people would mock this as laddishness. Whatever it was, it was overdue. Eventually it would be the paper's salvation. By accident almost, I was part of their sea change, their injection of new blood. I was delighted, not least because I soon found I was partial to a bit of rock 'n' roll. I knew about Foucault. I also knew and liked the bits of the biz that had Foucault to do with anything but high jinx.

I soon found out that there was no merrier way to spend an early evening than ensconced in a pub, part of a pack of young writers and subs, coaxing war stories of the great days of the British rock weeklies out of Alan Lewis. One in particular we would ask for again and again, like children demanding a favourite bedtime story. Lewis as a young reporter on the road with the group Japan in the country Japan, a half-hour odyssey rich with samurai sword fights with Okinawa promoters and late-night encounters with oriental groupies. One of the latter Lewis had, in a mad moment, written up as a bit of lurid, sensational copy, safe in the knowledge that his wife never read his pieces. On this one occasion, determined to make an effort to better understand her hubbie's chosen livelihood, she did.

I, then, was part of the class of '88 that was earmarked as the next generation of the paper, the Famous Flames to James Brown's Hardest Working Man in the rock business routine. Also, there was Steve Lamacq, the flyweight champion of all things indie. He had seen more gigs than I'd had hot dinners. He had certainly seen more gigs than he'd had hot dinners. Here was a man who lived off scampi fries and Diamond White cider and spent his holidays on Mega City Four's tourbus. There was the lovely Mary Ann Hobbs who, it was said, had once lived in a van with Saxon and liked heavy metal and motorbikes. Next to these I felt like some periwigged fop out of Sheridan. This was to become the folklore affectionately played up to by all of us. I would laugh at their grubby lifestyle. They would chidingly accuse me of spending my free time drinking tawny port in gentleman's clubs with Paddy MacAloon from Prefab Sprout. If only.

Most of my first year as an *NME* writer I spent explaining the difference between psephology and phrenology[1] to single mums and scallies. Even when I was really being a writer, my time was largely occupied, not in kicking back over cocktails with stars, but bashing out copy on a child's typewriter with four rigid fingers, unsticking keys, becoming the Jackson Pollock of Tippex and hoping that someone in Silicon Valley would hurry up and invent Microsoft Word.

---

1 One is the study of voting behaviour, the other is feeling the lumps on people's heads. The A level board were understandably keen on students knowing the difference.

20 Waiting for the Great Leap Forward

1989 was a year of revolutions. Half of Europe went nuts and mutinied and by the end of the year, Christmas Day in fact, when Mr and Mrs Ceaucescu were summarily executed with little regard for the festive season, all bets were off. The Berlin Wall came down and the Cold War ended in a continent-wide thaw.

I had some personal revolutions of my own awaiting me. They weren't in the same league as the redrawing of the map of Europe. But they were pretty major if you were me. Which of course I was.

I was a music journalist, a real one, for the world's greatest rock weekly, though oddly still in regular employment a couple of hundred miles away.

I was steadily getting into my stride though, passing with a shiver of pleasure and pride the small milestones that comprise the journo's life. Who knows what the career ladder may be on *Tunnels and Tunnelling* or *Hazardous Cargo Bulletin* – your first 'on the road' piece with a consignment of nerve gas perhaps or a review of a Siberian pipeline – but I remember every rung and handhold of this my own ascent.

I'd done my local live reviews. These included a few 'pic leads', the longer ones with a photo basically. Then you get the page lead, someone major who merits a big pic and several hundred words of thoughtful, considered analysis. This is written, if you're unlucky and deadlines are tight, on the back of a serviette coming home from the gig and then phoned through to the printers, always a Beckettian nightmare of frozen communication. 'Stop. New Par. Much of their new material is a corny pastiche … yes, will repeat, corny new word pastiche … no, not Cornish pasty, corny pastiche …'

After that come your first album reviews. Billy Bragg's 'Waiting For The Great Leap Forward' was my first pic lead. I raved about it. I'd always liked Billy and I still hadn't got over the unseemly thrill of getting free records, sometimes brought round by a large mysterious biker with a crackling walkie talkie and a clipboard whose face you never saw but who always seemed Australian.

There were two milestones that I had long fantasised about though. The first was the singles reviews. I had written my own singles reviews in the back of chemistry and German exercise books throughout my teenage years. Occasionally they'd be discovered and read aloud with loaded sarcasm by a gimlet-eyed teacher with handlebar moustache and tweed hacking jacket. Now all such embarrassments paled into insignificance. It all seemed worthwhile that day I was asked to 'do the singles'.

The singles page was one of my favourite parts of the paper. It was one of the pages I'd turn to first, and I later found out from reader surveys that thousands felt the same. The singles page was, in the right hands, a delight. Compared to the heavier fayre of the features pages, the singles reviews were canapés, choice, tiny, piquant morsels, eighty or so words that could cut to the quick or capture the very essence of a pop record. I could well remember particularly brilliant examples from down the years. Paul Morley on 'This Charming Man': 'This is not the kind of record that you find yourself in a corner with at a party, pressed awkwardly against it and fumbling with its buttons. This is the kind of record that you marry.'

Paul Du Noyer or perhaps Mat Snow on 'Walk Out To Winter': 'This is a bright, chilly spring day with fresh milk in the fridge kind of record.' John Peel on 'Aphrodite's Child': 'An abrupt fade adds to the record's charm. If you then leave this record on the turntable long after common sense has advised otherwise, you will hear a voice imploring you to "Do It".'

Then there were the various anonymous quickies I remembered. Some Eighties alternative types had released a tune entitled 'Don't Eat Bricks'. The review read simply 'sound advice'. Of a maudlin progressive ditty, 'One day in the late 1970s, all of the Mellotrons in the world were hunted down, collected together and burned. And it was good. But in the confusion one Mellotron escaped. This is the story of Mellotron.' Of Phil Collins's 'Can't It Wait Till Morning?': 'No, it can't, Phil. When are you going to stop making these bloody awful records?'

So my first singles column was a day of no small import for me. I planned it with military precision. That is, if the military have a division devoted to taking the piss out of Phil Collins. I arranged to make the trip to London and stay in the Ilford flat of my old college mate Stod, now seeking to make his way in the civil service. I touted two huge IPC carrier bags full of 12- and 7-inch vinyl along the Central Line to Ongar. As I hurried down Stod's street, I was aware of that uniquely uncomfortable feeling; plastic carrier bag handles gently stretching in the hands under a too, too solid weight of burden. Just before they snapped I got them indoors, upstairs and arrayed them on Stod's spare bed.

Given that only forty or fifty singles can broach the charts most weeks and that only about twice that number at best will ever get played anywhere, there are an evidently insane number of singles released every seven days. Thousands. Hundreds at least. Most get sent to the *NME*. When a hungry new rock writer gazes upon them, spread vulnerably about on a duvet in Ongar, eager to please, the sight inspires various thoughts. There is an involuntary judder of savage hot-blooded lust. For as Kissinger said, 'Power is the ultimate aphrodisiac.' Just look: Sting, Phil Collins, that bloke who used to be in The Alarm. Here was the chance for revenge; witty, penetrating, Pulitzer prize-winning revenge with a little luck. The revenge of the little guy. If along the way, we could find the new Beatles, new Clash, new Smiths, new China Crisis at least, then so much the better.

I remember only one of my first batch of singles. It was 'Big Fun' by Inner City featuring Kevin Saunderson. It was – and is – a remarkable record and I said so. The others are simply a blur of all-day and all-night typing, each review on a single sheet, the easier to facilitate the sub's gleeful cutting and hacking. Drifts of Tippex, lists of labels to check; I soon realised that the joy of 'doing the singles' was tempered by the fact that it was a total bloody pain. An overnight sneerathon fuelled by booze and fags, illuminated by the odd hysterical rave. So poor and thin are those weekly crop of singles that you would soon find yourself praying for something half decent to garland with the Single Of The Week accolade, XTC's 'The Loving' and Costello's 'Veronica' are two I recall, even if neither was the future of rock 'n' roll, the real quarry we were always in pursuit of.

But it wasn't quite a thankless task. For all the death-threats and irate rants you received there was nothing like the thrill of hearing a grudging 'Funny singles this week' from a passing sub or friendly PR.

The death threats and rants came, by and large, from the *NME*'s legions of correspondents. Every day, bulging mailbags would be hauled up to the 26th floor by a tiny, gnarled South Londoner called Jim[1] who 'used to play snooker with the Krays

---

1 We called him Jim the Crim. We were, after all, professional wordsmiths.

every Friday' and still like 'a spot of Eddie Cochrane myself'. Jim would often ask on arrival, panting and crimson-faced, 'What's in these bleeding mailbags?'

To which the correct reply would have been, 'Illiterate venom, corrosive hostility, praise that is somehow more disturbing in its shrill hysteria than abuse, stylised pastel drawings of Michael Stipe's head on the body of an ocelot, demands for Kate Bush's home address in turquoise ink,[2] incomprehensible rants about mind control messages on Chaka Khan albums, entries to long-forgotten Manfred Mann competitions from 1965, requests from squaddies for Barbara Ellen's old knickers and offers of accordions for sale. Life, Jim, but not as we know it.'

In terms of range, vitriol and sheer volume, the correspondence that the *NME* attracted made the other magazines in Kings Reach Tower[3] blanch with envy and awe. You could see the guys from *Practical Boatowner* and *Cage and Aviary Bird* hanging round the lifts as Jim arrived twice a day, their faces pictures of downcast inadequacy.[4] They were lucky if they got a couple of queries about salt-resistant varnish and parakeet moult a week.

The best stuff, which meant the weirdest, ended up pinned on the noticeboard by the editor's office. Two primary schoolchildren wrote in asking for dishevelled, veteran news editor Terry Staunton's picture. They ended their crayoned missive with a scrawled 'we can send munny'. A woman from Bratislava wrote fourteen longhand pages of foolscap denouncing The Sweet's bass player Steve Priest for his shabby treatment of her. It turned

---

2 Back in the days when I used to stalk Elvis Costello's dad, I was just as interested in Kate – more so in fact since as well as being clever, fascinating and making great records, she had the distinct advantage of being the most beautiful creature I had ever seen.

3 During my first year at the paper, it moved from the West End to an enormous brutalist skyscraper south of the river, thus reducing the already low glamour quotient.

4 Postal envy if you like. You too can have a mailbag like mine.

out that Priest's only crime was to be quite reasonably nervous of this woman who had tried to send him, get this, a live panther though the post: 'I had thought for a long time to find a gift that would represent Steve's personality and character. In the end I decided a panther but the Slovakian Zoological Society said there would be problems with the postage.' No slouches those boys at the Slovakian Zoological Society, I thought admiringly.

I once received a copy of a feature I had written on Birmingham girl group Fuzzbox, heavily, painstakingly anno-tated and appraised as if it were an academic text. In the same package, the correspondent ('Marcus') included a sheaf of petrol receipts, all his O level certificates and a slide viewer containing 3D pictures of raw meat and some people having a party on a yacht. Strangely, you sort of got used to all this.

Legend told of disgruntled acts and managers waging postal war on critics. Chinn and Chapman (the men behind The Sweet funnily enough) once sent Charles Shaar Murray a rotting cow brain. Well-known tramp-rock band The Levellers sent Andrew Collins some human faeces in a box after an unfavourable review. But mainly it was odd blurry pictures, items of clothing, maps, miniature bottles of whisky, badges, sandwiches, hair, poems and complimentary airline toiletries. A young woman once wrote to me saying that I was the best writer since Shakespeare and that she would like to be my unpaid Girl Friday. 'I am prepared to do anything … and I do mean ANYTHING!!' she ended, provoca-tively. She enclosed a picture of herself riding a Shetland pony in a blizzard.

Some of the letters were, of course, expressly intended for publication in our letters page. For decades, this had been called Gasbag and had featured the famous Benyon Lone Groover cartoon in which a cowboy would say 'wow' and 'man' a great deal. Now it was called Angst, a concession to modernity. The letters too had changed. In the early Sixties, the typical letter was a request for Adam Faith's inside leg measurement or a passion-ate defence of Acker Bilk over Chris Barber. In the Seventies, the staple became the angry rant from 'A Real Music Lover, Mansfield' stating that anyone who didn't realise that Jethro Tull's *Passion Play* was the greatest album ever made was a tone-deaf knobhead and a perve. In the Eighties, it was a partly digested bit of Camus and a reference to The Cure with lots of (extraneous) brackets.

From experience though, I quickly learned that whatever the music publication there are only really about five types of letter.

1. First, there's the optimistic and lazy student. This is generally a pale girl from Essex who has decided to do her A Level Media Studies on The Development of Goth Music from 1976 to the Present (purely because she can) and has no clear idea how to go about it. This is where I came in. Could I send her all the information I had about goth music: pie charts, graphs, slide transparencies and, if possible, the home address of Andrew Eldritch from The Sisters Of Mercy? No stamped addressed envelope of course, but she would generally include some little silver stars.

2. Secondly, there was the cheery foreigner. His missive went something like this: 'Hello!! I Am Gunnar, boy, 14, also from Malmo!! I am very much liking the British indie and alterna-tive pop rockers! My favourites are Pulp, Blur, Stones Roses, Barclay James Harvest and Jackdaw With Crowbar!! Perhaps I could write you especially if girl!! Perhaps I visit you in London!! Rock on!!'

3. Thirdly, there is the mad person. The envelope would often bear a clue, such as a curious address formation 'New Musical Express, Kings Reach Tower, London, EEC' or an unexplained

phrase near the stamp ('Dove soap' in one case). The letters themselves were characterised by an exaggerated, faintly chilling formality:

> *Dear Mr Maconie, I write to you in the hope that you can help me. I am the Perspex God Of Valhalla and I can see you wherever you go with my special television helmet. I need to contact Kevin Rowland of Dexy's Midnight Runners urgently as I have some of his cormorants and chessmen in my lung. I hope you can assist me in this. Radar, gouda, face slowly melting.*
>
> *Yours faithfully*
> *Mr D N Walters*
> *Taunton*

4. There was the Lonely Hearts; 'Hey, NME, I'm desperate to get in touch with a girl I met at Dudley JBs rock night last week. If she's reading this, I was the one in the Queensryche T-shirt who kept throwing beermats at her. She left really quickly without leaving her number. I think she was keen though. Is she out there?'

5. Finally there was the letter of complaint. Voltaire famously declared, 'I disapprove of what you say but I will defend to the death your right to say it.' If Voltaire had ever written to the *NME* he would have said, 'I think what Stuart Maconie said about Simple Minds was bollocks. Was he at the same gig as me?'

'Was he at the same gig as me?' Ah, the memories. This was one of the refrains that ran gently, vitreously, like a river of bile through the letters page. Whether it had been handed down through generations of irate letter writers, or encoded in their DNA or whether they had merely absorbed it by osmosis from years of Gasbags and Angsts, we shall never know. But certain phrases occurred time and time again in the writings of our very own Disgusteds of Tunbridge Wells. They would accuse us of 'lazy sixth-form journalism'. They would accuse us of 'building bands up to knock them down'. They would ask whether we were at the same gig as them.

On at least one occasion I wasn't. In '89, the paper sent me to review the Reading Festival. Nowadays, the Reading Festival is slowing down into a sedate and reflective old age but for many years it was a little section of the innermost circle of hell transplanted into the Thames Valley. It began life in 1960 as the National Jazz & Blues Festival, the sort of place where you could catch Long John Baldry and BB King, and harmonicas wailed night and day. By '89, the festival had long been mired in a literal slough of rotten facilities and even grubbier music. At least in the Seventies you might have got the Quo, Thin Lizzy or AC/DC. By the time I arrived on the scene in my unsuitable casualwear for a bill that 'boasted' Fields of the Nephilim, Bonnie Tyler, The Quireboys, Meatloaf and Jefferson Starship, it had reached what even its official website history now describes as 'its nadir'.

All day long I stood around appalled, drinking gassy yellow liquid from plastic glasses as revolting dirty hippy traveller kids called Gandalf and Placenta set fire to decent folks' sleeping bags. Then during the early evening as is customary, local Hell's Angels descended onto the site and began urinating feverishly into empty plastic cider bottles which they then proceeded to fling at the hapless Bonnie Tyler. I could stand it no longer and fled to the safety and warmth of my companion's car. I could not believe I had put her though this and was all apologies as we left the site well before headliners Jefferson Starship, who, if you remember, built this city on rock 'n' roll, took the stage. Radio 1 were broadcasting the whole event and so we listened in comfort, eating Murray Mints in the gathering dusk, as we began the drive back to civilisation.

I wrote a scabrous denunciation of the whole grisly affair and ended with what I thought was something of a flourish. I said that Grace Slick of Jefferson Starship née Airplane had seen first-hand the horror and carnage of the disastrous Altamont Festival, scene of widespread rape and beatings and murder, and so was unlikely to be phased by some beered-up greasers from Newbury and its environs.

The following week a letter appeared in the paper concerning my review. It was actually quite flattering, commending me on my robust assessment and chuckling a little at my jokes. The writer did feel though that they could not let the review pass without pointing out that Grace Slick had actually left Jefferson Starship.

Left them, in fact, a year and a half previously. I waited patiently for the sack but it never came. Perhaps placing the trans-Siberian pipeline in Wales gets you the heave-ho from *Tunnels and Tunneling*; maybe attributing the invention of napalm to Mother Theresa would lose you your stipend from *Hazardous Cargo Bulletin*. The music press was far less uptight about the facts and I was well on the way now to becoming a real hacker at the coal-face of rock.

21 Caravan of Love

It may be the repressed Englishman in me but I cordially dislike those radio DJs who are continually telling you about their farms/ex-model wives/children or celebrity mates. In the same way, I get uncomfortable with those journalists who invent cute names for their significant others and scatter mentions of them throughout their copy, or who pepper their music memoirs with gratuitous, indulgent accounts of their tormented emotional life, turbulent relationships and unresolved issues about showing affection to their dads.

But now it appears I am writing just such a memoir, and have to assume that, thus far in, you give enough of a toss to at least deserve an explanation about who the mysterious companion was I had forced to endure that Reading Bank Holiday.

She first popped up a few chapters back actually. The day I got the job at the *NME*, you may recall I went drinking with a woman who I mentioned (quite casually I thought) as being the subject of a monumental crush. Crush was putting it a bit lightly anyway, and by now it had grown and grown and been reciprocated. The trouble was that she was married with young children. It was a position very few young *NME* hacks found themselves in, and with the characteristic 'engaging cavalier attitude' first spotted in

English teacher Mrs Gregory's school report of 1977, we 'ran off with each other' as my grandmother would have put it. My new friend Mary Anne Hobbs thought it terribly romantic. So it was, but it was also a bit scary.

Eleanor had moved to her native Birmingham to begin setting up a new home. The plan was that I would seize the opportunity to set up home with her and continue my fast-track through the *NME*'s murky underworld, providing I didn't get sacked for making up gig reviews. Then we'd live happily ever after. The problem was that I still had several classes of students in Skem approaching their exams. I had to work a term's notice and even if I hadn't, I couldn't leave them in the lurch. They had become mates and many had university places riding on good grades. They'd have had to kill me. Some of them had done things like that before.

So, for a term, I lived a strange triple life, moving between three points of a Bermuda-ish triangle; the *NME*, Skem College and a new life in Birmingham. It was probably not how Nick Kent had spent his days but somehow it hung together.

My students, those of whom knew anyway, thought it was all very exciting. To the hipper ones, I guess there was a certain frisson in having a teacher who wrote for Britain's coolest rock paper. Some of them would bring copies into class and, with heavy irony, read out my latest reviews, passing comment on solipsism, litotes and instances of ugly ellipsis.

One Tuesday afternoon, I was taking a class of A level students. They (and I probably) were trying to get our heads around the various shades of phenomenological thought when the school secretary Andrea popped her head around the door. 'There's a James Brown on the phone for you.'

'Well, I'm teaching right now. Could he ring back later?'

'I told him that but he says it's rather urgent. He just needs to know if you can go to Seattle on Thursday with Michael Hutchence.'

A silence fell across the class. 'Could you read the chapter on Harold Garfinkel and ethnomethodology, I'll be back in a sec.' I walked with as much of an unconcerned air as I could muster to the phone. INXS were on the US leg of their Kick world tour. *NME* had never really covered them. James wondered if I fancied a shot at it. Naturally I did. But it meant being in Seattle on Thursday, in just three days' time. I was teaching tomorrow. It was impossible. Surely.

Back in the class they thought not. 'You've got to go, soft lad. We can cover for you. Set us some work, we'll take the register. They don't need to know you're not here. If anyone asks we'll say you had to go to the photocopier.'

I should say that I actually made a clean breast of it. My head of department, a wry, kindly man, said that they could cover me for a few days or so. It was the end of May, term almost over and everyone revising. I was part-time anyway. 'We'll say we've sent you on a course or you've absorbed lethal gamma rays.' He had read *NME* as a teenager he said, and once hitchhiked to Dundee to see the Incredible String Band. Somewhere in him was a kid who would love to be flying to Washington State with a load of rock 'n' rollers.

Julie Burchill claims that one day she was a schoolgirl in Bristol, the next she was sitting on Chrissie Hynde's knee and snorting amphetamine sulphate in the back of the Sex Pistols van as it drove along Oxford Street. I can't beat that. No one can. But I'm fond of my story. On Monday I rode the 632 Ribble bus home from Skem to Wigan; on Thursday I drank cognac in Seattle with Michael Hutchence.

The intervening fifty or so hours had been hectic, to say the least. For one thing, I hadn't bothered to tell the *NME* that I hadn't got a passport. The furthest I had ventured previously was Spain, twice, and both times on those funny, now extinct, one-year visitors' passports. Some kindly soul at the Foreign Office obviously thought that indolent perennial students, career short-termists and gun-runners had as much right to travel as anyone else. So these sheets of folded cardboard were their concession to them in much the same way that the 140 Caller Withheld function is BT's goodwill gesture to adulterers and perverts. Wednesday then found me queuing up in the Passport Office in Liverpool along with a thousand other desperate souls. Just as rumour had it that you could get married on a ship by the captain and that taxis should carry a bale of hay so urban legend had it that you could get a passport in a day if you were willing to turn up with the forms and plead. Straight away I decided that honesty was the best policy, particularly since for once honesty was way sexier than fantasy.

'You need it for what?'

'To go to America. The day after tomorrow. To interview INXS for the *NME*.'

'INXS? You mean Michael Hutchence?'

Thank God there was a woman on my counter. Quite what it was that Michael Hutchence had that made women go slightly damp and limp at the sound of his name we regular guys shall never know. Apart from the looks, the hair, the romantic swagger, the glamorous highly paid job, the exotic, intoxicating charm and the heady, musky tang of feral sex, he was just like one of us.

A mystery that I was mightily glad of that drizzly spring morning in Liverpool. Had I ended up in the next line, I'd have got the little fellow in the pullover. But I got Julie. Julie made me promise to send her Michael's autograph and then waved me away, passport clutched in my sweating hand. When I got to the door, I turned back. She was arguing with a family in topaz shell-suits. But she caught my eye and mouthed 'Good luck'. Why good luck? Because, of course, I'd ladled on thick that it was my big break with the paper, my first foreign trip, my baptism of fire. My lower lip may have trembled a little. I'm not ashamed. Michael

Hutchence had the heady, musky tang of feral sex and what have you. The rest of us have to play the hand we're given.

I caught a train to London that afternoon and did the same again at the US Embassy in Grosvenor Square. Another lovely generous woman (this time from Baton Rouge who'd never heard of INXS) gave me a multiple indefinite visa to the United States.

I went from there to the *NME* where I enquired after my airline tickets. 'The record company will bike them over later,' I was told. Something profound was dawning on me, something that was to upend my whole conception of every piece of on-the-road rock reportage I'd ever read. The *NME* didn't pay for the trips: the record companies did.

I had, stupidly, imagined that it happened something like this: the editor and a handful of his most trusted lieutenants are sitting around smoking pipes and sipping at pale cream sherries.

'I see INXS are touring.'

'Really? U2 without the whiff of irony I've always thought. Hutchence has the heady, musky tang of feral sex I'll grant you, but where is the style, where's the elan? A Sydney bar band, a successful one but a Sydney bar band nonetheless, if you ask me.'

'Fair point … and well made. But they are terrifically successful and representative of a particular strand of modern rock. I say we despatch someone to cover several dates of their US stadium tour, an ideal setting in which to evaluate them. Nadine, arrange flight, hotels and so forth …'

I now realised, with a powerful sense of deflation, that it was nothing like this. Trips to cover bands were paid for by the record labels with the paper acting as a wing of the PR machine. I now know of course that this is the standard arrangement throughout the press. But back then it came as a shock. But then I hadn't even realised at first that pieces in music papers were specifically geared around key releases for maximum publicity value. I had, with breathtaking naiveté, thought that they were models of pure journalistic enquiry, occasioned by nothing more than almost academic interest. Not so. Every time I had read some sneering denunciation of a rock dinosaur, some poison pen review, the poison had been paid for by the band. What a pillock I had been! What pillocks they had been, come to that. But as time went by, I realised that what mattered was not the fact that some waspish writer had mocked Mick Hucknall's terrible cap or Axl Rose's onstage pronouncements. No, what mattered was the coverage itself. The piece alerted people to the fact that Simply Red or Guns N' Roses had a new record out. Most people would never get to the third paragraph and the finely crafted character assassination. 'Don't read your press, weigh it' is the advice I would give to any young band.

As it was, my first rock 'n' roll trip bore no relation to the normal state of affairs anyway. It's customary to travel accompanied, usually by a photographer and a PR person, either working 'in house' for the record label, or an independent PR firm hired by the label. Fellow *NME* hack David Quantick described press officers as 'like drug addicts but less efficient'. This was funny but mildly unfair. She (and it generally is she) is there to facilitate contact, to act as a conduit between scribe and musician or – once the band has reached a certain level of fame – to prevent access. More importantly, they're also there to buy booze, drugs and Chinese food and arrange transport for the useless hack, to wake him up at noon, settle his hotel bill (with its mysterious 'Pay TV' charges and minibar demolition) and then take him to a really nice diner/patisserie/trattoria/whatever they have in Latvia for brunch.

The photographer's function is more straightforward. They take photographs. Thus the writer and photographer form a kind of creative team. Great rock photographers are celebrities in themselves. In some areas of magazine publishing, the writer also takes photographs. This has never caught on in the rock press. The

NME had tried it once when they asked Jack Barron, a useful photographer by all accounts, to provide pictures for his piece with Pop Will Eat Itself in Moscow, thus alleviating the hassle of getting an extra visa. In the snow at the airport, after several days of punishing vodka consumption and sleep deprivation, the band noticed that he was trying, with palsied hands, to take the much postponed cover shot with his Walkman. The experiment had never been tried again.

Photographers' lifestyles compare favourably to that of the average Kuwaiti sheik in terms of ease and luxury. What with album sleeves, posters and syndication, they live in Cotswold manor houses where they dine on swan toasties and mead. The snap they took of Paul Simonon smashing his guitar on the stage is a gift that keeps on giving right into their dotage, a pension scheme of the gods. They also have cooked up some incredible deals for themselves along the years. On one particular and distinguished single letter named rock mag that I've worked on, not only were photographers paid for the job they were on, they received compensation for the other jobs that they couldn't do because they were being gainfully employed on this one. It's a stitch up that Jimmy Hoffa would have been impressed by. If I sound bitter, well, that's because I am. I don't begrudge them their vast wealth. I've just spent half my life waiting for them at airport check-ins as they insist on every lens and filter going through by hand.

No problems on that first trip though. I was going alone. Completely alone; no photographer to envy, no PR to hold my hand. This has never happened on a foreign trip since but, of course, it was the case on my first trip.

I flew TWA. This should have made me even more anxious but fortunately I wasn't aware of that soon to be defunct carrier's terrible reputation among frequent flyers; the acronym was said to stand for The Worst Airline or Try Walking Across. I had nothing to compare it to though, and the whirl of the last few days meant I was just happy to be sitting bent double in economy row 27, eating pretzels and drinking gin and tonic. I was charged four dollars for a set of earphones and then the opening inflight attraction was *Mr Bean*, a silent comedy.

For the next eleven hours, I listened to INXS albums and pondered how exactly I would make contact with them. I knew that they were staying for one night in the same hotel as me, the Four Seasons, Seattle. Apart from that I had no concrete arrangements, rendezvous or contacts. I merely had a piece of paper and on it were written the words 'Bruce. Laconic. Tour Manager'. I had to assume that laconic was a character assessment rather than a surname.

Someone had quite a spectacular heart attack on the plane and we were met eleven hours later at Seattle Tacoma airport by a fleet of emergency vehicles, each with its own distinctive, shrieking siren. By the time I got to 'arrivals', my nerves were shredded like confetti. I took a taxi to the heart of downtown and its myriad coffee shops, found the Four Seasons hotel and strode to reception with as much of the seasoned international traveller about me as I could rustle up. Over the next few years, I would come to dread this little scenario, rich and pregnant with disappointments and confusion. Double bookings, no bookings, wrong hotels, bad hotels, credit problems, bad cheques; I would come to know them all. Perhaps my feelings all stemmed from this first time when the receptionist asked for my credit card in order to pay for any 'extras'. I wasn't sure what this meant. Even if she had mentioned the 'minibar', to me this would simply have meant a small pub, the Henhole on Gidlow Lane perhaps. As it was, slightly dubious about the whole notion of 'extras' (was it like 'something for the weekend'?), I told her that I didn't have a credit card in any event.

It was perfectly normal for an impoverished part-time teacher in Wigan in the late Eighties not to have a credit card. Like the mobile phone and CD, they had yet to become a de rigueur requirement of modern life. Not so in Seattle. The receptionist, and all the other staff and guests within earshot, looked at me as if I had said that I hadn't got any shoes or that I lived in a tree. Did I have any means of covering for extras then?

'Well, yes, this,' I said and produced a small wad of dollar bills. They reacted as if I had produced a nugget of uranium. People backed away in horror. It was a small useful lesson in America's touching ways. It's a country built on the vigorous pursuit and the healthy circulation of money, and yet the sight of a fistful of bucks in a swanky hotel reception goes down about as well as you dropping your trousers and brandishing your equipment around the lobby.

Some time later, I was lying on an enormous bed, drunk with jetlag, watching *Gilligan's Island* and eating a Reese's Peanut Butter Cup. The show I was meant to attend was tonight, in just a few hours' time in fact, at the Seattle Center's 17,000 Key Arena. As yet I had not had a whiff of the band. A little light-headed with fatigue, I wondered how it would go down back in London that I'd flown halfway around the world on my first major international assignment, not met the band, flown back again and wrote a piece about *Gilligan's Island*.

I conceived a plan that had 'desperation' writ large upon it. I would go downstairs and sit in reception until I heard an Aussie accent. If all of this seems hard to believe, well, it seems so to me as well now. But the inkie rock papers were different from real newspapers; they worked to a different agenda. It wasn't considered rock 'n' roll to have everything too much under control and nicely diarised. There would be the press officer to sort out the inevitable chaos and confusion.

But not this time. That's why I sat for two hours in the lobby of the Four Seasons listening for pungent traces of 'strine' among the passing businessmen. As afternoon faded to evening and showtime approached, just as the beads of sweat were starting to form on my brow, I heard it.

'Guess we ort ta mike a mowve soonish, sport.'

Two men in black Levis and leathers were moving through the lobby at speed. Scrambling over chintzy furniture and leapfrogging vacationing old ladies from Vancouver, I intercepted them by the lifts.

'Excuse me,' I said, 'are you Australian?'

'Yeahhh ...' came the hesitant reply.

'Are you anything to do with INXS?'

'Yes, I'm their tour manager,' said the better dressed of the two. 'Why?'

'I'm here to interview the band.'

'Ah, the *NME* guy. What kept you? I'm Bruce by the way,' he said, laconically I had to admit.

I was just in time for a lift to the venue. Bruce led me from the car park through subterranean passages to a dressing room deep in the bowels of the earth. The band were already there, munching on baskets of exotic fruit and admiring a bouquet sent by local FM rockers Heart. It could have been a tricky moment – I had as yet no idea of rock's backstage etiquette, of not diving into the kiwi fruit and cognac till offered, of not monopolising the singer and definitely not asking who the two fifteen-year-old girls are who look a mite under-dressed for Toronto in November.

There were no fifteen-year-old girls, though there were fruits and beverages of several continents. Trickiness was easily sidestepped as, fortunately, INXS are Australian with all the easy bonhomie that goes with the territory. Even so, when Hutchence entered the room a certain climactic change occurred, a slight but perceptible crackle of electricity. He was a sweetheart too, it turned out. He bummed a fag off me instantly ('Benson & Hedges! Real cigarettes, you beauty!') and took me into a corner for a beer and a gossip. If it was an act designed to charm the innocent abroad, it pretty much worked, I had to say.

The show itself was probably just your average arena show by a big MTV rock band, slick, larger than life, loud. But to me, who'd never actually been in an indoor space this big, a boy from Lancashire woozy from dislocated circadian rhythms and excitement, it was unutterably thrilling. Afterwards I drank quite a lot of INXS cognac, took the tourbus back to the hotel chatting to Hutchence, the gregarious keyboardist Jon Farriss and the excessively named bass player Garry Garry Beers. After that I fell into my hotel room and lay awake all night watching cable TV.

The next day, Michael Hutchence came to my room for breakfast and the arranged interview. We were both feeling a little fragile and bleary. He insisted on keeping the curtains drawn and we sent for pot after pot of jasmine tea. It was an unremarkable interview but contained the odd insight. He was nervous of the *NME*, he admitted. 'You guys in the UK, you're so obsessed with cool. You're more concerned with whether a band is wearing the right shoelaces than how good they are.'

Later he would die in a room just like this in the most desperate of circumstances. That morning though, he sipped his scented rock star tea and chatted and cheerfully autographed a backstage pass for the girl in the passport office in Liverpool.

INXS went on to Sacramento the next day. I flew back to Heathrow. Back in the 1970s, Ian Macdonald spent five weeks on the road for *NME* with King Crimson, sleeping with groupies, travelling on their bus, filing weekly tour reports from Spokane and Des Moines. Those wondrous days of brazen excess were long gone. By the time I became a rock hack, journalists enjoyed a massively compressed version of the touring experience, a day or two on the road, a lot of substance abuse and shenanigans, no sleep and a couple of mind-bending long-haul flights. Some journos, though, took full advantage of this; one famously flaky

NME writer failed to meet a deadline complaining of 'terrible jetlag, man'. The trip had been to Brussels.

By the time INXS got to Phoenix, I was back at Skem College clearing my desk. I settled some old debts: I paid for the curry I owed Steve after the controversial world pool series of 1988, he paid me the long overdue tenner he owed me for arguing that 'Caravan Of Love' by The Housemartins would not reach Number 1. My own Caravan of Love (and rock 'n' roll) was taking me to destinations new.

The principal – a cold, lizardy, arrogant man who we all kept at arm's length – gave a little speech in which he thanked me for all my help and warned me that as a freelance journalist himself (he had the odd piece in the *Times Education Supplement*), he had made £23 the previous year. I was thus giving it all up for the most precarious lifestyle imaginable. The staff and students, though, said what anyone with blood in their veins would have: risky or not, you have to do this. Go, go quickly and get us Morrissey's autograph.

They gave me a book token as a going away gift. I spent it on *Psychotic Reactions and Carburettor Dung*, the collected works of Lester Bangs, legendary gonzo rock journalist of the mid-Seventies. Bangs was addicted to pop music and Romilar cough syrup, got drunk and insulted his celebrity interviewees and once clambered onstage with the J. Geils Band to type a supposed review in real time and in the full audience view. He died aged 33 from an overdose of painkillers. With a few minor reservations, I liked that job description. And with that I was gone.

22 I Am Kurious, Oranj

At parties, people would ask me what I did for a living and I would make vague little noises, half-formed sentences in which buried somewhere were the words 'music' and 'journalist'.

It always felt uncomfortable. It either felt as though you were showing off, engaging in a flourish of one-upmanship or, conversely, like a euphemism for being unemployed. I didn't fully understand it myself so I could hardly expect others to.

By and large, they didn't. When you told them you were paid by the word (7p when I joined) they would ask earnestly why you didn't just write more words. I had one lengthy, hard-to-follow conversation with a wannabe rock writer who thought that freelance meant working for nothing ('Tony Parsons is freelance? Well, he's a mug then! And so are you! I've had loads of offers of freelance work. Who needs it!').

My mum and dad didn't actually say, 'When are you going to get a proper job?' To be frank, they had enough to be going on with with my other little upheavals. They must have thought it though. As far as I was concerned I had a proper job. Somehow I had become a writer, though that sounded a little grand for what I did, rock journalism being, to quote Frank Zappa, 'people who can't write talking to people who can't speak for the benefit of people who can't read'.

Frank Zappa could sneer – in fact, some would say that's about all he could do – but I was a writer and, as Paddy MacAloon sings on 'Jordan The Comeback', 'two things you should be slow to criticise, a man's choice of woman and his choice of work'.

It seemed like I'd chosen well. Eleanor got a job in a special school and did the real work while I hung around the *NME* acquiring more of the trade's very particular skills; taking the piss, reviewing at (and sometimes with) speed and taking pop music way too seriously.

I also began to learn, slowly, gingerly, what actually happens on a newspaper. Even though I eventually became Assistant Editor, I would never presume to be a dyed in the wool newspaperman. I never 'set' anything on 'the stone', never handled a 'slug', never spiked a nutgraph on the offset roller. But I did learn a thing or two about 'pars' and 'nosing' a story. Some say that music journalism is a contradiction in terms, like military intelligence. In fact, whether you're writing about fishing or drum and bass or military build-ups in North Korea, many of the principles of the newspaper business are ubiquitous.

A sub is a sub, for instance. Before I'd worked on newspapers I assumed a sub-editor was an assistant or underling of the real editor. In this assumption, I was sort of right but sort of wrong. The editor has a deputy and an assistant. The subs are the production team; the people who chase up the copy, prod and hack it mercilessly, check it for house style, mark it up for printing, set it, think up the headlines and the captions, deliver it up for public consumption in 9pt Helvetica or Franklin Gothic Medium. Subs are often journos themselves and can turn their hand to a feature or review but, on a day-to-day basis, subbing is their stock-in-trade. At heart, all subs think that all writers are ponces. On one of those early visits to New Commonwealth House, the then chief sub Jo Isotta marched through the main office waving my Railway Children feature.

'Ah,' she cried, spying the new boy responsible. 'The man himself. Good. We need to lose about a hundred words from the intro. You can do it yourself.' Half an hour later, she strolled back into the office to find me still poring over the text, agonising over which judiciously chosen words and phrases could possibly be excised without damaging the elegance and structural beauty of the whole. 'Oh, give it here!' she exclaimed. 'Writers! Married to every fucking word!' With that, she parked herself at a vacant nearby desk and proceeded to slash at my masterpiece with a red biro, till it emerged razored, bleeding and shorn of 100 words of extraneous fat.

The sub-editor's relationship to 'copy' is a bit like a butcher's attitude to brisket; yes, it's the raw material of their craft, vital, tasty, but completely, endlessly choppable, minceable and reheatable. All that said, I soon learned that the subs are the paper's engine room and they're often the best people to hang out with – funny, tough, reliable.

Subs could make or break a piece of writing. Good subs would gently (or, just as often violently) rein in your excesses. They would know instinctively that your ill-chosen joke about a dead rock star or uncalled-for diatribe against world capitalism would be regretted by all in a week or two and perceptively remove it before it ever got to print.

Bad subbing though could ruin your day. An elegantly constructed sentence of Wildean cast could be wrecked by a red pen wielded inexpertly the morning after a long night. Bill Prince, a sub himself, knew all about the frightening power invested in him. As a cub writer on *Sounds*, he'd interviewed Phil Collins and turned in a piece that was a model of reason and fair-mindedness. Unfortunately, legendary sub Sandy Robertson was of a more bilious frame of mind when he began work on it and the end result was littered with new and acrimonious interjections after most of Collins remarks such as, 'Well, he would say that, wouldn't he, the talentless bald prick' and 'God, what rubbish'. Collins was incandescent, almost as incandescent as he was when Paul Morley, in one of the great asides of pop writing, remarked that he looked like he was permanently wearing a stocking over his head.[1]

In time, when the paper moved to its vertiginous eyrie 26 floors up on Kings Reach Tower on the South Bank, you would often find me in the subs room. I enjoyed the brisk work ethic and salty good humour of the place and made good friends: Brendan Fitzgerald and Andy Fyfe, the gregarious kiwis; Bill Prince, formerly of indie hopefuls The Loft; Betty Page and Cathy Ball; the dapper, lugubrious, hilarious Ian McCann whose business card featured a logo of a monkey wrench and a spanner and the words 'Ian McCann. Aluminium Cladding. Attentive. Courteous. Reliable. Also Music Journalist'.

A couple of times a day, someone from the subs room, Brendon, Andy or Bill, would pop their head around the partition into the main office and call out 'we need headlines; Costello, Pet Shop Boys Live, Jesus And Mary Chain in New York'. And the favoured few, of which I became a member, would troop off to the subs room.

Here the music press had been genuinely influential. Once upon a time, music paper headlines were predictable fare: 'Clapton For Reading. Van Der Graaf Split? Marley Live Is A Double', that kind of thing. But at some point, headline writing developed into an art form in itself. Elaborate puns, in-jokes, running gags. By the time I arrived at the *NME*, good headline writing was regarded as one of the most valued skills on the paper. We would sit for what seemed to outsiders – the suits from accounts and advertising – a wastefully long time choosing just the right headlines. We knew that the time was well spent. A good

---

1 This is almost as good as my friend Geoff Stokes's classic observation that Pete Townshend looks like everyone does when they look in the back of a spoon.

headline – funny, thought-provoking, shocking – made the difference between a read and an unread feature. That, as we would remind the shiny-suited Essex boys in advertising, made the difference between whether anyone saw their tacky ads for chrome cassettes, bottled beers and student bank accounts.

Glance at *The Times*, *Guardian*, *Sun* or *Observer* today and the headlines are directly influenced by the music press style of the Seventies and beyond. Before that even the *Sun*, now regarded as the last word in robust, memorable captions and heads, thought that 'Phew, What A Scorcher' was a humdinger of a strapline. Without the example of the rock press, I believe no one at the *Sun*'s sports desk would have ever dared come up with what may be the greatest headline of all time following Celtic's shock defeat by minnows Inverness Caledonian Thistle or 'Cally' in the Scottish Cup: 'Supercally go ballistic, Celtic are atrocious'.[2]

I can't beat that but I had my own minor triumphs. I once sat for half an hour trying to magic up something for a Bruce Springsteen lookalikes convention before coming up with 'You Wait All Day For The Boss And Then Three Come At Once'. I was carried from the room shoulder high, as I recall.

Every Wednesday, the headline writers' cabal would congregate in the subs room for the compilation of the 'funny chart'. Tucked away on the charts page each week was a humorous variant on the regular Top Forty inspired by and themed around something in that week's paper. Ten songs you might hear in an Indian restaurant? How about Girlfriend In A Korma? Paperback Raitha? Curry Up Harry? Of all the sections of the paper, the 'funny chart' was the most labour-intensive and disproportionately time-consuming. Six or seven of us would sit around in the

---

2 My personal favourite though has to be the headline allegedly found in the *Liverpool Echo* when a local hero and noted explorer embarked on his famous polar expedition: 'Sir Vivien Fuchs Off To Antarctica'.

subs room shouting and chortling all Wednesday afternoon to produce something the readers casually devoured in three minutes while waiting for the rest of the bus queue to board. We enjoyed it though. That was pretty much the point, I think.

For my birthday that year, El treated me to a week away, even though money was tight. We stayed in a tiny caravan in the Cotswolds, lit by gaslamps and with a TV powered by a car battery. Towards the end of the week, freelancer to the core, I thought I ought to check in with the office. It was a glorious morning as I strolled down to the phone box in the village and called James Brown. Anything doing?

Well, yes, there was actually. 'How do you fancy doing your first cover?'

Of all the rock writer's landmarks, the first cover is the most special. It's our first *Top of the Pops* appearance. 'Holding the front page' is part of newspaper folklore and in the milieu of the rock mag or paper, the cover has a powerful and unique place in the scheme of things. It's the first thing a reader sees as they scan the shelves in Menzies or WH Smith and so it must grab them by the lapels. If you've got a Madonna or Oasis interview, you'll put it on the cover. If it's a slow week, you'll put them on the cover even if you haven't got an interview so long as you can work up some 'think piece' or bit of froth; a live review dressed up as a feature, a ten-minute phone call puffed up into an exclusive.

During the early Nineties, we put Morrissey on the cover whenever the occasion demanded and many times when it signally didn't. The result was always the same; the paper flew off the shelves. In fact, and this is curious, the *NME* when adorned with the (usually shirtless) Morrissey regularly sold more copies than the current Morrissey single that the piece was pegged around. This led one to the inescapable conclusion that there were people out there who were fans of Morrissey's entertaining pronouncements who couldn't give a monkey's about his records.

So I did fancy doing my first cover. Very much so. I walked back through the lanes, late August sun warming the Cotswold stones of the pub and the church and the thatched cottages, hoping that Eleanor would understand that I'd have to cut short our trip. She did and so a day later, she put me on the train to Edinburgh.

The Edinburgh Festival has, in terms of public profile at least, become a stand-up comedians' festival over the last few years. For every genuinely funny turn, there are twenty Cambridge graduates doing their 'don't old people smell funny' routine. That's a pity as one of the joys of the festival is its charming, eccentric diversity: the church halls full of amateur groups from Penge doing T.S. Eliot verse plays on stilts, the one-woman shows about female circumcision set to the music of Boney M.

In 1989, one of the toasts of the fringe of the Fringe was a new ballet by Michael Clark, the enfant terrible of English dance. The ballet was called *I Am Kurious, Oranj* and concerned sectarianism in British life and the lasting legacy of the accession to the English throne of William of Orange. It had a rock score, and the moment you were apprised of this fact, you knew that only one man could have been responsible for it. History, weird spellings, conspiracy theory. It could only be MES.

Since there will never be a blue plaque on his wall in Prestwich nor will he (worse luck) ever be inducted into Cleveland's Rock 'n' Roll Hall of Fame by Roger Daltrey in wing-collared shirt, let us talk here a little about Mark E. Smith. He has never sold a great many records though he has made hundreds; yet people across the globe revere him. Mark Edward Smith was a smart young working-class Mancunian, bored with his job at the Docks office, devoted to Can and the Velvet Underground, who, when punk erupted like acne across the face of the North, saw the creative possibilities. He formed a group called The Fall, named after the Albert Camus novel; a punk group in theory but maintaining all the while a sardonic distance, expressed in a predilection for wilfully uncool clothes, a deadpan Lancastrian sullenness and a bloody-minded refusal to play the game.

Legendary early gigs included a supermarket's staff Christmas party and several traditional working men's clubs, where they were not immediately appreciated by audiences who were expecting one of the many touring versions of the Brotherhood of Man. Their records were queer, curmudgeonly ditties about bingo callers, container drivers, football administrators or the Third Reich, delivered in a bluff drawl with the infamous, much imitated 'Uh' at the end of every word. Sometimes, in his songs, he would declare his intent clearly. 'Pay Your Rates', he'd demand, or 'Leave The Capital' or 'Eat Y'Self Fitter'. 'The North Will Rise Again', he announced, or 'We are The Fall, the white trash that talks back'.

Mostly though, the Fall's song titles were fabulous and exotic, works of elliptical, surrealist poetry: 'Hexen Definitive/Strife Knot', 'Prole Art Threat', 'Pilsner Trail', 'Fortress/Deer Park', 'Spectre Vs Rector', 'Who Makes The Nazis?', 'Jawbone And The Air Rifle', 'Gut Of The Quantifier', 'Muzorewa's Daughter' and the greatest of them all, 'To Nkroachment: Yarbles'.

'Sounds like a Fall song,' would be the standard response among *NME* staff when faced with some weird, macabre, absurd mangling of the English language. Except of course that there was nothing silly or undergraduate about his wordplay, nothing Pythonesque. His songs were all rooted in the Northern proletarian experience, and all 'about' things. It was just that few people other than MES had the faintest idea what those things were.

I Am Kurious, Oranj – an odd, vague pun on an infamous experimental movie from Sixties Sweden – was 'about' the events of 1688 when Dutch Protestant William of Orange and wife Mary deposed the Catholic King James from the throne of England. The

NME, at this point hugely supportive of The Fall, decided that the piece and accompanying album were worth a cover story. Photographer Kevin Cummins and I were duly despatched to Edinburgh post haste.

The production itself was just as you'd imagine a challenging late Eighties ballet to be. Lithe, shaven-headed young folk in nappies and slashed T-shirts thrashed about to the sound of The Fall's angular, abrasive art punk.

Blue-rinsed ladies from Morningside who had come for a little modern culture looked at each other in fear and dismay. Despite the noise, Cummins fell asleep within seconds, the kind of pure, deathlike, head-lolled, drooling sleep that babies and the elderly are prone to. He perked up briefly during a set piece featuring an Old Firm derby game but then slipped back into insensibility. I felt the same way I felt about all ballet, i.e. numb with incomprehension. I was still really looking forward to meeting Mark E. Smith though.

I went backstage and found him in his spartan dressing room, smoking a fag and drinking from a can of McEwan's Export. His first words to me were, bullishly, 'Hey, I know you. Haven't you made a record about me?' After I'd assured him that I hadn't he suggested that we repair to a pub to continue the conversation, a suggestion I felt Smith had made many times before in his life.

I produced my cheap Dixons cassette recorder and Smith, though quaffing deep of a pint of 60 shilling, stopped and sat upright. 'Where d'you get that from?'

'Dixons,' I replied, truthfully.

'That's just the kind of gizmo I want. For me lyrics when I'm on the road. A little recorder that takes proper cassettes, not those micro cassette things. I went to buy one in my electrical shop in Prestwich. Bloke offered me one of those Dictaphones that take those stupid little cassettes. I said, "No way, pal. I'm on tour a lot. I could be in a hotel in Oslo, Budapest, Eindhoven. I get an idea for a song, I want to be able to use ordinary cassettes. Not have to go traipsing round Tel Aviv or Brisbane for them stupid little ones."

'He said, "Don't be daft, mate. You're living in the past. Everywhere sells these little tapes now. Everywhere. Get with it, man."

'So I said, "OK, I'll take the machine. And I'll take ten of the little tapes as well."

'And he said, "We don't sell 'em."'

MES laughed long and hard and then drank his beer in much the same manner.

Over an astonishing variety and quantity of drinks, we talked of the events of 400 years before. 'Wasn't James the second a little mad?' I asked over a Drambuie.

Smith pulled on his cigarette and glanced furtively and anxiously around the room. 'That's as may be, Stuart son. But I'd watch what you say round here.' With a quick nod of his head, he indicated the almost deserted snug bar. A man of around eighty with a West Highland terrier was doing the *Daily Record* quick crossword.

The day went on very much like this. I came home from Edinburgh with a great cover story and, like all the journalists who have ever met him, a fixation with Mark E. Smith.

I could easily fill the rest of this book with MES stories. The journalist David Cavanagh has dined with Smith on a number of occasions. After one interview, Smith asked him if he'd care to come out for dinner, adding, 'Do you like Turkish food?' David hungrily agreed and ended up eating a doner kebab and drinking a Diet Coke on the plastic stools in the window of an all-night Salford kebab shop. On another occasion, Smith invited him back to his own home for a spot of dinner. Cavanagh was surprised; the offer came mid-evening after a day of Herculean drinking but again readily agreed.

'Make yourself at home while I rustle something up,' said

Smith, disappearing into the kitchen. For the next half-hour came the sounds of taps running, cupboard doors opening and closing, gas rings being lit and saucepans being stirred.

Finally Smith appeared, beaming proudly and said, 'Get that down you.' He handed Cavanagh a plate on which sat a crisp sandwich. 'Do you want a pickled onion with that?' he asked, mouth full of Mother's Pride and Walkers Cheese and Onion.

As I write these words, The Fall are touring the States in support of their 36th album. But back in 1989, as a new decade hove into view, it was a much earlier MES song that had new resonance. From Droyslden to Dukenfield, Eccles to Delph, from Oldham to Ancoats, the music was getting louder, the drugs wilder, the trousers wider. The white trash were talking back. Oddly, they seemed to be saying, 'Top one, nice one, sorted.'

The North had risen again.

23 24 Hour Party People

Little Hulton lies on the north-eastern rim of Manchester, between the urban sprawl of Walkden and Farnworth and the scrubby badlands where Atherton peters out just beyond the quaintly (and aptly) named Hag Fold. I knew Little Hulton well. During the mid-Eighties, I'd spent a lot of time in the area with my then girl-friend, who lived in nearby Boothstown, inexplicably later chosen for his residence by Eric Cantona.

Little Hulton, from my experience, had seen better days. Chloe's auntie did a pools round there and sometimes we helped out, not a job to lighten the spirits. It had been a stolidly proud working-class district in the not too distant past, a close-knit mining village. Now the 'back to backs' and cottages were gone. Smack and unemployment were taking a chilly hold. You chose your pubs with care, some were good-humoured, some were good places to get glassed. The mad mile from the Antelope down to Walkden was no place for the faint-hearted of a Friday night. But it had a certain something. I liked its bolshi-ness and salty humour. I just never expected a genuine rock 'n' roll revolution to start here, one that would affect teenagers in Osaka and Madrid, one that would occupy many of my waking hours for the next year; surely not here, among the 'everything a pound shops', the streets full of boarded windows and smashed bus shelters.

Technically speaking, some would say that Madchester, the temporary insanity that gripped youth culture at the close of the Eighties and dawn of the Nineties, actually begins quite a few miles west of Little Hulton in the nightclubs of Chicago and Detroit, where Steve Silk Hurley and Frankie Knuckles were pioneering the thumping hedonism of House and Derrick May, Juan Atkins and Kevin Saunderson were developing the eerie, unearthly, robotic grooves of techno. In fact, Madchester owes its existence to a complex nexus: DJs such as Graham Park, Mike Pickering and Dave Haslam who introduced house music to the city's white youth; the Hacienda Club itself; the German chemists who synthesised MDMA and gave the scene its drug, although Madchester was always as much to do with Boddingtons and drizzle as E and Ibiza.

I like to think that Madchester really begins in Little Hulton when all these various factors were refracted through the grimy, distorting prism of a gang of urchins and ne'er-do-wells who became the Happy Mondays. As Dave Haslam described them 'more likely to become stars on CCTV than MTV'.

In November 1988, the *NME* had put house DJ Todd Terry on the cover next to a graphic of a smiley, the Seventies feelgood icon. The smiley was the new face of Acid House, a deep, weird intense hybrid of techno and house that had become the sound of the times. There was talk of a Second Summer of Love. Illegal warehouse parties proliferated, Radio 1 DJs like Phillip Schofield, as was their role at times such as these, made blustering disapproving remarks about the drug element of this new and dangerous scene. A moral panic was brewing and the next week's cover featured a policeman – in reality art editor Justin Robertson dressed up in an outfit we got from a fancy-dress shop in Blackfriars – tearing up a smiley T-shirt. The *NME* had its own hardcore lobby of ravers led by Helen Mead and Jack Barron, who took to beginning each of his features with the salutation 'Greet the new dawn, bubs' until the subs had a quiet word.

Acid House was something of a misnomer really. The new drug that was central to the scene was Ecstasy. To quote the *Whole Earth Review*'s technical description, E brought on 'No visual effects (but) ego softening; neurotically based fear dissolution; feelings of emotionally based love and empathy. Lucidity retained, in-depth communication facilitated. Present-moment awareness heightened.' Users concurred but put it another way, 'loved up' or 'getting on one, matey'. All agreed Ecstasy was an excellent choice of brand name. E could bring a rush of warming euphoria to the coldest, darkest corners of the far North. Little Hulton, for instance.

I first came across the Happy Mondays before I joined the *NME*. In 1987, they'd put out an album with the striking title *Squirrel and G-Man Twenty Four Hour Party People Plastic Face Carnt Smile (White Out)*. I'd be lying if I said that I was so prescient that I could tell then they were the next big thing. It all sounded a bit ramshackle. The title track '24 Hour Party People' wasn't even included on the record at first. I got hold of it on a budget indie compilation where it shone like a grimy diamond in among Tallulah Gosh and the Mighty Lemon Drops. I played it again and again, each time simultaneously appalled and delighted.

It sounded like jazz funk played by drunken embittered Labour club musicians, all cheesy keyboard fills and ragged syncopation. The vocals had the bellowed tone of a headcase arguing with his wife at a bus stop and the words were creepily intriguing: 'How old are you, are you old enough? Should you be in here, watching that?' You didn't want to know what was being watched. You felt like having a shower actually. But it was sordidly invigorating stuff.

Since joining the paper, I'd been aware via the bush telegraph that something was afoot in East Lancashire. I knew that the Hacienda's club nights were booming, I'd been several times myself over the past year, caught the authentic 'buzz' on the burgeoning nude nights as DJs like Haslam (the man who ran the Playhard label that I'd done one of my earliest pieces on) mixed in indie rock, psychedelia and the new house and techno sounds out of Chicago and Detroit. People were dressing strangely and dancing freakily, blokes as well as girls and all with a kind of wild-eyed abandon. That was down to the drugs to a degree, yes, but there was also a groundswell of, to use the rock hacks favourite word, zeitgeist. There was something in the air.

Wednesday was meeting day at the *NME*. Staff and freelancers, some seeing daylight for the only time in the week, would cram into the editor's office and thrash out an agenda of sorts. Down the years this had become a much-loved bearpit. The various factions would fight their corner, demanding more coverage for Washington Go Go, Hip Hop, Shambling, Shoegazers or whatever had energised them that month. Freelancers would punt stories and projected articles, scenes would be championed, even created. That particular Wednesday when the call went out for ideas and it was asked who we should be covering that week, I suggested the Happy Mondays.

There was much entirely natural suspicion. The Mondays' first album had made little impact outside the North; south of Watford, it was chiefly known for its unwieldy title and general air of unkempt seediness. Several people thought that they'd split up or that they were being kept alive artificially as a situationist prank by their label boss at Factory records, our old friend Tony Wilson.

But I'd seen them twice in quick succession that month, in Birmingham and Newcastle. I'd raved about them in the live pages. Not only that, I'd had an advance cassette of their new album *Bummed*, had listened to it that morning on my schlep down the West Coast Main Line from New Street to Euston. Even on first listening it sounded fabulous; a Martin Hannett production, woozy, seditious, funky and faintly menacing, like Sly Stone jamming with Joy Division or Can auditioning for *New Faces*. 'Wrote For Luck', 'Mad Cyril', 'Lazyitis', great songs written in a secret language, a code decipherable only to the impure in heart. There was something happening here, honest. Others weren't so sure and – maybe rightly – suspected me of regionalist bias or of over-egging what was essentially a bit of a joke. For both reasons, I didn't mention that the first track was called 'Some Cunt From Preston'.

Fortunately, I had a few powerful allies. James Brown always liked a bit of Northern rough and he too had caught the sulphurous whiff from up the M6. Two pages then, 2,000 words by Tuesday, some colour pics from Cummings, tell the story of this new scene then, if there is a story to tell.

Up North, there was none of London's reticence. Something was happening, even if it was still operating at a largely subterranean level or within the neo-brutalist grain silo that was the Hacienda. That week, the Happy Mondays were appearing on *Celebration*, a Granada TV arts show hosted by Tony Wilson airing in the North West. I was to meet them there. By the time I caught the train for Manchester Piccadilly two days later, I was convinced that *Bummed*, with its dyslexic street poetry, catchphrases, ranting, limericks, playground ditties and swagger, was the best thing I had heard in years.

The fable of the gang and the notion of the outlaw is central and undying in the mythos of rock 'n' roll. Be it The Clash or Guns N' Roses or The Strokes or whoever is searingly 'now' by the time you read this, every generation throws up four or five skinny young men, leaning on a wall in a back alley, all cheekbones and self-possession and desperate glamour. This is Nature's Law and I'm reasonably happy to go along with it.

But in most cases, it's patently clear – why shouldn't it be? – that these are really musicians who look like a gang, dress like a gang, act like a gang, trying on those bits of outlaw chic that look good and leaving the rest – the pimples, poverty, probation officers, the methadone, income support and hotwiring – for the genuine scallies. Only once have I ever come across a group who were obviously a gang first and a band second, who were clearly in this just as much for the perks, camaraderie and 'doss' as they were for the music.

I couldn't quite believe them. The five of them were having a crafty fag in the car park outside: Shaun and Paul, siblings obviously with their hook-noses and shark eyes, Cow, the guitarist, tall, absent-minded, good-natured, an ex-postman it turned out, Gaz, the drummer and, astonishing in view of this fact, the most ostensibly glamorous of the band with his suntan and ringlets, Paul Davis or 'Dickhead' as he was known, small, almost mute and wearing an expression of sheer vacancy. Finally, of course, Bez.

Bez's wild eyes rolled in his head, looking anywhere except the person he was talking to. He jabbered endlessly, meaninglessly, chiefly to Shaun, giggling to himself all the while and dancing on the spot or moving from side to side like a goalkeeper awaiting a penalty.

I quickly decided Bez couldn't possibly be in the band. Instead, I thought – I'm not proud of this – that he must be another Ryder brother, sibling to Paul and Shaun, and obviously mentally handicapped in some way. They were letting him hang out with them and I thought this was admirable. Bez, by the way, was wearing an olive drab waterproof poncho, the sort that professional carp anglers wear for night sessions at the gravel pit.

Every other 'gang' in rock history, from The Clash to Dexy's to the Manic Street Preachers, have worked hard on the look: a dash of Robert De Niro here, a soupçon of *Apocalypse Now* there, a drizzle of James Dean or Brando. The Happy Mondays had, by contrast, arrived at a style that is best described as crackhead Mountain Rescue Team or Mujahadeen Rod, Jane and Freddy. There were big fishing anoraks, dungarees, at least one kaftan, jeans the dimensions of tents, Goretex outdoor jackets with the collars pulled up Bash Street Kids style to obscure most of the lower face, walking boots. Then there was the way they communicated. At first, they might have been speaking in Congolese for all the sense I could make of it. It was Stanley Unwin meets thieves' cant, phrases like 'double good', 'snidey', 'banging' and 'nish' peppering their speech. They also spent most of their time baiting each other. Shaun was particularly vindictive and reserved most of his vitriol for Dickhead who absorbed it all with a look of inscrutable, ineffable melancholy. Fortunately I seemed to get on well with them; just as well, as I would be spending an awful lot of time with them in the next year or so.

That was the Happy Mondays. Insular, bickering, whiny, menacing, funny, magnetic, and somehow unutterably cool. It was as if the Mafia had merged with the *Last of the Summer Wine* mob and decided they had the makings of a really great rock group. And make no mistake, they were, at their '89 peak, a really, truly great rock group. Even in that deserted Granada backlot on that mid-week in Piccadilly, in front of three desultory cameramen, a girl with a clipboard, Tony Wilson and me, they had that pungent whiff of the real thing.

Up in the gallery I watched the last few songs with Wilson and Rob Gretton, the New Order manager. Both were heroes of a kind to me. Wilson could barely contain himself at the glorious racket his charges were making down on the studio floor; the Mondays recording as they did for his label Factory, part-owned with Gretton. I can't recall what they played but I can remember the endless bantering and badgering:

'Are you on one or what, you fucking nonce, get sorted.'

'My voice is shagged! Was that the 96-inch remix, Eric fucking Clapton?'

At the end of the set Gretton turned to me and beamed. 'I've only got two words to say about them. One's Sex … and the other one's Pistols!'

We spent all night in the bar of Granada TV. Ryder wanted to see 'if any fit birds off the telly came in'. They didn't. Inevitably, our conversation turned to drugs. The Happy Mondays were enthusiastic proponents: 'Count Basie was a skaghead, Alan A Dale did mushrooms to get those great tunes for his lute,' said Paul Ryder. The Mondays were far from stupid. A little later though, as Paul started very visibly to droop and loll, Shaun turned to him with a compete lack of filial love and barked, 'You're in a mess, mate. What do you take that fucking shit for anyway?'

I went back to London the next morning, head pounding, and wrote up my story. I began with the Rob Gretton quote and ended by concluding 'double, double good'. It was catching, it seemed. In between, I said that the Happy Mondays were the best band in Britain and that Manchester was buzzing. In the office, I fought long, hard and loud for the piece to be the cover story, not just because it was my story – though obviously that had crossed my mind – but because something was happening here and I felt the *NME* should nail its colours to the mast sharpish.

It didn't make the cover. But it did get two colour pages inside. The headline read 'Some Cult From Manchester' – a reference to the city's new-found cool and to that outrageous opening track on *Bummed*, a meaning that was lost when the album appeared and the track's title had been changed to the much more anodyne 'Country Song'.

The piece appeared in November 1988. It would be a year later exactly, with the release of the Happy Mondays *Madchester Rave On* EP, that this scene, this movement, this 'thing' would be named. By then, of course, it was pretty much dead. Something about the rather tackily self-mythologising title of the *Madchester* EP suggested the Mondays knew that. By then the clothes were commonplace everywhere, the slang was used self-consciously in Camden as much as Chorlton, the cultural commissars had descended on Manchester and appropriated it. More importantly, all the great records had been made. But what great records; and what a year it had been.

1989 belonged to Manchester, to the Happy Mondays and the other mooching, tousled, zonked-out, freaky dancing crowd. I spent most of that year in Manchester it seems. Drinking in Dry bar, hanging out in Central Station Design, the team behind the Mondays' artwork run by Shaun Ryder's cousins, the room heavy with the fug from huge bongs and the sound of Rhythim Is Rhythim's 'Strings Of Life' or A Guy Called Gerald's 'Voodoo Ray'. Whacked out of my gourd – all in the name of research – in the Gay Traitor bar of the Hacienda. Or watching Clint Boon of the Inspirals gleefully packing 'cool as fuck' T-shirts into mailers and yelling, 'We can't make 'em quick enough' at the band's Sackville Street base. Or listening to Brian Auger Trinity and Northern Soul in a Vauxhall Astra with The Charlatans driving between the studio and a Monmouth pub.[1] Or interviewing Shami Ahmed, head of Joe Bloggs, the clothes label renowned for their voluminous flares and vast psychedelic hooded tops, and coming away with armfuls of free gear, some of which still gets used when creosoting the fence.

Or, stranger still, watching thousands of kids in baggy blue and red T-shirts sit down on the floor to James. James were a strange act; their music sounded like sea shanties played by punks who liked folk music. I liked them a lot, not least because

---

[1] Keyboardist Rob Collins drove, a little scarily for me I have to say. A couple of years later, it was making this trip that he crashed the car and killed himself.

the personalities involved were so diverse. Singer Tim Booth was otherworldly and mysterious, a former public schoolboy who loved Patti Smith and Iggy Pop and who had cured himself of a mystery liver disease by alternative therapies. Bassist Jim Glennie was a whippet-like former football hooligan from Moss Side. After years of wildly vacillating fortunes and line-ups, Madchester made them stars and stars on their own terms with a new seven-piece line-up. One of these seven was a trumpeter called Andy Diagram. Yes, one of those Diagrams. A Diagram Brother. Late at night in hotel bars across the world, I would pump in for information about 'Bricks' and 'There Is No Shower'. He would humour me, amused that his silly former band could inspire such insane devotion. That's pop music for you. Again.

That mad, mad, double, double, good year of Madchester ended on a real high point. It ended for me in Grindlewald, a village nestling between the ice and rock peaks of the Jungfrau and the Eiger, the highest point in Europe, with the other band of their generation, The Beatles to the Mondays' Stones. They were the Stone Roses.

The Stone Roses had been plying their trade, with little success, since the middle Eighties. Their trade was a kind of gothic romanticism, and there were embarrassing pictures of them in the file looking like Lord Byron's awkward cousin and trainee gypsy violinists to prove it. Even that year, 1989, had begun with their management company showering free tickets like confetti and imploring journalists to go to their gigs. Fortunately I had done, and thus had seen early and first-hand what the mounting fuss was about. They had changed. They had arrived at a sound that was thrillingly both old as the hills and younger than yesterday, vintage and vibrant. Some Led Zeppelin, some Byrds, lots of funk and Hendrix, bags of self-possession and a very faint trace of MDMA generation shape-throwing, though the thought of John Squire's dancing to 'Ebeneezer Good' was risible.

That was in January. Less than a year later, they were having their picture taken on the roof of a continent, in the high rarefied air and virgin snow of the Swiss Alps with the mountains glistening in the distance. You may have seen the famous pictures by Tim Jarvis. Dressed in their Madchester finery, they link arms that are held aloft like a cup-winning team, behind them a vast, awesome panorama of mountain, valley, brilliant blue sky, dazzling snow and fearsome rock architecture. Somewhere, just out of shot, is me, sitting picking gingerly at a croque monsieur, groaning and regretting last night's third pitcher of cognac.

We had flown to Switzerland, purely to get that Olympian shot. The band had just released 'Fools Gold', a totemic seven minutes of psychedelic grooviness which you knew was their masterpiece even then. They were on everyone's lips, top of every end-of-year poll. So the mood demanded something a little flamboyant. It was a joyously, recklessly extravagant gesture, cooked up by Cummins and the wonderful, much-missed Philip Hall, the independent PR who also nurtured the fledgling Manic Street Preachers. The original intention was to nip up to Aviemore in the Scottish Highlands (as some of you may remember, the scene of my thirteen-year-old school pal Mark Lowton's failed seduction to ELP). I'd arranged to meet the others at Manchester Airport. Very late, they bowled up, Philip sweet and apologetic, the band charming, roguish, clearly a little stoned. Philip handed me my airline ticket. I couldn't help noticing that it was a Swissair voucher and was headed for Zurich.

'No snow at Aviemore, cock. We're only going to the Alps,' said Mani, all schoolkid mischief and excitement.

We sat at the back of the 737, just like the skivers and scamps do on the school bus. They lit the first joint before the seat belt signs were off. Nothing happened. A tall, cool, blonde stewardess did venture down at one point but she ended up staying for a chat. Something about the Roses simply disarmed people. Without any malice or braggadocio, it was clear that normal rules did not apply to them. They carried themselves then with the uncontrived, unmistakable élan of the natural rock star. I was to remember this a few years later, after it had all gone sour and Ian Brown was charged with threatening to chop a stewardess's hands off on a flight to Japan.

On the train from Zurich to Interlaken, perhaps emboldened by the presence of some English weirdos, a young Swiss lad started to make a bit of an arse of himself, swearing and lighting fags which he tried to give to us. The train grew palpably tense until a businessman berated him and then turned to us. 'I am sorry about this young man. I hope you do not behave like this on your English trains.'

I wanted to say, 'This train, sir, is on time to the very second. An English train would by now be four hours late, in a siding at Derby, and the heating and lights would have failed. We would have resorted to cannibalism and started our own rudimentary religion.'

But Ian Brown beat me to it. 'Chill out, mate. He's only getting excited. Have some of this.' With that he passed the businessman a huge bottle of cognac, one of many that had been purchased at duty-free. After a moment's pause, during which silence fell with a sharp intake of breath throughout the packed carriage, the businessman wiped the bottle and drank deep of it. The cognac got passed around, people smiled and had a quick pull as they did the crossword. Then another joint was rolled. I'm not making this up.

We arrived in Interlaken as night fell, as far as I remember. We banged on the door of our picturesque lodge and finally stirred the only staff member, a bloke of about 23 who spoke no English and had the air of the amenable but clearly demented manservant in Boris Karloff movies.

We seemed to be the only other people in the hotel. The porter – let's call him Igor – remained cheerfully impervious to our attempts at French, Italian and German. These are three of Switzerland's four official languages; the fourth is Romansch, a strange partly gypsy tongue spoken by two per cent of the population. Depending on whether you were a comparative linguist or a starving pack of rock trash, Igor was either a dead loss or a really lucky find.

Via elaborate mimes and such, we acquired several pitchers of beer, several more pitchers of cognac and doorstop ham and cheese sandwiches. We sat in front of the log fire by the Christmas tree and drank and ate. Igor sat with us and drank and ate too, saying nothing but smiling broadly.

When the booze and food ran out, Ian and I went in search of more, in what was feeling more and more like the hotel in *The Shining* with every moment. We stumbled on the kitchens and, as we switched the lights on, saw that every surface, but every one, was covered with fat but surprisingly speedy cockroaches.

When it got light we left, leaving Igor asleep in front of the dead fire, with francs shoved into his apron pockets and a wad more bundled into the hands of the Father Christmas mannequin in the lobby. No one had felt much like bed and breakfast after the roach floor show. Bleary and bamboozled, we made our way further into the mountains by tram until we reached Grindlewald, an out-of-season ski resort at the foot of the Eiger. We found another hotel, took some pictures in the deserted streets beneath the sheer rock face and then slept till it was time to go to the only open bar, drink more cognac and do the interview. When it was over, we smoked cigars on the balcony, looking at the stars over the silent peaks and the lights in the farms in the valley below.

'It's all right here, innit,' said Mani, quietly. No one else spoke.

The Stone Roses stand neatly poised on the edge of immortality. They are electric with potential, alive with the threat of greatness; they are already too big to be smothered by some tired and shabby theorising about the 'chemical revolution of the new dance scene' or, for that matter, about the 'boiling swamp of youthful creativity' that is (ahem) 'Madchester'. As the Roses themselves are the first to admit, people have danced to pop music from Elvis Presley through the Sex Pistols to Acid House.

To say the Stone Roses are a dance band is true, but only as true as saying they are a pop group or a rock group. What is most exciting about them is their cocky, undaunted ability to delve into different idioms and, more importantly, different eras and fashion something all their own and everything to do with now. Too much of what has been written about the Stone Roses could have been said about The Shamen, about The Beloved, about any one of those minor dilettantes. The Roses are too sharp to be dragged down to this level; too bright and possibly too beautiful.

That's part of what I wrote when I got back to London. I don't blame you if you think that it has the distinct whiff and sound of guff about it. It looks suspiciously that way to me too. All I can say is that you might have written it too had you been on that balcony below the Jungfrau, with the most exciting group in the world, having not slept in any meaningful sense for three days.

I still have a pair of blue woollen gloves lent to me by John Squire as I hung around shivering in the snow while they had their picture taken, always a slow process. When I got home they were still in my luggage. Somewhat cheekily, I hung on to them, thinking that if the Stone Roses did become as big as The Beatles, they would be a piece of rock memorabilia of rare magnificence, like having one of John Lennon's knitted ties from the Cavern era, or at least a balaclava of Ringo's.

It didn't quite work out like that. But I have them still. Unlike those Joe Bloggs jeans, I won't be using them when I'm creosoting the fence.

24 Rich and Strange

Even back then, when I was in the thick of it, I never laboured under the illusion that music papers were the section of journalism of most world import. I would – and still will if you furnish me with a premium imported lager or two – argue that pop music is globally important, that it brought down the Berlin Wall, ended the Vietnam War and that Elvis Presley and The Beatles are more significant figures culturally than every Conservative Party chairman put together. But I know that the pop press is not as serious as real newspapers. This is by design and part of its charm. Pop writing doesn't have its Bernstein and Woodwards, but it does have those who at least try to be Kenneth Tynan or Dorothy Parker.

I spent a lot of time trying to make people laugh. I didn't consider this an ignoble calling although some of the more severe members of the staff did. For them, music writing was a deathly serious business, all about teasing out mystical references in the works of Van Morrison and feeling Kurt Cobain's pain second-hand. I thought pop music was so self-evidently the most important thing in the world that it didn't need a lot of over-serious young men's windbaggery to confer some legitimacy on it. I leaned more towards Bob Dylan's attitude when he said that Smokey Robinson was 'America's greatest living poet'. It was a kind of whimsical joke but he obviously meant it, and it turned attention away from the self-righteous and self-important auteurs of rock in favour of a pop songsmith. Dylan I like to think was having a sly dig at the kind of people who get obsessed with Dylan.

After a year or so in the job, Alan Lewis asked me to edit the Thrills section of the paper. Whatever the original intention of this page had been, it had now become a drip-tray for stuff that wouldn't fit anywhere else, a ragbag where you'd find a uselessly small piece on some Taiwanese film director next to three hundred words on the new Cabaret Voltaire remix album. I decided to model it on *Private Eye*, adopting the same scurrilous, irreverent tone about pop music that it did about politics, and began stealthily introducing spoof items.

Very early on in my tenure, I ran a piece to coincide with the Nelson Mandela tribute concert at Wembley stadium celebrating his release. I claimed, untruthfully of course, that the great man had slammed the organisers of the concert for the poor line-up. According to the piece,

> *Mandela, who has kept in touch with modern music via John Peel's world service show whilst incarcerated on Robin Island, reacted angrily to the announcement of the line-up for his tribute show. Mandela stormed, 'Aswad! The Neville Brothers! Simple Minds! What a parade of bland, obvious, '80s leftovers. Where is the reflection of the Madchester scene? Where are the Roses, Inspirals and Mondays? Not to mention today's shoegazing bands such as Slowdive and Chapterhouse. Tracy Chapman? I ask you.*

This gave a few people a moment's mirth I hope and then was forgotten. Until a week or so later, I received a letter from an expatriate reader in Holland. He enclosed the front page of *De Telegraaf*, a leading Dutch broadsheet. There, splashed across five columns was my Thrills piece, reprinted almost verbatim as a genuine news story.

NELSON MANDELA HEEFT CRITCISED NAAR DE ORGANISEREN VAN ZIJN SCHATTING CONCERT. 'ASWAD? WAARHEEN ZITTEN NAAR DE ROZE? DE INSPIRALS EN DER MONDAYS? TRACY CHAPMAN? MIJ VRAGEN U!'

I imagined a baffled Mandela being questioned about it all when he was next in The Hague, and a faint glow of pride came to my cheeks.

This, though, was not the most famous case of one of my Thrills squibs being taken a little too seriously. I also introduced a column called Thrills Believe It Or Not. This was a skit on the ubiquitous newspaper columns which tell you – usually wrongly – that more people are kicked to death by donkeys each year than die in plane crashes or that the Great Wall of China is the only man-made object you can see from the moon. Each week, I would print four or five small, patently untrue items of pop trivia. I said that David Bowie had invented the game Connect 4, that Neil Tennant was a fully qualified rugby league referee and that Billy Bragg could breathe underwater.

In one column, I also 'revealed' that Bob Holness, host of TV's long-running *Blockbusters* quiz, had played the famous saxophone solo on Gerry Rafferty's 'Baker Street'. Quite why, out of all the fictitious items I invented, this one should have caught fast in the public imagination, I have no idea. I have heard it reported back to me in pubs and over dinner tables ('Being in the biz, this might not be news to you but did you know that Bob Holness …'). I've seen it asserted in national newspapers. I've even heard other people claiming to have started the rumour. It's actually Rafael Ravenscroft. He also played the lesser known but equally lounge-lizardy sax break on Hazel O'Connor's 'Say Goodbye'. That's about Midge Ure by the way. No, it is really.

Alan Lewis called me into his office one day and said, 'I see that you've been introducing a fair bit of, errm, humorous stuff to Thrills.' Expecting the worst, I mumbled something about shaking things up, not taking ourselves too seriously and the shortage of Taiwanese directors to write about.

'Well, the serious stuff, if you can call it that, looks a bit out of place now so drop it all. Make it all funny. Go for broke. I like it. I don't suppose Bob Holness really did play the ... no of course not. Well, keep up the good work. Fancy a pint?'

So Thrills got sillier and sillier, and became a little enclave where David Quantick, Andrew Collins and I would indulge ourselves. We ran a series called God Help Us If There's A War (after a remark by Mark E. Smith) where current pop stars who looked particularly flaky and dissolute would be held up for scrutiny. Most weeks this was the splendid Richard Ashcroft from The Verve, who, top man that he is, took it in good spirit. We ran a regular feature called Bismillah where particularly poor lyrics were held up to mild ridicule.

There was a weekly column called Not The Alice Cooper where readers were invited to send in pictures of relatives who had the same name as rock stars. It was a simple idea but a charming one. There was something undeniably hilarious about these pictures of balding men washing the car who were called Jimmy Page or twinkling white-haired grannies called Janis Joplin. I particularly enjoyed it when, after a while, readers would muck about with the whole format and send me a picture of a smiling grey-haired chap of about 65 pruning roses with the note, 'This is my dad. Believe it or not, he's called Captain Beefheart.'

The section of Thrills that gave me the biggest headache was called The Material World Of – a modern variant on those fan questionnaires that formed the staple of pop and footie magazines in the Seventies, the ones where Francis Lee and Peter

Marinello would reveal that their favourite film actors were Dustin Hoffman or Susan George and that their favourite meal was Steak Diane. The footballers would change but the answers rarely did. So it was with bands. I faxed off lists of questions to pop stars, the principle being that you could sometimes learn more from seemingly trivial questions (what can you cook? who's your favourite comedian? what was the last book you bought?) than through the more lengthy process of the interview. Most weeks, I was proved wrong, though, and I'd receive, scribbled on hotel stationery from Rod Stewart or the Jesus and Mary Chain, barely legible and absurdly short scribblings that would read 'Beans. John Cleese. Don't like books.'

One week, though, I ripped the reply from the fax and had to sit down and swallow hard. The group in question had not just answered the questions fully and properly. They had answered each one with an apposite, brilliantly chosen quotation or remark from a whole range of cultural figures; Mao, Philip Larkin, Marilyn Monroe, George Best, Flaubert, Andy Warhol, Dostoevsky, Heidegger, R.S. Thomas. It was a breathtaking gesture of self-confidence, one that elevated the whole rather silly section into something profound. I ran it as a full page rather than the half or quarter it usually merited and I determined to watch these people closely. The band were the Manic Street Preachers.

When we weren't inventing facts about Bob Holness and Neil Tennant, or making fun of Mad Richard Out Of The Verve or marvelling at the Manics, we were inventing movements. Inventing movements is a noble and long-standing tradition of the music press; in fact of critics in general. Dylan Thomas spent whole interviews denying that there was something called New Apocalyptic poetry and that he had any part of it, Debussy hated being called an Impressionist. Up on the 26th floor of Kings Reach Tower, we were aware that Madchester was dying down (the Mondays had gone mental on drugs in the Bahamas and the Stone

Roses had disappeared completely) and the world, or certainly the *NME*, was waiting for the Next Big Thing.

On a good day, Steve Lamacq could invent three fiery, short-lived movements before his cider and scampi fries in the Stamford Arms. He tried to get something called Fraggle off the ground. This consisted chiefly of the Mega City Four and anyone else who wore baggy shorts, played loud, lumpy indie rock and lived in a van. The paper's Irish contingent replied with Raggle-taggle, a kind of Celtic knees-up or 'music to sell pegs to' embracing The Waterboys and, well, The Waterboys mainly. Not taken with either of these, I countered with the defiantly silly Lion Pop. Pop was the operative word here; I tried desperately to find bands who represented style, glamour, a dab of irony and good tunes. I came up with St Etienne and Cud and a bunch of serial no-hopers from Sheffield called Pulp though I may have invented some bands to fit the thesis. Lion Pop had ridiculousness built in at the design stage and was mentioned about four times in the paper. It did, however, form the basis of something else that came along a little later, something that packed much more cultural clout.

Cud came from Leeds and were, as *Trouser Press* magazine succinctly described them, almost 'parodically obscure' ('the drummer from Cud' had become one of the paper's in-jokes, a shorthand for the quintessentially third-division indie musician). They were actually a splendid group of people, led by chunky, leather-trousered frontman, Carl Puttnam. Their music had a definite strain of daftness – songs included 'Only A Prawn In Whitby', 'Leggy Mambo' and 'When I Rome, Kill Me' – but they could make a half-decent record when they wanted as in their finest moment, the minor hit 'Rich And Strange'.

To coincide with this single's release, we decided to do something rich and strange. Carl Puttnam and I went to a health farm in Leicester for a detox weekend. We hung around poolside on sunloungers with cucumber slices over our eyes, drank carrot juice in Jacuzzis, played tennis and in the evening drank a bottle of smuggled Johnny Walker Red Label and played Trivial Pursuit with some glamorous, toned, well-heeled fifty-something ladies from Melton Mowbray.

I remember all the rich and strange little outings as well as I remember the more obviously glamorous and cosmopolitan stuff. I got stuck in a lift with Iggy Pop in Paris and when we were rescued, as we prepared to do the interview, I asked Ig if he minded if I smoked. He looked at me with a wry, gentle smile and said, 'No, I don't.' Afterwards I realised what the smile really meant. It meant, 'I am Iggy Pop, grand vizier of debauchery and ungovernable noise. I have lived in a Berlin bedsit with David Bowie where we weaned ourselves off a daily diet of kilos of cocaine. Onstage I cut myself with broken glass. I wear clear plastic trousers the better to display my famed old fellow. I have seen things that would make your hair curl; dark, dangerous things that no man should see. And I have come through it and attained a kind of wisdom forged in excess. I don't think your having a quick B&H is going to phase me, do you?'

Two days after meeting Iggy Pop I went to Rotherham to interview Jive Bunny. You may have forgotten Jive Bunny. You may have paid money to trained psychological heath professionals in order to forget them. They were a family outfit from the arse end of South Yorkshire whose simple but effective shtick was splicing together old rock and roll and Glenn Miller tunes over a moronic dance beat with an accompanying video of a simplistic cartoon rabbit. They were massive briefly, presumably all the records bought by old school mobile DJs to revitalise wedding receptions when they've put the lights out again after the chicken leg and sausage roll buffet. They were universally despised (except by the millions who bought their records), though in truth they were no more unpalatable than Westlife. In a nice reversal of expectations, Iggy Pop was kindly and modest while Jive Bunny were bolshy, unapologetic and contemptuous of their peers. I liked them for that.

Rich and strange. I interviewed Motörhead in the chi-chi bar of an exclusive London restaurant. Guitarist Wurzel – a large, bovine man with a shambling gait – arrived first and placed a copy of Dylan Thomas's *Collected Poems* on the table.

'You're a Dylan Thomas fan,' I asked, a little surprised and delighted.

'Yes,' he growled. 'I was first introduced to him via the prison library service.'

The others – Lemmy and Phil Campbell – arrived and, at Lemmy's suggestion, we began to drink copious amounts of Jack Daniels and Coke. Every now and then, their press officer would appear from behind an ornate rococo pillar. 'Ten minutes, guys,' he'd interject brightly and the band, who obviously had little respect for him, would ignore him.

After several hours we got on to politics. Lemmy is a man of robust views, more apolitical than right-wing in truth but certainly no Polly Toynbee. We became embroiled in, of all things, an argument about whether essential public service employees should be allowed to go on strike. Lemmy thought not. I thought this was harsh and undemocratic. By that stage, I probably said, 'That's a bish hart and undemotic.' Lemmy began to explain his reasoning, waving a tumbler of JD around for emphasis, when the PR appeared again. 'Going to have to wrap things up, guys. Your car's here,' he chirruped.

With this Wurzel lifted him into the air by the throat and pinioned him against the ornate rococo pillar. 'Will you fucking fuck off, you nonce. Can't you see we're enjoying having a bit of a chat with the boy?'

The boy. I kind of liked that. Coming from Motörhead, there was nothing patronising about it. It was a good-natured, entirely reasonable remark. Motörhead have seen things I will never see, things I do not want to see, terrible hair-curling things. By comparison I was a boy soldier, a cadet in the company of these warty, raddled old berserkers of rock.

The PR went home. And we hung around sloshing it back and discussing firefighters' conditions of service until they threw us out of the hotel.

It should be said that this was the same useless PR who had also once overseen a meeting with Alice Cooper. Before the interview got under way, the PR asked what I thought of this 'cool' idea for a picture: 'Alice reading a copy of the *Sun*, kicking back, relaxed, laughing.'

I said, as placatingly as I could, that I thought it was a fairly shit idea. 'But Alice is such a big fan of the *Sun*, and the readers would love it,' he insisted. We'll talk about it later, I said, and went into Alice's hotel room. He was sitting with his feet up looking out of the window. A copy of that day's *Sun* lay on the bed. We shook hands. I had a bad feeling.

For the first fifteen minutes, it was a very strange interview indeed, the sort that might occur in a dream. The kind of dream where you're back at an old school with no trousers on, or your hair turns to grass in the supermarket.

I would ask a detailed, thoughtful, analytical question about the lyrics to 'The Ballad Of Dwight Fry' or the dynamics of the celebrated twin guitar line-up of Michael Bruce and Glenn Buxton. Alice would begin to answer, haltingly, giving me a strange look and then chortle and start to talk about Samantha Fox or 'that crazy George and Lynne cartoon. Sheesh, do they ever get dressed?' I'd bring up *Billion Dollar Babies*, he'd bring up Freddie Starr Ate My Hamster.

We went on for a while, chit chatting through a thin mist of mutual incomprehension before Alice leaned forward quizzically and said, 'You are the guy from the *Sun*, right?'

'No, the *New Musical Express*.'

'The *NME*?' Alice seemed nonplussed. 'He told me you were from the *Sun*,' he said, indicating the PR who was chatting gaily to the photographer in the next room, perhaps outlining his plans for a shot involving Richard Littlejohn, Jo Guest or Garry Bushell. 'Stupid jerk,' muttered Alice, after some time, and tossed aside the copy of the *Sun*.

'OK, "The Ballad Of Dwight Fry", lemme see …' After that, we got on famously.

Like drug addicts but less efficient. Perhaps Quantick was right. On the other hand, some of their tactics were little short of inspired. When Supergrass were set to make an important appearance at Scotland's T In The Park festival, their PR at EMI let it be known that Danney Goffey was a devotee of Tunnock's Caramel Wafers, a local delicacy. This wasn't exactly true but it was worth many pieces in the local papers. In fact, more, it was worth a VIP guided tour of the Tunnock's factory from Mr Archie Tunnock himself.

As we left in the car provided, a bloke in the street outside spotted us and shouted out to a friend, 'Look, it's that band.' Supergrass smiled modestly to themselves. 'That band, you know … M People.' As M People's most prominent member was a tall black woman with a bouffant hairdo, you have to marvel at the fellow's grasp of pop culture. He would have made a fine music journalist.

Rich and strange. I'm at the Liverpool training ground watching John Barnes rapping. We're here for the making of the New Order England World Cup Squad video for the fabulous 'World In Motion'. If you look closely, and use the freeze-frame judiciously, I'm just visible for a nanosecond playing keepy-uppy with Kevin Cummins behind Keith Allen's head. For some reason, Barney Sumner was dressed as Elvis and when later we went off to do the interview, we found two young urchins admiring Barney's lovely red convertible.

'You can have a ride in it if you like,' he said amiably and then immediately corrected himself. 'No, sorry, lads. Sorry, you can't. See you.' As we drove away he explained, 'I suddenly saw the headlines, "New Order star dressed as Elvis lures small boys into car." It wouldn't look good, would it?'

New Order were involved with one of the most fun, rich and strange off-the-wall days out I can remember. This happened to be a tradition I started – still part of the paper I think – of organising boozy Christmas forums, me and a few voluble pop stars who'd get together in a hotel room and review the year's most notable singles for a piece in the Xmas double issue. The inaugural session took place at the Ramada Hotel in Manchester with Paul Heaton of the Beautiful South, Peter Hooton of The Farm and, of course Mark E. Smith. We met at midday in the downstairs bar and MES had downed four pints before we got to the room. Once in the room, more and more drink was called for, casually, with waves of the hand Roman emperor style. It came again and again, brought on hostess trolleys by disbelieving hotel staff. We played MC Hammer, and MES, by now far gone, said, 'You know, you've got a bit of a look of MC Hammer yourself.' In the end, the carnage was so great that The Farm had to cancel that night's gig in Liverpool.

The next year, we relocated to a soulless high-rise hotel in London's Docklands. This time the panel were Miles Hunt of the Wonder Stuff, Graham Massey of Manchester's 808 State and Peter Hook of New Order. Hookie has been an icon for years now; bearded, imposing, bass slung low around his knees, producing the subterranean growl at the heart of Joy Division and New Order's music. He was the last to arrive. Massey, Hunt and myself sat in the lobby sipping beers until we decided that it would make more sense to find the room, order drinks and generally set up. I strolled over to reception: 'We're going to be joined by a third gentleman in a while, I hope. Would you send him up to the room?' The concierge asked for a name. This was a problem. Rock stars never use their real names in hotels. It is an ingrained defence mechanism against detection by stalkers, journalists and hotel managers. Paul McCartney checked into American hotels as Paul Ramon which is why The Ramones were so called.

The trouble was that I had no idea what Peter Hook's hotel pseudonym was. So how to tell the concierge how to recognise Hookie? A fellow Mancunian musician, Graham Massey, knew Hookie's style well. He smiled at the concierge, 'Look out for a man dressed as a German U boat captain.' We chuckled as we headed for the lifts and decided to ring down at intervals to locate him.

About ten minutes later, as we were organising chairs and such, there was a knock on the door. I answered. It was Hookie. He stepped briskly into the room. He was wearing a full-length leather trenchcoat, black motorcycle boots to his knees and a white Aran polo-neck sweater with a huge rollneck. He was, as usual, bearded and wore shades and a peaked cap.

'Did you have any trouble finding us?' we asked.

'No,' he replied, a little puzzled. 'I walked into the lobby and, before I said anything, the guy on reception said, "Ah, you'll be the gentlemen I'm expecting. Your friends are in room 301, sir."'

I'm not sure we ever told him.

25 A New Career in a New Town

Ranked high on the list of why provincial misfits want to become music journalists, up there with the sex, drugs, little laminated passes and free records, is travel. Join the navy and see the world, join the *NME* and see World of Twist.

All areas of artistic endeavour seem to find travel innately romantic. Robert Louis Stevenson said, 'It is better to travel hopefully than to arrive', suggesting he often used the Virgin West Coast mainline. Thom Gunn said, 'one is always closer by not standing still'. Byron went to Greece, Graham Greene went to South America, Auden and Macneice went to Iceland.[1] Our titular muse Laurie Lee wrote *As I Walked Out One Midsummer Morning*, the tales of a young man's penniless and ragamuffin wanderings with a battered violin in the Pyrenees, which in itself has all the hallmarks of an 'on the road' piece with The Levellers.

Pop music shares this fascination with going places. David Bowie's 'A New Career In A New Town' speaks volumes, without

---

1 The land of geysers and austere primal beauty, not the land of gateaux and chicken dippers.

words actually, of the intrinsic beauty of uprooting. 'Trans Europe Express' evokes the shadowy elegance and charm of crossing the continent by train and mentions David Bowie in passing. Electronic music has found glamour and mystery in the unlikeliest places: motorways (Kraftwerk), flyovers (The Clash's 'Westway'), underpasses (John Foxx). Simple Minds sang 'I Travel'. I travelled with them once actually, to Frankfurt where I stole the mayor of Frankfurt's place at dinner and dropped my overnight bag into a Jacuzzi. This is where the rock journalist's fund of war stories and tall tales emanates from; the rock hack and band in their natural milieu. The trip.

If you're the kind of person who spends your summer making your way (slowly, via public transport, face-painted, skin-peeling, carrying a blue Karrimor backpack the size of a walk-in wardrobe) between Glastonbury and Reading, then trips are little squares of blotting paper bought from a small, walnut-faced Mancunian in a balaclava that when ingested make you think you're Cardinal Wolsey or Cher. 'Trips' to rock journalists are something else entirely. They are excursions with a pop group to a foreign country, normally accompanying them on tour or 'on the road'. You are naturally expected to return with a few thousand words of copy but no rock journalist (unless he worked for one of those terribly over-efficient American magazines where they have fact checkers and 'bureau chiefs') would ever call a trip an 'assignment'. Assignments are things junior school kids do over half-term. Trips are trips. Junkets, freebies, blags, jaunts paid for by the record company and thus, ultimately, the band.

The band never realise this though, unless they are particularly old or cynical or in the unlikely event that they are composed entirely of record company accountants and lawyers. And no such band has ever existed or will ever exist. No, bands, bless them, are so happy and grateful to have a record deal and be going to New York/Tokyo/Prague/Frankfurt/Antwerp or even the Rockzkrungalinezeski Festival, Tirana, that they do not care that the schnapps, lobster and hotel porn the journalist is consuming with gusto will ultimately be deducted from their royalties ('promotional costs'), or, even worse, be written of as a bad debt by the label just before they are dropped and trudge back to their old jobs at the cash and carry.

Rock journalism was for me a kind of national service. A sort of Dutch national service though. The Merchant Navy run by freaks. The VSO on drugs. Because of rock journalism I got to see the world which I would never have done otherwise. Moreover, I got to see it slightly drunk and at someone else's expense, an experience denied most people unless they win *Family Fortunes*.

I wouldn't want you to think that it was a picnic though. It was free. But then so it should be. No holidaymaker in their right mind would pay good money – their own money – to spend three sleepless days in Alabama with short-tempered, alcoholic members of a heavy metal band who hate one another. Or a week in the worst hotel in Leipzig waiting for Van Morrison to calm down. Or in a leaking tent at a rave festival in Bulgaria run by the Balkan Mafia. On his national service, my dad climbed Mount Kenya and organised a football team of local youths. On mine, I spent four days stuck in a very small van driving from Kings Heath, Birmingham, to Les Mans with Napalm Death. One of us really knew the meaning of hard work and trial; far from home, trying to forge bonds of friendship and responsibility with unskilled, grudging, suspicious natives with little in the way of formal education whose language and way of life was a mystery. My dad, on the other hand, had it bloody easy from what I can see.[2]

To say I saw the world is an exaggeration. I didn't see the Middle East or China or Africa. Despite the best efforts of Peter Gabriel and Andy Kershaw, the rock press by and large has yet to

---

2 Rimshot, cymbal, thank you.

be convinced of the 'happening' nature of the Kinshasa music scene or the 'buzz' around Ulan Bator. I would have loved to go to these places. It would have made a change from O'Hare airport, which I visited so often I got to know the duty-free assistants by name.

That sounds ungrateful and blasé. So let me say at once that I never, ever took for granted the pampered luxury of jetting around the globe for free and staying, gratis, in pretty good hotels and personally establishing one of the world's premier collections of shower caps and tiny bottles of foaming bubble bath. I did see most of Europe, Scandinavia, Japan and the United States of America. It wasn't travel that became a routine, it was rock travel. Rock travel is very much like what Robert Mitchum said about film-making: hours of tedium enlivened by minutes of sheer terror.

Rock travel is never routine. Or rather, it is routine but not in the routine sense. Because everyone in the business regards efficiency, forward planning and calm as the mark of boring old farts, nothing must be allowed to run smoothly. Generally you will miss your plane because someone – a journalist usually – will oversleep. This, he will say, is because he was with Liam Gallagher or The Strokes in the Soho House till four a.m. And this could conceivably be the truth. But it may equally because he was playing Mickey's Magical Kingdom Racing on his Playstation till two and hasn't worked out how to set the alarm clock yet. If, by some fluke, you arrive at Heathrow in good time, don't worry; the long, fractious argument the photographer will have about what constitutes hand luggage will easily eat up another half an hour. Plus it will antagonise the ground staff who will relay the message to the flight attendants that you are arrogant vermin and not to give you the tiny packet of pretzels.

Actually it can work out a lot better than this. Cummins and I were travelling to New York once and, as was customary, asked for an upgrade without much hope. But we were upgraded 'all the way up', as the check-in girl said with a cute smile. All the way up. Club class. A mythical kingdom at the edge of the world, where Richard Branson and Elton John live.

Club class is better than most rock journalists' houses. It's a wonder more upgraded passengers don't squat, just refuse to get off the plane, seek asylum, and live in the air for the rest of their lives. There are beds and computers and pyjamas. There's a little room where you can go and (back then) smoke a Peter Stuyvesant lying in a futuristic beanbag thing and feeling like Hugh Hefner. On my first – and, to date, only – sojourn in the world they call 'club', the steward offered me an Armagnac that was older and more costly than the house I grew up in. A little woozy by now, I politely declined.

'Oh go on, sir. Can't I tempt you?' The look he gave me was chummy, knowing, conspiratorial even. It said, 'Look, sunshine, you've been upgraded, and it may never happen again. Enjoy it. You're as entitled to all this as much as that fat German over there who laid off a thousand steelworkers this morning. We have cruel inhuman pâtés, deep muscle massages and vintage booze here that you wouldn't believe. And it's free. Therefore I say to you, fill your boots, for verily you are at your granny's.' And he poured me a pint of Armagnac.[3]

However hopefully you travel, you have to arrive. When you arrive, it helps if you really like hotels. I adore them. I love everything about them. My heart beats a little faster at the very mention of the words Hyatt, Four Seasons, Malmaison and Landmark. Of

---

3 What I am about to say is terrible, wrong and a vile act of class treachery but it is what I thought both then and now. The only thing that could improve club class is if they had little seat-back screens showing you what the people in economy were eating and how little legroom they had. Naturally the arrangement shouldn't be reciprocated, not unless you wanted the events of Moscow, October 1917, to be re-enacted on every transatlantic flight.

course, it shrinks a little at Novotel and Ibis. Hotels are a holiday from real life to me; a dream world of endless hot water, free newspapers, Japanese news channels, massive beds, fluffy pillows, tiny chocolates, laundry bags, peanuts, shampoo, towelling robes and 'sending down' for a club sandwich and a Chivas Regal that you just know will come cascading down the slopes of a Matterhorn of crushed ice and with a little plastic stirrer.

That's the theory anyway. There is a darker side to hotels of course. There is the dreaded 'It doesn't actually say here sir that the company are picking up the account' conversation. There is the breezy, voluble vacuuming chambermaid who comes into your room at seven a.m. There's the intense, cloying heat, the international micro-climate of hotels.

There's the fire alarm. All hotels are subject to the curse of the random fire alarm. But some have turned this into an art form. There is a famously dubious, shabby, genteel hotel in central Manchester where there is never a need to book an alarm call as all regulars know that wailing sirens will go off at frequent but unpredictable intervals throughout the night, keeping you in a state of light, damply anxious cat-napping. Booking an alarm call is not recommended anyway because of the staff's positively Ecuadorian approach to time-keeping. A friend of mine staying there booked his alarm call to make an early train back to London. The call came and he dashed through the oddly empty streets to Piccadilly to find that the alarm call had come three hours early, that it was barely dawn and that the trains hadn't started running yet. According to legend among BBC employees at New Broadcasting House on Oxford Road, a researcher had once booked a room there for an elderly academic travelling up from Oxford to take part in a radio programme. Mindful of the professor's age and lack of worldliness, the researcher asked the hotel to 'look after him' during his stay. On checking into his room, the elderly professor found a strange woman lying on his bed. The hotel had simply assumed that 'look after' meant provide the guest with a prostitute. Needless to say, it was the Happy Mondays' favourite hotel in the whole world.

The rock journalist soon becomes au fait with hotel protocol. Soon too he or she becomes well versed in the personnel of the touring rock band. The PR we have met. Then there are roadies. There are two types of roadies. One is a young bloke of 23 with a very short indigo mohican, baggy combat shorts with seven hundred pockets and a Biohazard T-shirt. You will never have a conversation with this roadie as he lives high up in the lighting gantry and, like a lemur, only descends to earth to feed and procreate.

The other type of roadie is a tall, warty man of about 48 with a greying ponytail and tight black jeans. This man is called Gripper and he has been a roadie since 1969 when he 'rigged the backline' for Led Zeppelin.[4] Since then he was worked with Supertramp, the Amazing Blondel, Elton, Rod, Smokey, Sailor, Faust, the Angelic Upstarts, Cabaret Voltaire, Tina Charles, Black Uhuru, Ultravox, the Brotherhood of Man, Megadeth, Musical Youth, Corrosion of Conformity and Gareth Gates. There is no rhyme nor reason to this because there is no rhyme nor reason to the roadies' career curve. It is a case of 'Have Maglite, Will Travel'. Invariably you will end up drinking liqueurs with this man very late one night and when you ask about any of his previous employers, be it Bowie, Jagger, Ted Nugent, Sting or the bloke from Metallica with the teeth, his answer will be the same: 'He's a really nice bloke actually.' Gripper could have worked Hitler's Sudetenland tour and his verdict would have been, 'Hard-line politics, yes. But he's a really nice bloke actually.'

The tour manager is King of the Roadies. The roadies fear and worship him as he is one of their primitive kind who has made it into long trousers and his own hotel room. He had a mobile phone

---

4 'Percy Plant still sends me a Christmas card actually.'

in 1978, a laptop in 1982 and a PDA in 1990. Like Japan, tour managers get technology two years before everyone else. In fact, they normally get it from Japan, where they were tour-managing the High Llamas last spring. Right now, tour managers are using hover jet packs and Internet browser eye implants that won't be commercially available till 2013. Get to know the tour manager. Remember his name. He dispenses money, drugs, backstage passes and luncheon vouchers. All tour managers are a paragon of zenlike calm and wry serenity – organising bail, paying for wrecked hotel rooms, getting a connecting flight to La Paz from Leeds Bradford at midnight – until the day they have a massive, horrible nervous breakdown, change their name to Luminar, dress in white and go and live in a commune in the Brecon Beacons.

Returning to trips, perhaps the reason Mark E. Smith thought I 'had a look of MC Hammer' was that something of Hammer's personality, outlook, style, perhaps even physical appearance had rubbed off on me during the time we had spent together. The quality time. The famous trip to Dusseldorf. The brief, glorious holiday in Hammertime.

Hammer was, I'm sure you recall, a pantomime rapper with a career as hectic, glorious and fleeting as a mayfly's. In the early Nineties his one proper hit, 'You Can't Touch This', made him a household name from Detroit to Derby to, as we shall see, Dusseldorf. He was, even by the standards of the art form that brought us Dave Hill and Milli Vanilli, ridiculous. He wore gigantic golden harem pants like a comedy caliph in an old *Crackerjack* sketch and, at the other extreme, really sensible glasses as sported by independent financial advisers. It's a measure though of how successful he was, however briefly, that on the same trip to Dusseldorf to meet him, there were representatives from *Smash Hits*, *Time Out* and the *Guardian* as well as myself.

We caught up with him in Dusseldorf. When I say 'caught up with him', it wasn't a race, nor was he avoiding us. It's just one of those things journalists say to make their professional lives sound more exciting when they consist largely of going to places like Dusseldorf. Kraftwerk come from Dusseldorf and this is by far the sexiest thing about the city. That's pretty telling, even if you're as big a Kraftwerk fan as I am.

We spent the afternoon in cake shops and admiring the one-way system. Later MC Hammer was playing in a forbiddingly grim concrete and glass building on the outskirts of town. From the look of it, it was usually used for storing unsold copies of *Auto Trader* or as a place where forklift trucks come to die. It was actually a leisure centre, we later learned. Suddenly, you felt a brief pang of pity for the leisure-hungry Dusseldorfer.

With all the exaggerated self-regard of the one-hit wonder, Hammer decided once we had all arrived at the building ahead of that night's show that access to his imperious self would have to be seriously curtailed and rationed. He needed more time to himself, perhaps to perfect his characteristic dance style which made him look part Cossack, part natterjack toad. Sheepishly the PR told us that our interview times would be rather brief.

I got fifteen minutes because I was chummy with his PR, Debs, a warm, easy-going Scouser. 'Don't tell anyone else. They're hardly getting fuck all,' she said as I was ushered into the drably functional dressing room. Hammer was seated in the centre of the room on a plastic chair. Facing him was a vacant seat, clearly intended for me. Behind that was another seat, in which sat one of Hammer's retinue of large black men of obscure function. Obviously this one was going to 'sit in'. Weirdly though, he wasn't going to do this from where I could see him but directly behind my back. Why? I thought. Was he going to pull faces to entertain his employer?

All became clear after quarter of an hour or so. In the middle of some pointless enquiry or other, I felt a gloved hand tap me on the shoulder. I turned round. The lackey was sitting back in his chair expressionless. Maybe I'd dreamed it. I carried on. A minute or so later, he did it again. I turned again. He sat sphinxlike. I continued. Seconds past. He did it again. 'Stop doing that,' I wanted to say, quite forcefully. But then it dawned on me. This was my signal to stop. To have simply said, 'We need to wrap things up now' or 'Hammer, you really should be climbing into your preposterous trousers' would have been too casual, too sane. In order to project an entirely false sense of intrigue and mystery, the flunkey was tapping me gently. With a gloved hand. It felt vaguely reminiscent of the emergency stop bit of the driving test. I missed the first couple, but on the third stroke I was more than happy to perform the emergency stop. I didn't skid or lose control of my vehicle. Fifteen minutes would be a cruelly short space of time to speak and share and debate with Brian Eno or David Bowie or Kate Bush or even The Stereophonics. But, believe me, it is ample time to get to the very essence of MC Hammer's life and art.

I stepped back into the soulless holding corridor where my journalistic colleagues sat in despondent array. They had just been told how the remainder of the time would be apportioned. *Smash Hits* and the *Guardian* would get eight minutes each. Nick Coleman of *Time Out* would receive four minutes.

'Four minutes!' I sympathised. 'What on earth can you do with that?'

'Oh well,' he said philosophically. 'I suppose I could get him to boil an egg.'

Every other week I seemed to be in flipping Germany. Cummins and I 'caught up' with The Pixies in Berlin. This time we shared the trip with a *Melody Maker* journalist, one Graham Linehan.[5] We stayed in Berlin's little-known ironmongery district. All the shops boasted giant window displays of pliers, wrenches

---

5 Later to become justly famous as co-creator and writer of *Father Ted*.

and sandpaper. It was like *Eraserhead* and it gave the area whatever the opposite of a sophisticated and rakish air is. No, actually, it gave it a very rakish air. An air of rakes and wire brushes. Venturing out one afternoon Cummins and I saw a middle-aged gentleman in full Bavarian garb: leather shorts, high woollen socks, little cap with the feather in, dungaree bib-type shirt. He looked completely ridiculous, in much the same way that a man dressed as a morris dancer would strolling along Deansgate or sporting one of those buckled hats in a Swansea discotheque. Berlin seemed to me a curious place to come to live with Iggy Pop if you were trying to give up drugs, as David Bowie had famously done.

The actual interview with Black Francis (or Frank Black as he is now or Charles Thompson as he is really) went pretty well, considering Frank's tendency to talk about UFOs and mind-control experiments for twenty-five minutes at a stretch. Later we all went out for dinner and Graham, for reasons now unclear, passed out in the strudel.

Back at the hotel, Graham and Frank chatted animatedly about alien abduction while Cummins and I went to get the beers in. We asked for four pints of the local brew.

'I will serve you in seven minutes,' barked the barman in a clipped and officious manner as he tinkered absently with a pump.

'Can't you be more specific?' I asked with, admittedly, a shade of irony.

This it turned out was a bad move. He slammed down the metal shutters of the bar and came out from behind the counter shrieking and violet with rage.

'Right, now, for your rudeness, you will have no beer at all. You English are all the same and thinking you are funny but I tell you that you are the hooligans!'

This found a raw nerve somewhere deep in Cummins's psyche. He delivered himself of a short but powerful speech still imprinted on my memory.

'This is the worst fucking country in the world. And you, pal, are the worst person I have ever met in the whole fucking country. Congratulations, Fritz!'

It very nearly came to blows. Luckily it remained at the level of the trading of deeply felt but purely verbal nationalistic insults; I think cabbages were mentioned and possibly a World Cup or two. All the while, Frank Black looked on in horror and bewilderment.

I once spent a night on the Reeperbahn with Erasure. Everyone loved it except me. They all thought it was 'colourful' and 'edgy'. I thought it was cheap and sordid. A little tragic too, watching those washed-our Romanian teenagers trying to look seductive by the light of a salmon-pink 40 watt bulb. Maybe it's the Lancastrian prude in me. Fortunately something happened the next day that really cheered me up. We sojourned to Hamburg docks to take some atmospheric pictures. There was an old guy there walking his dog. He watched as we tried out various combinations: Vince Clarke looking moody by a tugboat, Andy Bell staring at a crane. As we were packing up, the old chap came over.

'And now, one of you all together, ja?' he offered helpfully, completely misinterpreting the situation. This is how I have in my collection a photograph of myself, photographer Derek Ridgers and both members of Erasure smiling broadly and giving the old thumbs-up by a hydraulic dredger.

Ridgers is a legend among the rock press fraternity. He combines Peter Cook's E.L. Wisty with Johnny Rotten: downbeat, lascivious, melancholy, inscrutable. His gnomic utterances rival those of Chauncey Gardener in *Being There*. On one famous trip to Los Angeles with the Beautiful South, we were all frolicking in the famous rooftop pool of the Hyatt Hotel, the venue for the end-of-tour party in *Spinal Tap*. Indeed, the hotel as a whole is steeped in rock 'n' roll folklore. Little Richard keeps a suite there permanently and Led Zeppelin christened it the Riot House, scene of much Seventies debauchery.

We got out of the pool, towelled down and stood on the edge of the roof sipping tequila sunrises. LA lay vast, smoggy and weirdly beautiful before us, all steel, glass, flaring sunlight and distant blurry mountains. We fell silent. Then Ridgers spoke. 'Doesn't seem like a Thursday, does it?'

The four days I spent on the West Coast with the Beautiful South were perhaps my favourite trip of all. Yes, we got into a fight with pool cues with a nutcase called Chief in a Mexican bar called Spartacus. Yes, our shuttle bus driver went mad and abandoned us on the freeway, literally ran off down the road screaming. But it was a hoot. In the interests of balance then I should tell you about the worst trip of my career. Indeed – unless I am ever thrown into a Burmese jail or go on a Club 18–30 holiday – it will remain the worst few days of my life. This was the time I lived in a van for four days with Napalm Death.

Napalm Death were, still are probably, a band from Birmingham. They may be hardcore or death metal or grindcore or sludgecore or thrash. I forget to be honest. They came to fame in the late Eighties playing a kind of music from hell; songs lasting three and four seconds, not songs at all in any accepted sense but fragments of appalling noise that sounded like armageddon or tank warfare or a really big scary robot vomiting up some Meccano and nails. Perversely I quite liked them. I like difficult music, and, besides, it annoyed some of the ersatz soul boys on the *NME*.

Napalm Death were travelling by van from their home city to Le Mans in order to headline some terrible festival. The idea was that I and a photographer would accompany them and get to know them. Implicit in the general scheme was the prospect of humorously subverting readers' expectations. Four days in a van with Napalm Death? It sounds like a living hell. But guess what? They turn out to 'be really nice guys actually' who like fine wines and cheeses, golf, Truffaut and the short stories of Raymond Carver.

No, right first time. It *was* a living hell. It was one of those Hieronymous Bosch paintings that reek of human suffering and unspeakable torments but with baguettes and strawberry milk cartons and twenty-nine screenings of the film *Robocop*. None of Napalm Death would be my first choice of companion on, say, a canal-boating holiday. Individually you could talk to Barney, the dopey but approachable singer/vomiter, or Shane, the complex, brooding, plump bassist with the Afro and the nervous tic that made him pat and straighten it constantly. But the drummer was something else. The drummer – small, dark, goblinish – radiated evil like a handful of weapons grade plutonium. He was boorish, he was whiny, he was loud and vulgar and hateful. He smelled bad. After twenty minutes in his company Gandhi would have kicked him in the throat. Naturally, he was the most opinionated of the lot; spouting half-digested Animal Liberation Front slogans all the way to Calais. He was just the kind of person Jean Genet must have been thinking of when he said, perceptively I think, 'I really like animals. I just don't like people who like animals.'

All bands have on-tour catchphrases. The astute journalist will quietly, speedily assimilate them and use them when appropriate. Napalm Death had one catchphrase – 'I'm seriously weakened' – and the drummer used it in every sentence, with the bullish confidence of the truly unfunny. He clearly thought this was up there with the remarks of Shaw and Wilde and each time he said it he would gurn and nudge, as if to point up his wit. Before we had got to Newport Pagnell services, I wanted to kill him. I thought of little else. My hands twitched.

There were eight of us in the very small van. My associate from *NME* was Peter Walsh, a Mancunian photographer who had embraced his home city's new-found culture with gusto. He wore flares, a Jackson Pollock Stone Roses T-shirt and a floppy fringe.

'Top one,' he would drawl, 'sorted!' The band took an instant jokey dislike to Peter. They called him a Sonic, their dismissive catch-all term for anyone who didn't like grindcore music, who could string a sentence together and who washed their hair more than once a month. The *NME* was a paper for Sonics, I was a Sonic, Peter Walsh was the biggest Sonic of them all.

'Nice one!' Walsh would say.

'I'm seriously weakened,' the drummer would counter.

Someone would fart and put *Robocop* on again. It was, I repeat, a living hell of mindless repetition.

Once in France things got worse. For all their vegan windbaggery and anarchic gloss, the band were old-fashioned, small-minded conservatives. They pulled faces at the food on offer in the service stations.

'I'm seriously weakened by this Roquefort shit,' the drummer would say, and ask for pizza or Heinz tomato soup. He made you ashamed to be English. I remembered that the French took a lenient view of crime passionnel, and wondered if that included being driven mad with rage and disgust at thrash metal drummers.

We arrived in Le Mans as dawn was breaking and found the little hippy family-run pension where the festival organisers were putting us up. Bleary-eyed but generous to a fault, the owners ushered us into a large sunny room with a patio and rustled up some breakfast: coffee, croissant, scrambled eggs.

'What the fuck's this?' asked the drummer, holding up a croissant as if it were a live snake. 'Ain't yow got no normal toast?'

Some normal toast was found. We ate in relative silence – 'I'm seriously weakened by these eggs' – for a while until even this was broken by a loud splatt and a chortle. The drummer had thrown his plate of eggs at the wall; the yellow amorphous mass slid down to the skirting board. The owner looked like she was going to cry. I completely lost it.

'What is your bastard problem, you ignorant peasant? These

people are feeding and housing you for nothing, moreover they are paying you good money to play your stupid, childish, tuneless drivel. We are covering it for the *NME* and it is, rest assured, the only half-decent publicity you will ever receive. No one gives a flying fuck about your Peel sessions or your half-baked politics. You are a wanker of the first order and you should go down on your hands and knees and thank God daily that a dimwit and an arsehole such as yourself is being pampered like this rather than cleaning toilets or some other job more suited to your station.'

I'd like to think at this point that I turned to address the room and apologised to any toilet cleaners having breakfast but I can't be sure. I finished with a flourish. 'Go and apologise to that nice lady over there, then clean that mess up and come and finish your breakfast, you pathetic knobhead.'

He did. I think he knew from the shaky tone of voice and cold glassy look in my eyes that I had gone mad and was capable of anything. There is nothing more frightening than a truly unhinged person, and my gate was completely off at this juncture.

We got along perfectly for the next few days, in that we never exchanged another word. The band played, it was awful, and we came home. Somewhere around Limoges, delirious with fatigue, booze and claustrophobia, Walsh made them stop the van while he vomited on the hard shoulder. 'Sonic's chooking oop,' they crowed and took pictures of him.

The next day, we arrived back at my house at five a.m. The sky was just beginning to streak with light. Without a word, Walsh and I went into the kitchen and I poured us both a half-pint of brandy, which we drank in a single draught. Then I went to the shelves and took down the Napalm Death CDs the record company had sent by way of research. Next, I rummaged under the stairs until I found a hammer, a saw, some pliers and a wrench. We proceeded to smash the CDs to glittering shards

26 He Knows I'd Love to See Him

Shakespeare didn't do interviews. This is a pity. I'd like to have known what his favourite colour was, or what his influences were, or whether *Taming of the Shrew* was his difficult second play, or whether he was just writing his plays for himselves and, in sooth, if other people liked them, then that was verily a bonus.

If you've read any rock interviews, you'll know what I mean. Perhaps because rock bands serve apprenticeships as readers, when they become famous enough to be interviewed, they slip into Interviewese, a lingua franca rich in cliché and ripe for translation.

We feel it's our best album.

We feel it's our latest album.

We feel it's our *Sgt Pepper*.

It's got a brass section on one track.

Our manager? He's a pussycat really.

He's a criminal psychopath but he dishes out the drugs and money.

And so on. Probably only once in the course of rock press interviewing did any band, no matter how candid or unaffected, actually not talk up their new record to me. That was the La's. Having scoured West London for somewhere to eat that fulfilled their many curious criteria vis-à-vis spiciness, region and composition, we settled down in Pizza Express (they ordered ham and eggs, the first and last time I have seen anyone order this menu item).

'So tell me about the new album,' I asked jauntily with a mouthful of American Hot.

'It's shit,' said frontman Lee Mavers in thick, catarrhal Scouse.

'Pardon?'

The other members of the band, including future Cast leader John Power, shrugged noncommittally.

'It's shit, la,' continued Mavers. 'It's last. It's sad. Nobody should buy it.' The PR blanched. Mavers's attitude to the band's only album is now famous. But this was the interview in which he revealed his loathing for the 'plasticky' sound and lack of genuine warmth. He was particularly scathing about producer Steve Lillywhite who he accused of cobbling together the finished album after the group had abandoned it. In Lillywhite's defence, Mavers was far from the ideal producee. He had demanded a vintage mixing desk which The Beatles had used. He had, it was said, refused to use new guitar strings and asked for antique Sixties strings 'with Sixties dirt on them'. This type of behaviour is not unknown among the more temperamental artiste but at least Brian Wilson, Phil Spector et al. waited till they'd become legends first. As it is, Mavers's intransigence made him legendary; that and a clutch of fabulous tunes on an album that's really very good, whatever he thinks.

The meeting with the La's was a particularly curious interview but really all interviews are fundamentally odd. They bear no relation to real human discourse. The more I did, the more I became convinced of it. They are falsely intimate, strangely choreographed, a kind of courtship ritual. First, you are pitched headlong into an absurdly intense and personal discussion of subjects you would normally only dare raise with an extremely close and valued friend: sexual relationships, formative childhood experiences, politics, drug habits. Secondly, only one of you is disclosing. However much you delude yourself that this is a conversation not an interrogation, the truth is that it's not and nor should it be. The readers don't care what you think. They want to know about the Nazi salute at Victoria Station or just exactly what was the deal with Marianne Faithfull and the Mars bar. Thirdly, the person being interrogated is often extremely rich, famous or weird, sometimes all three. Finally, you will probably never see them again. It is a heady cocktail designed to produce bizarre results.

Bad interviews are the stuff of nightmares. Moments from them come back unbidden in the middle of the night or during a pleasant lunch. I have had a few, and not too few to mention actually. Sometimes they are doomed from the outset. Ray Davies of The Kinks gave me the runaround for weeks, twice refusing to speak at the last minute, though I'd trailed after him to Wolverhampton and Manchester and sat through his set full of whiny, sneering songs about ordinary people not special enough to be pop stars. Eventually, I 'caught up' with him at his Konk studios in Notting Hill. He claimed to have flu and wore a scarf over his mouth for the whole interview. He was needlessly sour and had borrowed the terrifically irritating tactic from former Labour leader Michael Foot of laughing mirthlessly in mid-answer as if to, ha, imply that though he had never been, well, ha, asked a more stupid and asinine question in his life, he would, oh dear, ho ho, deign to answer it. At one point I suggested that 'All Day And All Of The Night' was the first heavy metal song and he said, sniffily on several levels, that, no, 'You Really Got Me' was the first heavy metal song. Then he walked out.

Some bad interviews hinge on a single pivotal moment. This is what happened when I interviewed Mick Hucknall on the radio. Everything was going, if not well, then acceptably (come on, what would you desperately like to know about Simply Red? Exactly) until I mentioned his new single, a collaboration with The Fugees, then one of the hottest acts in the world. Jokingly I said, 'Well, you never know. It might be a hit.'

'What do you mean?' asked Hucknall, suddenly stern.

'I was being mildly sarcastic,' I replied cheerily. 'You and The Fugees. How can it not be a hit?'

He grew sterner still. 'What, are you saying I should have recorded it under a pseudonym?' he asked techily, looking around to his entourage for support. They all shook their heads and tutted obsequiously, of course.

This should illustrate a point about 'sitting in'. If the PR asks whether they can 'sit in' on the interview, say no. They'll probably insist and you'll probably have to back down but it's worth a try because 'sitting in' is the scourge of the half-decent interview. PRs approach the subject breezily ('Hey, Stu, you don't mind if I sit in do you. Might be fun. I'll stay schtum, of course') but don't let the levity fool you. 'Sitting in' turns every PR into a Guatemalan secret policeman. They are there for one reason only: to stop you asking their celebrity charges about their predilection for wife battery/heroin/ladyboys of South East Asia/or their rotten new album.

It would be lovely if one day and in one interview when the big star turns in petulant pique and flappery to his retinue looking for sycophantic support, the PR would pipe up and say, 'Just answer the boy's questions, you big girl's blouse and stop making a fuss. Your new record is shite, actually.'

This didn't happen with Mick Hucknall. The interview pretty much fizzled out there and then with both both of us now chippy, belligerent and puffed up. The PRs huddled around him, wrapping blankets around his wounded ego, ushering him away to the haven of his tinted-screen limo.

I should have learned my lesson about jokes. Don't try them.

The bigger the star, the less likely they are to get irony. I once asked Paul McCartney whether there had never been a moment, not just for a second, when he'd rather have been in Gerry and the Pacemakers. 'Gerry and the Pacemakers?' He looked at me as if I'd gone mental. 'What do you think?' Suddenly, blindingly, I saw his point and spent the rest of the interview telling him how great he is, which is both true and less open to misinterpretation.

Through working for a weekly music paper, I got to meet most of my musical heroes ('heroes' is a terrible word here with all the wrong connotations but no other quite fits the bill). This is quite an amazing thing when you think about it. Naturally it could have been a disastrous and deflating thing. But it wasn't. In their many different ways, none of them let me down.

One day in the summer of 1990, Julian Cope came to the *NME* to meet me for an interview. I know it was towards the end of Thatcher's reign because of what Julian was wearing. He was dressed in a capacious sky-blue knitted Mickey Mouse sweater, fawn ballet tights, aviator shades, leather motorcycle boots and a First World War pilot's helmet à la Biggles. It was the hottest day of the year.

'I'm dressing stupidly on purpose,' he confided, 'in order to create positive crazy vibes and bring Thatcher down.' He came up to the 26th floor to meet me and we rode the lift down together along with the polyester suits from Accounts and their giggling secretaries. Julian was oblivious to their stifled giggles and mockery. I glared at them, thinking, 'This is Julian Cope. You aren't fit to buckle those boots, pal.' We picnicked in the park. Thatcher was gone by autumn. No coincidence I reckon.

Late one afternoon, working at home in Birmingham on some story, or possibly eating Hula Hoops and watching *Fifteen to One*, I got a call from Danny Kelly.

'There's a six o'clock flight to Dublin. Can you be on it to meet David Bowie?' There had been a last minute dropout by one of our staff writers who we suspected had faked a fainting fit on the tube rather than meet the man whose then current Tin Machine project he'd heaped abuse on in a recent review.

Bowie was all charm incarnate and quicksilver mind even if the interview (with all the band) was naturally unsatisfying. Bowie would start to answer every question, enthusiastically and entertainingly and then remember he was in a band and defer and then one of the Sales brothers would say something quite dull. Tony Parsons, an old *NME* man of course, put it best if a little harshly in a magazine article when he said, 'Interviewing David Bowie and Tin Machine is like finally getting a date with that gorgeous girl you've always fancied and finding out she's brought her three ugly mates.'

Bowie was, appropriately, a hero, if not as much as his old sparring partner and muse Brian Eno. When I was struggling with French irregular verbs, Eno was dressing in feather boas and applying the philosophies of experimental music to the pop chart of The Sweet and Lieutenant Pigeon. Then, saying that 'there's only room for one Brian in Roxy Music', he quit.[1] After that he made a series of records that were enormously important to me. I'd used *Discreet Music* as a valium to get to sleep after another bad day at Courtaulds. I'd done college essays at three a.m. with *Music for Airports* lending the room a reflective gentle chill like air conditioning. I'd sung along in my cups to 'Kings Lead Hat' and 'Backwater'. I'd tried to fight his corner at the *NME* in a variety of ways; obliquely, by introducing the character Professor Eno as Thrills resident expert on all matters, and once, in a grand gesture,

---

1 He actually reckons that he knew he had to leave when he was onstage in Sheffield and found himself, during 'Virginia Plain', wondering how he would get his catsuit dry-cleaned for the next night.

I also called him the most important man in pop, claiming that he'd invented glam rock, hip-hop, ambient music and, for better or worse, U2.

I can't now remember why we first met, what project he was up to, what album he may have been promoting. The details have been lost in the overall thrill. He remains the most interesting human being I've ever encountered. If we ever get that world government that loony American survivalists in Montana think is just around the corner, then we could at least make the best of a bad job by electing Eno president. For one, he is liberal, agnostic, humane. For another, it would be nice to have a world leader whose interests include Victorian pornography and perfume. At one point during the interview he mused, 'Ten years ago, the new Calvin Klein scent could never have been successful. It's so determinedly non-floral.' This is not the kind of thing Ozzy Osbourne says often in interviews. Nor Napalm Death for that matter.

Meeting heroes is always problematic. There's always the worry that your heroes will not resemble the character that exists in your head, not be the personality you have constructed and come to love through their words and music. Happily though, they often are. Elvis Costello was quick-witted, entertaining and nicely spikey, minnow flashes of truculence beneath the silvery surface. Roddy Frame and Edwyn Collins, first met in yet another soulless German hotel bar, were genial, quirky, fun. At no point during our meetings did I say, 'I used to be obsessed with you, so much so that I hung around with your dad for a while.' Or in Roddy's case, 'I once impersonated you for a weekend in Bangor. Is that a C diminished just before the chorus in "Oblivious"?'

No one wants to hear this kind of thing. It's not flattering. It's scary. However sincerely and admiringly you mean it, however much to you it says, 'Your art means a great deal to me and I have always taken a great interest in your professional and personal development,' it inevitably sounds to them like 'At home I have constructed a shrine to you made of my own hair. I also have your face tattooed on my tongue. Look! Good, eh,' When meeting heroes, rein yourself in.

This was tested in 1993 when, after a decade and a half of puppy-dog devotion, I got to meet Kate Bush. It was in the untidy office of a rehearsal studios in West London. An intimate little restaurant on the Via Montale might have been nicer but you can't have everything. She was lovely. She gave me a kiss too. I don't remember one word of our conversation. But I do remember the kiss. At the *Q* awards, some years later, Phil Jupitus presented Kate with the Lifetime Achievement award. She got a standing ovation and seemed genuinely touched. As she left the podium, Phil ran a finger under his collar. 'Fifteen years ago now … but I still feel slightly guilty.' Voices, mainly male ones, rang out with laughter.

With Paddy McAloon I smoked cigars, drank brandy and sang Jimmy Webb songs at the grand piano in a Newcastle cock-tail bar. Phil Oakey of the Human League bought me an ice cream in the Yorkshire Dales. Scott Walker was more nervous than me: some achievement given that I was almost catatonic with appre-hension. To err is human, to err … um … err is unforgivable. The interview tape sounds like a convention of *Beano*-style comedy Red Indians.

One day, James Brown tossed a pre-release tape onto my desk. 'You like Chic, don't you. Disco and all that. There's a new album. Fancy doing them?'

Disco? Disco? I said. Disco was too small a word for it. Chic are one of the greatest groups in the history of recorded sound: Nile Rodgers and Bernard Edwards are to the world of club music and black pop what Lennon and McCartney are to the world of white music. No, more than that. Because Rodgers and Edwards are not just great writers and arrangers, they are musicians of the very highest … James had glazed over, like people do when they're being shown slides of traction engines at vintage car rallies.

'I'll do it,' I said.

Photographer Kevin Cummins had often been the bane of my trips and jobs. He once caused me to miss the last flight home from Copenhagen querying nugatory items of expense on his hotel bills: 'Three kroner for a croissant. Flippin 'eck,' he shouted and what's worse he did it in a beany hat and comedy shorts in a lobby full of sharp-suited Danish women. I hid behind a large pot plant. His refusal to fly United Airlines – he is a steadfast Manchester City fan – made many an American jaunt reassuringly complex and stressful.

For all that, he was a man of excellent taste: I forgave him all his faults for having the foresight to make a Chic compilation tape which we played as we cruised in his very nice car for an hour getting ourselves childishly excited about the meeting with two of our heroes. I had brought with me a copy of my prized 12-inch single of 'I Want Your Love' to be autographed if, please God, they were as delightful as their records. 'I Want Your Love' was on the compilation tape. They all were: 'Happy Man', 'My Feet Keep Dancing', 'Le Freak', Carly Simon's 'Why', Sheila B Devotion's 'Spacer'. Heard together with the top down that summer's morning in Kensington, they convinced us that we were about to meet gods, not men. Some people feel like this about UB40, astonishingly.

Cummins sussed out photo locations. I went up to the hotel room. I knocked on the door. I could dimly hear music.

'Come in,' came a familiar voice.

Nile Rodgers was perched on the windowsill of his room. He was cradling in his arms a beautiful white Gretsch semi-acoustic with gold pickups that flashed in the sunlight streaming in through the lace curtains. Events were taking on the unmistakable character of the dream. Perhaps in a moment I would wake up and find I had nodded off while interviewing UB40 in a greasy spoon in Kings Heath.

But no. 'Oh hi,' said Nile Rodgers, smiling his big famous smile. 'You're the magazine guy. Hey look, I'm thinking of buying this guitar and I need a few minutes to check it over. Make yourself comfortable. Pour yourself a drink. I won't keep you long.'

I muttered something meaningless, possibly in a language unknown even to me and sat down.

'Happy Man', 'Le Freak', 'I Want Your Love'. Like the tape, they were all there. He didn't do Sheila B Devotion's 'Spacer' or 'Why' by Carly Simon. That really would have convinced me that I was dreaming. But it was still a wonderful few minutes.

'Nice guitar,' he said finally. 'I may buy it.'

As I groped for something to say, Bernard Edwards entered the room looking Studio 54 immaculate in a three-piece Armani suit. We began the interview. Again, I don't really remember a word of the conversation. I remember that it was cordial and funny. I remember that they were cheeky, even laddish, and told tales about the 'ladies' they'd worked with down the years. But the bit that sticks in the mind is, again, the unexpected detail: Nile Rodgers playing the guitar in a veil of white lace and West London sunshine, a moment of cinematic perfection. I got them to sign my 12-inch of 'I Want Your Love' too. Driving away from the hotel, I glanced at what they had written. It read 'To Stuart from Bernard and Nile. Yowsah, yowsah, yowsah!' Perfect.

Mark King of Level 42 was not really a hero but I'd always been a sucker for that slap bass thing. And he is a gentleman of the old school. Maybe they're all like this from the Isle of Wight. I went there to his lovely rural pile and he bounded out to meet us dressed in an apron.

'Hurry up, I've made pizzas for lunch.' Later, we were chatting about formative musical experiences and the Mahavishnu Orchestra came up. I mentioned the shock of seeing that *Whistle Test* show back in the early Seventies. 'Would you like to see it again?' he asked. It turned out that it had had much the same effect on him, and that he had used his influence to get a copy made of the original tape, now languishing in a vault at the BBC. We sat in his den and watched it on his huge, state-of-the-art home cinema system. It was still completely mental.

From that very first day at the *NME* I was aware that there was one meeting above all the others that loomed tantalisingly in the future always just out of reach. One day it would come, though, and I'd be ready. It would be my High Noon. But when it came it wasn't at noon but at about eleven o'clock at night in a swanky hotel room high above the Kurfürstendamm in Berlin. Morrissey's hotel room.

Morrissey is simply the best interviewee in the world. He has turned it into an art form, to the extent that, as stated previously, editions of the *NME* boasting a Morrissey cover story would sell more than his records did. Morrissey had fans who weren't actually that wild on his music. They were fans of Morrissey the interviewee.

I'd been waiting in Morrissey's Berlin hotel room for a while. He was somewhere in the building, I'd been assured of this. For a while I thought he was just shy. Then I began to think that it was an elaborate Lou Reed-style plan to unnerve the hack. But at just this point, a vertiginous quiff appeared around the door.

'I expect you'll be wanting a drink,' he asked in his uniquely wounded and Lancastrian version of camp.

A significant decision, this. I decided to test him out. 'I'll have a Jack Daniels and Coke please,' a provocatively and deliberately Aerosmith-style rock 'n' roll beverage for such a sensitive chap. He rolled his eyes. 'Then you shall at least have it in a champagne flute. Do you have champagne flutes in Wigan?'

Naturally I don't remember what we talked about. I remember chancing my arm and asking him to come downstairs for a pint afterwards. He did, and we ended up taking in a few of Berlin's worst nightclubs. He had me sussed I think. During that first conversation, he began one answer, 'If you've studied my career in detail,' and then leaned forward and muttered, sotto voce, secretive, 'and I know you have, Stuart,' with a wry smile.

We didn't become friends. Moz doesn't operate like that. But Morrissey was so routinely bad-mouthed and lampooned while being simultaneously factory-farmed by the rock press that I think he knew he had an ally in me. I was Northern. I was a music writer. I was a fan but not a frightening fanatic who would come and live in his garden. Although of course I'm glad he didn't know that I had once made the car in which I was travelling (in the boot to boot) pull over on a desolate hillside to listen to 'This Charming Man'.

We met regularly over the next few years. I interviewed and wrote about Morrissey at length in various publications. He never let me down. One time we met, at his insistence, in a rough locals pub in a decrepit corner of Vauxhall and did the interview, bizarrely, seated at one of those ancient tabletop space invaders machines while a band in the back room played obscure Eddie Cochrane numbers (which he recognised instantly).

But our most memorable meeting was in Camden. He kept a house there on a private road, perhaps still does, and early one gorgeous summer's evening, we sat on the grass under a tree outside his place. As we talked, a young woman – clearly an American backpacker, clearly lost – wandered up to us.

'Hey guys, I'm trying to find this pub where they have the indie shows, the Dublin Castle. You know it?'

As we directed her, the realisation of who she was talking to dawned on her. Morrissey, I mean, not me. Her face froze in a kind of delighted horror. She began to babble.

'It's you, it's you, isn't it. You. You're him. You're you …'

Morrissey smiled at her, and with just the briefest of glances in my direction, said, 'I'm not the man you think I am.'

It's a line from 'Pretty Girls Make Graves', one of the less well-known songs on their generally overlooked first album. A good joke – one that you would only get if you'd studied his career in detail. And, as we've established, he knew I had.

But even Morrissey had started to lose his way in the early Nineties. It was a thin time all round. Useless scruffy grunge acts whose songs roughly translated as 'Oh mom, do I have to tidy my room?' filled the rock press. It was time for something new, something with a bit of of pep, vim, British humour and savvy. Something that celebrated the virtues of the mods, of Sixties pop, Northern Soul, glam rock. Proper pop, the stuff that we were good at, the mood abroad in the songs and style of groups like Blur, Suede and Pulp. But what to call it, this new British pop.

I've got it.

Lion Pop!

No, tried that. Stupid name.

Oh, well, something would occur to me, I'm sure.

27 To the End

By 1993, I had risen, without really understanding how or why, to Assistant Editor of *NME*. If you know me at all well then the fact that I was seen as a born manager, a good organiser, a dedicated team player, unflappable, a tough-minded realist and a shrewd business head to boot shows how fantastically flaky and erratic most music journalists must be, at least then.

George Orwell, yes him again, said that to take a freelance writer and make him an editor was like taking a prisoner and making him a gaoler. I knew what he meant. But for the most part, the arrangement worked. I was happiest when writing about pop music and least happy when discussing budgets with the 'suits' in publishing upstairs. No young boy or girl, the light of revolutionary fire in their eyes, has ever dreamed of one day discussing ad ratios, cover-mounted CD grab-bags or promotional 'shelf wobblies'. But I didn't have to do this too often. Generally, my editorial duties ran to thinking of funny headlines about Slowdive and chasing Dele Fadele and Barbara Ellen for their ovedue singles reviews.

Then, one day that spring, our little world high above the greasy reek of Waterloo was turned upside down. Danny Kelly called for Brendan, assistant production editor, and myself to join him in his office. He asked us to close the door. Danny was 'hands on' before the term was invented, so the closing of his door could mean only a couple of things. A bollocking of titanic proportions. Or another thing that hadn't as yet even occurred.

This was that other thing. Danny was leaving the paper. He couldn't tell us why except that he had been offered another job. He couldn't say what job for legal reasons. We were stunned. The *NME* was volatility itself but there were some individuals whose lives were seen as bound up with the title. We were, after all, the world's biggest rock weekly. Where else was there to go?

The answer was obvious actually: *Q* magazine. For a long time, some of us had been admiring this monthly competitor's rise from being a rather drab, starchy thing about boring rock aristos à la Collins, Hucknall and Gabriel into a slick, witty, grown-up read. Danny himself used to get quite techy about this. If he caught me reading *Q*, he would fly into one of his much-loved and characteristic irrational rages, waving his arms and shouting, 'If you like *Q* so much, why don't you go and work for it?' Then, one day a week or two back, he had asked to borrow a raft of Andrew Collins's back issues of *Q*. Now it was obvious why; he had been head-hunted by *Q* and had been doing a bit of swotting. If we liked *Q* so much, why didn't he go and work for it?

The news of Danny's imminent departure ran around the 26th floor like proverbial wildfire. The effect was extraordinary. There were tears, rage, desks and photocopiers were kicked. There was hysterical laughter and theatrical astonishment.

At the risk of sounding like a cold fish, I didn't feel any of this. I was shocked and saddened but I understood completely. Some of us did feel intensely loyal to the paper: we had all been regular readers and we were mostly proud to be working for a title of such significance. But I couldn't share the feeling that Danny had somehow let us down. Loyalty is for friends and family; the idea of being loyal to a private company is innately ridiculous, particularly ridiculous when the company was IPC, a wing of publishing giant Reed International. There was nothing particularly malign about the company. But it was a multinational business enterprise which, like all of them, would skin your loved ones alive and make toddlers work on giant spiked treadmills if it meant a percentage market-share increase. This is not a political diatribe, just a matter of fact. Danny was merely taking the ball and chain of his wage slavery elsewhere. The old sociology is still in the blood somewhere evidently.

But there was more shocking stuff to come in Kings Reach Tower. It was decided that, as a mark of collective endeavour and solidarity, all of us on the editorial tier below Danny – myself, Brendon, Andrew Collins, Steve Lamacq and Mary Anne Hobbs – would apply for his vacant seat. There were rumours that an outsider would be appointed and we wanted to show that we were more than capable of running the show ourselves. After all, we had turned the paper's fortune around, halting and reversing a decade-long slide in sales.

In truth, I was about as keen on being the editor of *NME* as I was of running the Todmorden branch of B&Q. And probably about as equipped to do so. I assumed though that this would become apparent at the interview and so didn't worry unduly about getting the job. Showing willing was the important thing.

I didn't get the job. None of us did in fact. That was what caused all the trouble. The management of IPC instead appointed one Steve Sutherland, a seasoned music paper hack, an IPC company man and an obvious choice in many ways. Except one, namely that he worked on the floor above for *Melody Maker*.

The relationship between *NME* and *Melody Maker* was a fierce tribal hatred so virulent that it could sometimes infect even those of us who kidded themselves they were rather more worldly and mature than the average overgrown schoolkid of the music paper milieu. Once, after an all-night boozing session at the Columbia hotel, a rather shabby but much-loved 'rock 'n' roll' gaff at Lancaster Gate, David Quantick and I broke into – or should I say, gently pushed open the door of – the *Melody Maker* offices and wandered vacantly around in the thin, early morning light, vaguely intent on some industrial sabotage such as wiping all the computer hard discs or tossing the photo library into the Thames that flowed softly and brownly 26 floors below. Thank God that, even through our dense cloud of bourbon, we had seen sense in the nick of time. We staggered down the stairs to *NME* instead where I fell asleep under my desk. First in at nine, editor's secretary Karen Walter found me there and, touchingly, covered me up with the only thing to hand, a large Stars and Stripes flag that had been a promotional freebie from the last Bruce Springsteen album campaign.

Appointing a *Melody Maker* man editor of *NME* was not, as was often said at the time, like a Labour Party stalwart joining the Tories. Politicians being what they are, slippery and uglier than lampreys, that happens all the time. It was far, far more bizarre and unnatural than any parliamentary floor crossing. It was more akin perhaps to the Reverend Ian Paisley becoming the editor of *Heat* magazine or India and Pakistan agreeing amicably to merge into one secular, relaxed, fun-loving country run jointly by Dale Winton and Michaela Strachan.

Alan Lewis told Brendan and I privately of the board's decision. 'I'd be grateful if you could try and smooth the way for the announcement this afternoon. Keep things calm.' Brendan raised an amused eyebrow (his own) and we exchanged meaningful looks. My thoughts returned to the strike of a year previously and the enthusiasm with which chaos had been embraced then. Starved of the kind of genuine problems that afflict most working folk – children, wholesale redundancies, tiles blowing off the roof in high winds – young music writers tend to fly off the handle at the first sign of trouble. I'd been on strike as a teacher over the government's swingeing further education cuts and it had been messy and difficult. I could not tell you for the life of me what the 'great *NME* strike' of nineteen ninety something was about. It was a bit of a laugh really. When word got around that you weren't actually allowed to go on free trips to the States with bands when you were technically on strike, everyone slunk back to work grumbling at the unfairness of it all.

Thus I knew we had a top-notch afternoon in store. In preparation, many of the more dedicated dipsos on the staff spent an hour or two in the Stamford Arms topping up the alcohol levels. By the time the meeting assembled, the mood was part boardroom drama à la Dallas circa 1983 and part public execution at Ludgate circa 1600.

The atmosphere was heavy with cigarette smoke – still allowed in music paper offices in the mid-Nineties – and the rank tang of exhaled lager. I can't remember the exact order of events. I do know that there exists somewhere a tape of it, recorded by Andrew Collins with his little reporter's cassette recorder tucked in his jacket pocket. As bootlegs go, it may not have the cultural charge of Bob Dylan Live at Manchester Free Trade Hall in 1966 (the one where the crowd get angry at Dylan's electric set and the guy shouts 'Judas') but if you were there, it's a cool souvenir. The bit where Sutherland himself enters the room is particularly good, the acrimony goes up a gear and some of the drunker staffers start to make that low, abstract growl of generalised rage and dissatisfaction popular with early morning Special Brew imbibers at Euston and Edinburgh Waverley stations. I perhaps ought to have said that Sutherland himself had been the author of the infamous 'Diamonds and Dogshit' spiel. It didn't take long for this matter to arise. Sutherland said, not unreasonably, that while he was a *Melody Maker* guy he was totally committed to them and perforce had to bad-mouth the opposition. But that was history. Now he was an *NME* man and he hated *Melody Maker* with all his heart.

On this particular bootleg, this would have been the point for someone to shout 'Judas'. But no one did. Several of us in the room though were thinking, '1993? Already? I think it's about time I was leaving.'

A wave of resignations followed. Many of the papers editors upped and went in quick succession: Andrew Collins, Steve Lamacq, Mary Anne Hobbs and myself. We all had our various reasons. I can only speak for myself.

I was fed up with a desk job, even one as irregular as being assistant editor of *NME*. I wanted to write and, increasingly, talk on the radio. Then there was the not inconsiderable matter of what to write about.

In 1993, grunge held foul, odorous dominion over the alternative music scene. As mentioned above, I absolutely hated grunge music. I found it styleless, graceless, charmless. I could see the sheer visceral power of Nirvana. I could feel Cobain's excoriating pain and rage. I just didn't fancy it myself. I didn't hate myself and I didn't want to die. I actually was quite happy staying alive. I had a nice walking holiday in the Lake District booked for one thing, and I'd just got a West Highland terrier. These were not the sort of things music journalists were supposed to be interested in, I knew. Actually, I was feeling less like a music journalist and more like a regular human being every day. Things were soon to come to a head on this front.

In the meantime, though, I couldn't reconcile the music I liked with the plaid-shirted dullards, self-righteous windbags, gangster rap misogynists and the like that we were in the thrall of at *NME*. In 1990, I'd met a band called Blur. They had recently changed their name from Seymour and had signed to Food Records. I'd gone to see them in a tiny basement club in Stoke-on-Trent to review them for the live section. A visit to Stoke is never, in my experience, without its horrors, but this was more enjoyable than most. They were excellent: punky art rock, a dash of Wire and Syd

Barrett, a soupçon of classic British pop and a thrilling, unhinged stage presence. We stayed up late in the bar of the hotel drinking and became friends. I began to champion them, which must have been useful when the lean years almost immediately arrived. Drinking, fighting among themselves and losing ground to newer bands like Suede, they had gone into a black decline.

A second studio album had been rejected by their record company, only being accepted after singer Damon Albarn had come up with the two new songs for it, 'For Tomorrow' and 'Chemical World'. I was sent this album, the evocatively titled *Modern Life Is Rubbish*, and loved it; now there were touches of Bowie, Teardrop Explodes, British psychedelia. I went to Japan with them and had the time of my life. Every night they played 'Pop Scene', the criminally overlooked single of the year previously, and played it with a buzzy, adrenalised passion and sparkiness that showed up just what was wrong with Alice In Chains, Tad, Mudhoney, Soundgarden, Pearl Jam and all those lumpy interchangeable grease monkeys. I stood there every night grinning from ear to ear, drinking my imported Seagrams, smoking a cigarette called, implausibly, Keith.

At some point in some piece, I used the phrase Britpop – someone must have used it before I'm sure, possibly about The Hollies – and it stuck. Unlike Lion Pop and a thousand other legless youth cults contrived by rock hacks like me, this one actually flourished if only for a while. Tony Blair still has the records.

But for all the fun of the daily inkie round, I felt more and more a general sense that it was no longer a suitable sole daily full-time job for a bloke in his thirties to be doing.[1]

I had a kind of epiphany in New York with Primal Scream. I was covering some sessions they were doing with funk legend and general nutter George Clinton. The Scream were and are led

---

[1] Talking rubbish on the radio: now there's a job for a grown-up.

by Bobby Gillespie, the whippet-thin, dissolute, affable Scot who I'd been meeting off and on for years. I'd liked Bobbie and his music since the middle Eighties when he'd worn polka-dot shirts, played the drums standing up and I'd first heard the wonderful 'Velocity Girl' on the *NME*'s famous, era-defining freebie tape C86. Since then, Bobby had defined an era of his own with Primal Scream's *Screamadelica*, the first genuinely groovy album to find its way into student record collections since Michael Jackson's *Thriller*.

Some may think that Nick Hornby introduced the notion of Compulsive Male Pop Curatorship Syndrome to the world. Not so. Guys like Bobby Gillespie have been around for ever, trying to buy every album ever recorded at Muscle Shoals studios, Alabama; compiling tapes of Joe Meek's flop singles; hiding in Curtis Mayfield's mother's shed. That kind of obsessive fandom is charming up to a point. But if it goes too far, you end up like Comic Book Guy from *The Simpsons*: aloof, hair-splitting, losing interest in your appearance, a bit tragic all told. Bobby and the Scream walk that line and, if they'd had a few of anything, they are inclined to wobble.

The weekend I spent with them in New York brought home to me the perils of being too 'rock 'n' roll'. I've always tried to bear in mind that famous Kipling line (Rudyard not Mr, obviously) about patriotism; 'what do they know of England, that only England know'. Substitute pop music for England and you have very sound sentiments. If you only know about B-sides and acetates and line-ups and serial numbers, then you are merely a statistician. To understand pop music fully and completely, you also have to know and care about families, cooking, holidays, sport, trousers, literature, transport, fishing, all that stuff. There is a lot more to it than sex and drugs and rock 'n' roll. The greatest pop song ever composed, 'Wichita Lineman', written by Jim Webb and performed, emblematically, by Glenn Campbell, is a kind of love song. But it's really a love song about work. The job the tele-phone maintenance guy has to do is playing on his mind quite as much as his enigmatic, ambivalent relationship.

Myself, Primal Scream, George Clinton and various unsavoury hangers-on spent all weekend going to rotten parties full of antisocial nitwits trying to find the exact formulation of crystal meth that the Velvet Underground used to get zonked on. We talked about nothing except comparative drug potencies and the horn arrangements of Deodata. The interview, conducted at midnight in Clinton's hotel room (or possibly Bobby's or mine or maybe even a complete stranger's) was a farce, a boring farce that finally dissolved into a circular discussion about who'd writ-ten some long-lost Stax B-side. It suddenly struck me that, persona, location and sundry trappings of rock 'n' roll aside, this was no more entertaining or vital a discussion than the ones that chaps sipping tankards have in Berkshire pubs on Sunday lunchtimes, the ones about laminated wood flooring or the Six Nations decider or the quickest way to get from Slough to Hendon. The fact that George Clinton was wearing a feathered head-dress and smoking the biggest joint I had ever seen was neither here nor there. It may just as well have been a turquoise Pringle sweater and a tin of St Bruno.

I clicked off the tape, said, 'I think I've got enough here' and walked back down the corridor to my room and immediately proposed to Eleanor over a transatlantic phone call. She said yes. I couldn't wait to get home. I heard it singing in the wire, I could hear it through the whine.

Like the rest of the departing class of '93, I left the *NME* quickly and without ceremony. The day I left I took something and left something behind. As a leaving present Kevin Cummins framed an enlargement of one of his classic shots of Morrissey. It was a sweet thought, and a terrific picture. On my last day I thought I had it with me in the car. When I got home it wasn't there. It was still in Danny's office, or rather the new editor's office.

I waited until the end of the day, till everyone had sloped off to the pub or a gig and then went back, showing my IPC pass for the last time. I couldn't find it. Maybe someone had moved it for safe-keeping or I'd misremembered where I'd hidden it. But it wasn't there. I never took the Morrissey picture home. I'm as ashamed of this as anything I've ever done. Mentioning it now is a small, belated attempt at assuaging the guilt I still carry around about it. No act of kindness is ever forgotten they say. Well, maybe the same goes for acts of thoughtlessness and ingratitude. Sorry, Kevin.

Standing there a little drunk in the gathering gloom, unable to find my Morrissey picture, I decided to take something else instead. Two, maybe two and a half years previously, Bernard Sumner of New Order had donated the Gibson Les Paul junior he had used in Joy Division as a competition prize. As was often the way at *NME*, the competition had never run and the guitar, in its battered case, had lived since then, gathering dust, above a wall cupboard in the editor's office. I glanced up. It was still there. I couldn't stand the thought of it staying there for another two, three, five, ten years, unplayed, unloved. Or worse, being swung around at Christmas parties as a superannuated prop.

That's why I stole it I guess. It's in the corner of the room as I type this. That's where it's staying too. A couple of years later, I was having a cordial cocktail with Bernard on the terrace of a restaurant in a London park. Suddenly I felt the need to unburden myself.

'You used to play a Les Paul junior in Joy Division occasionally, didn't you? A black one.'

'Err, did I? Oh yeah, that's right. God knows what happened to it, though.'

Thoughtful sip, pause, then as casually as possible, 'I've got it, actually.'

'Pardon?'

I explained. He didn't mind. Glad it had gone to a good home. Said if he ever needed it, he'd give me a ring. If he ever does though, he owes me a hundred and fifty quid. That's what it cost me to have it restored and repaired. Bloke at the guitar workshop said it had been treated abysmally. 'Solvent sprayed on it, dropped and scratched, neck broken off and cackhandedly glued back on. Whose was it? Not a proper musician, that's for sure.'

Perhaps not. Certainly there was little propriety in the way that the guitar guy came to be handling it. Half-inched, half drunk, from a publication that should have given it away as a prize years before. Would a proper journalist working for a proper paper have behaved like this?

But then music journalism isn't proper journalism. There were times when I used to be embarrassed by this. But now I'm rather proud of it.

True, no music journalist has ever laid low a corrupt government or awoken the world to famine and disease. No music journalist, though, has ever followed a child home from school, wheedling out a few sentences while pretending to be mummy's friend. No music journalist has ever banged on a door at midnight, screaming 'We know you're in there' through a letterbox at a woman in tears. Music journalism has no Bernstein and Woodwards, no Pulitzer Prizes. But then again, it has no entrapment specialists, no smear campaigns, no sleazy pictures of naked sixteen-year-olds run alongside frothing bug-eyed hysteria about paedophiles.

No music journalist has ever properly invaded the privacy of anyone. We're just not together enough. We get jetlagged going to Brussels. Rest assured, your privacy is safe with us. We'll go to the wrong house. At the wrong time. And when we get there, we'll try to take the compromising pictures with our Walkman or we won't have any batteries for the tape recorder. Or we won't have brought enough of the little cassettes, the ones that you can buy anywhere. It is the daftest, most innocent, maybe the most honourable branch of journalism.

We're incorrigible romantics, sleepwalking from crush to crush, stuck in an infatuation that began all those years ago in an upstairs room in Swinton. We don't want to know about the sordid truth, the lies, the addictions, the breakdowns, the payola, the double-crossing, the 'issues'. That's for the proper journalists.

All we want is to add our little thumbprint to the wet cement of the avenue of stars. To hang out with heroes, to drink champagne with legends or, at very least, cider with roadies.

That and, with a bit of luck, to find someone who's swapping a fishing rod for a Doctor Feelgood album.